Advance Praise for THE Evolving
Significance of Race

"As the contributors to this volume demonstrate, there are few myths as dangerous as the one about a 'post-racial America.' These are the times we most desperately need fresh angles on questions of race and racism in schooling. Sherick A. Hughes and Theodorea Regina Berry, in their refusal to soften or depoliticize injustice, have assembled a volume of important reading for anybody who believes that all students deserve the best possible education we can offer them."

—*Paul C. Gorski, Founder, EdChange and Board of Directors,*
*International Association for Intercultural Education*

"Immensely engaging and boldly written! *The Evolving Significance of Race* offers sharply analytical narratives that are grounded in personal experience, representing critical race theory at its best. This book provides compelling tools educators can use to incite productive dialog and to move their work forward."

—*Christine Sleeter, Professor Emerita, California State University Monterey Bay*
*and President, National Association for Multicultural Education*

# THE Evolving Significance of Race

This book is part of the Peter Lang Education list.
Every volume is peer reviewed and meets
the highest quality standards for content and production.

PETER LANG
New York • Washington, D.C./Baltimore • Bern
Frankfurt • Berlin • Brussels • Vienna • Oxford

# THE Evolving Significance of Race

## Living, Learning, and Teaching

EDITED BY
Sherick A. Hughes & Theodorea Regina Berry

PETER LANG
New York • Washington, D.C./Baltimore • Bern
Frankfurt • Berlin • Brussels • Vienna • Oxford

Library of Congress Cataloging-in-Publication Data
The evolving significance of race: living, learning, and
teaching / edited by Sherick A. Hughes, Theodorea Regina Berry.
p. cm.
Includes bibliographical references and index.
1. Race—Study and teaching—United States—History.
2. Racism—Study and teaching—United States—History.
3. Multicultural education—United States—History.
I. Hughes, Sherick A. II. Berry, Theodorea Regina.
HT1506.E96    370.1170973—dc23    2011044172
ISBN 978-1-4331-1670-4 (hardcover)
ISBN 978-1-4331-1669-8 (paperback)
ISBN: 978-1-4539-0526-5 (e-book)


Bibliographic information published by **Die Deutsche Nationalbibliothek**.
**Die Deutsche Nationalbibliothek** lists this publication in the "Deutsche
Nationalbibliografie"; detailed bibliographic data is available
on the Internet at http://dnb.d-nb.de/.

# CONTENTS

## I: Living, Learning, and Teaching Youth

## II: Living, Learning, and Teaching Teachers

# III: Living, Learning, and Teaching for a Political Future

# Foreword

MARVIN LYNN

Writing about race and education in the current sociopolitical context is both a challenge and an opportunity. At this moment in history, we are more than a year into the presidency of Barack Obama—the first African American elected to the office of President of the United States. Many of us, especially African Americans who have long been concerned about the nature of racism in the United States and around the world, didn't believe we would ever see this moment. We were incredulous; we just didn't think it would happen in our lifetimes. Well, it did. Now, the question becomes, "What does this really mean?" Many have tried to explain the phenomenon by putting forth propositions regarding the nature of a postracial society.

There have been two major postracial theses or propositions put forth. These propositions are meant to explain how and perhaps why the United States was able to elect an African-American president for the first time in its 233-year history. The first argument is that it signals the end of racism. The second postracial proposition is that it suggests that race, as an identity category, is becoming less significant in our society. Both of these propositions, if they penetrate the social and political landscape in major ways, could possibly create a context in which it will be even more difficult for critical race scholars to (a) establish research agendas that focus exclusively on racially marginalized peoples, and (b) put forth claims about the systematic nature of racism and its impact on the lives of racially marginalized people.

A recent poll done by *Essence* magazine published in May 2009 suggests that African Americans are more optimistic. Nearly 70% of African Americans believe that the election of Mr. Barack Obama as president signals significant social progress. The report also suggests that they believe that racism is less prevalent now than it was before Mr. Obama was elected. It seems that there is widespread agreement among the public that Mr. Obama's presidency signals the end of racism. I would argue, however, that this belief rests on an underdeveloped and therefore inaccurate notion about what constitutes racism or, better put, White supremacy. If one understands racism as negative behavior or actions based on the prejudicial attitudes and beliefs of White people about non-Whites, then it might be easier to make such a claim. But even then, one would need evidence to show significant decreases in the number of race-based hate crimes and lawsuits alleging racial discrimination in the workplace and elsewhere. But if one accepts Critical Race Theory's framing of the concept of racism, then it is understood as a deeply entrenched system of social, economic, and political privileges afforded to Whites based on their skin color. In this view, race is based on a socially constructed notion designed not only to categorize people based on certain immutable characteristics but to argue that these "races" present "ideal types" that must be segregated and sorted according to their racial status. Drawing on this understanding of race and racism, one would need to examine not only racial discrimination lawsuits and hate crimes, but other indicators such as relative rates of unemployment, educational attainment, income, relative rates of imprisonment, and housing in order to claim that significant racial progress had occurred. Additionally, one would have to show that there is parity between Blacks and Whites in all these areas. One does not need to conduct a major research study to show that this is indeed not the case. Assuming that racism is or will soon go away, one then has to naturally assume that the overall conditions for Blacks and other people of color in the United States have significantly improved. This widespread belief in these false assumptions of the nature of race and racism will present significant challenges for critical race studies in education scholars that will have to be strategically fought against.

An even more insidious claim made by some political pundits is that the election of Barack Obama as America's first African-American president signals not only the end of racism but also the end of race as a social phenomenon. According to some, President Obama's widely acceptable racial hybridity signals an important turn away from the kind of racial labeling required in a racialized social system (Bonilla-Silva, 1997), where race is the defining feature of the society. This claim is more insidious because it could lead to broad levels of support for Ward Connerly's "national campaign to end the consideration of race in the public arenas of education, employment and contracting" (http://www.acri.org/). Not only is the American Civil Rights Institute opposed to Affirmative Action on the basis that it wrongly punishes otherwise qualified White applicants from education and employment for the wrongs of the past, but they are interested in eliminating the notion of race and racial difference altogether. The view is that if races no longer exist, then racism would magically disappear. The problem, of course, is that racial minorities would no longer be able to claim that they are being discriminated against on the basis of race. While the courts have not provided an adequate response to claims of racial discrimination, the courts have historically been an important site for the advancement of equal opportunity in our society. *Brown v. Board of Education* is a key example. We will have to be more vigilant as the debates about the disappearance of race become increasingly more commonplace in the media or other social arenas such as schools.

In light of these arguments about the end of race and racism, critical race studies in education scholars continue to argue forthrightly that schooling inequalities—particularly those that negatively impact the lives of Black and Brown youth—are the result of complex processes of racial inclusion and exclusion of children based on their proximity to Whiteness—both in terms of their racial phenotype and what I would call "school place identities" (Carbado & Gulati, forthcoming). Carbado and Gulati use the term *workplace identity* to talk about how people enact their racial identities at work. Blacks with acceptable or nonthreatening workplace identities do not inhabit their Blackness in obvious ways. Children with White school place identities could be characterized as kids who "act White" (Fordham & Ogbu, 1986), but a more apt description would suggest that they, in fact, do not "act Black" except when it is safe to do so. Although Fordham and Ogbu (1986) claimed that the "acting White" phenomenon was the source of social isolation for so many gifted African-American students, it could also be argued that it is one of the main sources of success for students who might otherwise be targeted for failure or recommended for special education. Fordham's research could also suggest that African-American children who look and act like typical White middle-class children reap the rewards of academic success and are afforded opportunities not afforded to children who look and act Black. Academic success is not so much the product of effort, raw talent, and focus as it is the product of racial submissiveness and compliance. The following excerpt from a brief counterstory illustrates this concept:

Olamide and Chris are both middle-class African-American boys who attend a local private school in a large Midwestern city in the United States. The school, started by a prominent political family, boasts nearly 30% African-American enrollment. Another third of their students also hail from moderate- to low-income backgrounds. Both Olamide and Chris' parents are well educated. Olamide's mother is from West Africa—the daughter of a wealthy businessman—and his father is an African American who overcame poverty to become a successful scholar and educator. Chris' father is a well-established attorney, and his mom is a real estate broker who manages and owns several high-profile properties in the area. Both families turned from the public schools in their city because of their concern about what happens to Black males in the public school system: 63% of Black boys failed to graduate on time in this school system. In addition, they lead the way in terms of suspensions and expulsions. These students are extremely bright with advanced reading skills. Both boys are very active, gregarious children who enjoy socializing with other boys of their own age. Although the boys share many similarities, their parents have begun to notice appreciable differences in the responses they are getting from their teachers.

Olamide typically gets praised for what is often described as cooperative and respectful behaviour, whereas Chris is often described as unruly. In fact, Chris's parents were called into the principal's office and told that Chris suffered from significant emotional problems that would need to be addressed immediately if he was going to remain in the school. According to their teachers, Olamide consistently models excellent behavior because he is quiet and soft-spoken and always follows school rules. Chris, in contrast, is said to talk out of turn and to move around the classroom without permission. In meetings with teachers about the boys' academic progress, teachers focus mainly on the boys' behavior—good or bad. Chris' parents have taken a bold stance against the characterization of their son as "emotionally disturbed." They have pointed out that the school lacks African-American teachers who might be better equipped to handle their son's active nature. They have also pointed out that their son is disproportionately punished by school authorities for engaging in behaviors that are similar to and, in some cases, not nearly as severe or problematic as that of White boys who manage to avoid getting into trouble and being labeled "emotionally disturbed." Somehow the phrase "boys will be boys" becomes an appropriate way to frame the misbehavior of White boys, whereas "emotionally dis-turbed" is the way to frame that same behavior of Black boys. Olamide's par-ents agree and disagree with Chris' parents. They agree that he should be treated fairly and that the school should hire more Black teachers. However, they believe that Chris' parents should put more pressure on their son to com-ply with school expectations for his behavior given the unfair ways that Black boys are treated. In that sense, Olamide's parents have accepted that Black boys will not be treated fairly in this context and have placed the burden on them-selves to put undue pressure on Olamide to behave in a way that will be accepted by his mostly White teachers. Although Olamide's parents recognize that this is probably unfair to Olamide, who should feel free to express himself in school and in life, they want him to understand that freedoms afforded many Whites are not afforded many Black males. To that end, they have called for their son to behave accordingly. Despite Olamide's relative successes in school, both families have experienced a level of frustration with the teachers' constant focus on their children's behavior. In meetings with teachers, both groups of parents have asked teachers to focus less attention on how good or how bad their children are behaving and talk more about their children's aca-demic abilities. Whereas one boy is lauded for his passive behavior, the other boy is demonized for being too active. Chris—regarded as overly active—is on the verge of being kicked out of school. Meanwhile, Olamide's parents are con-cerned that their son is not being challenged because the teachers are so happy that he is not misbehaving. In their view, it says much about the school's pri-orities and fails to support their effort to expose their son to an intellectually stimulating learning environment.

As the brief chronicle illustrates, African-American boys are evaluated pri-marily on their willingness to comply with White, female, sociocultural norms that call for conformity and passivity. Olamide's behavior could be character-ized by some as "acting White," whereas Chris' behavior has been character-ized as "typically Black" behavior—aggressiveness, gregariousness, playfulness, and defiance at times. Chris is threatened with exclusion from school, where-as Olamide is praised by his teachers. There is no discussion about whether these boys' teachers might find better ways to accommodate academically gifted children who are active, creative, and social. In short, the punishments for dis-playing typically "Black" behaviors and attitudes in school—even when you are academically gifted—are severe. While Chris is the clear loser in the battle, both boys may eventually lose the war. Because African Americans are expect-ed to perform a certain kind of "school place identity" that is unrelated to their attainment of academic knowledge and skills, they ultimately get short-changed. When teachers emphasize behavioral conformity over intellectual development for particular groups of children—in this case, Black boys—these students, both conforming and nonconforming, ultimately get short-changed. To that end, schools—even expensive private ones—seem primarily interested in controlling and containing Black male bodies, not the developing their minds. This is still true and will probably remain true even with an African-American president in office.

Critical race counterstories such as this one pay close attention to the often hidden racial politics that dominate the educational landscape. Operating within a postracial narrative, the story of Olamide and Chris could easily be viewed as a story about a boy who misbehaves in school. Although that is part of the story, it certainly does not explain the underlying issues impacting both boys. The postracial thesis does not and cannot explain why White boys in this school with behavior patterns that are similar to Chris' manage to stay out of trouble. The deracialized version of the story does not ask questions about why there are almost no African-American teachers in a school with almost 30% African-American student enrollment. The postracial narrative—whether it be a story about the end of racism or the end of race—completely belies the history of schooling in the United States for African-American boys of all socioeconomic backgrounds. Critical race studies in education as a growing field will continue to bring attention to the experiences of children such as those described earlier and help to explain why race is such a critically important factor in shaping their experiences in school.

In this important volume, Theodorea Regina Berry and Sherick Hughes have continued the important critical race tradition of giving voice to students such as Olamide and Chris, who may be privileged in many ways but are still stymied by the school's commitment to enforcing White social norms that limit the ways in which African-American boys can grow and develop as human beings in a nurturing learning environment. Berry and Hughes, like so many others, are drawing on the foundation of early pioneers of first-generation scholars such as Gloria Ladson-Billings, William Tate, Daniel Solórzano, and Laurence Parker who introduced Critical Race Theory to the field of education in the early and mid-1990s. They are elaborating on and continuing the work of second-generation scholars such as myself (Marvin Lynn), Tara Yosso, David Stovall, and others who have worked tirelessly since the late 1990s through their writing, activism, and organizing to maintain and further develop this tradition in education. Like many of the authors among this second generation of critical race scholars, Berry and Hughes are doing their part to keep the fire burning in what may prove to be some fairly dark days ahead.

—MARVIN LYNN
UNIVERSITY OF WISCONSIN AT EAU CLAIRE

# References

Bonilla-Silva, E. (1997). Rethinking racism: Toward a structural interpretation. *American Sociological Review, 62*(3), 465–480.

Carbado, D. G., & Gulati, G. M. (forthcoming). The law and economics of critical race theory. *Yale Law Journal.*

Fordham, S., & Ogbu, J. U. (1986). Black students' school success: Coping with the "burden of 'acting white.'" *The Urban Review, 18*(3), 149–217.

# Acknowledgments

I battled the crippling effects of Lyme disease while completing this volume, and my part could not have been completed without prayers, a loving family, a thoughtful doctor, and patience from Barbara Bernstein at Hampton Press and Chris Myers at Peter Lang Publishing. Therefore, I thank God. I thank my earth angel mother, Maiseville Victoria Hughes, my resilient father, Jessie Hughes, Sr., my six siblings, and the rest of my North Carolina Hughes family. I thank my wife, Megan Hughes, her parents, Don and Trish Hoert, and the rest of my Ohio Hoert family. I am grateful for the brilliance of my family doctor, Dr. Jennifer Rabenhorst, MD. A special thank you is also extended to my colleagues, Dr. Theodorea Berry and Dr. Marvin Lynn, for their ongoing academic critiques and social support. Gratitude is extended to my worship families at Takoma Park Presbyterian Church of Maryland, to New Sawyer's Creek Missionary Baptist Church and Philadelphia Missionary Baptist Church of Camden County, North Carolina, as well as to the United Church of Chapel Hill. I thank my academic family of past and present peers, students, faculty, and staff who continue to challenge and inspire me. I am sincerely grateful for the work of Hampton Press Education and Policy Series Editors, Dr. George Noblit and Dr. William Pink and Peter Lang Publishing Series Editors. Finally, I owe much appreciation to Chris Myers, Patricia Mulrane, Heather Boyle,

Bernadette Shade, and Frank Liska of Peter Lang Publishing. They have supported my work from day one and their professionalism is unprecedented. I dedicate my part in this volume to my 6-year-old daughter, Micah Victoriana Hughes. Each day my soul is lifted by her thirst for learning, music, athletics, crafts, and humour, coupled with her early passions for fairness, forgiveness, fun, and friendship. When I grow up, I want to be more like her.

SHERICK HUGHES

Similar to the chapters included in this volume, my continued journey as a scholar-activist has included various chapters of enlightenment, tribulations, and accomplishments. I foremost attribute my ability to live and learn through these chapters of my life through the power of the Holy Trinity, who makes all things possible. It is with sincere appreciation that I acknowledge my family, past and present. Special thanks are extended to my colleagues, Dr. Sherick Hughes, Dr. Christine Sleeter, and Dr. Marvin Lynn. Gratitude is extended to my parish family at Saint Philip Neri Catholic Church and my beloved sorors of Delta Sigma Theta Sorority, Inc. Most important, we wish to thank all of the contributors of this volume. Your willingness to contribute works of scholar-activism is appreciated. May your tremendously powerful, spiritual, thought-provoking words not only provide fuel for such burning activism but also ignite new flames for change.

THEODOREA REGINA BERRY

# About the Cover

The cover art is intended to portray the evolving significance of race through a tree metaphor that perhaps, becomes most evident after a brief introduction to the tree: Emancipation Oak. Circa 1907, the smaller one of the two photos in the top left corner of the cover, allows us to see the oak as it likely appeared to the local Black community of Hampton, VA in 1863. That year the function of the oak evolved from a meeting place for Black teachers and students into a site where local Black folks gathered to hear the first Southern reading of the Emancipation Proclamation. It was this reading that earned the tree its Emancipation Oak namesake. The larger photograph centered on the cover was taken in 2007 and it portrays this live oak as it most likely appears today in its original soil at Hampton University. While the tree has not evolved scientifically into another species, it has arguably shown signs of an "evolutionary" adaptation not only through its longevity and changing form, but also in its changing function overtime. With the abolishment of slavery, Emancipation Oak now caters largely to a global Black community of the Black Diaspora, their allies, and the faculty, students, and staff of Hampton University. Contemporary visitors of the oak do so virtually and in person to find reflection, inspiration, and spiritual guidance.

# INTRODUCTION

Sherick Hughes, Theodorea Regina Berry, & Rod Carey

President Obama (then Senator Obama) aroused a sense of urgency regarding the evolving significance of race on March 18, 2008, in his "A More Perfect Union" oratory. He spoke to the issues of structure, culture, and their interactions while "taking on the tough topic of race in America . . . [with] the kind of careful political framing . . . we need in this country in order to move forward" (Wilson, 2009, p. 3). William Julius Wilson (2009), author of the groundbreaking article *More than just race: Being Black and poor in the inner city* and the book *The Declining Significant of Race*, was drawn to President Obama's speech while he was considering a "change of frame—indeed, a change of mindset on race and poverty" and politics (p. 11). In his previous seminal writings on race, Wilson called for color-blindness and race neutrality. Within the evolving significance of race and U.S. public education, one can juxtapose a president self-identifying as African American with incessant forms of educational inequities that disproportionately plague African Americans, Latinos, and the impoverished. The newness of the significance of race in the Obama era is replete with new manifestations of old racial problems such as disproportionality, as well as new opportunities. For example, although K-16 education remains a site of racializing, sorting machines, it is also a site of critical race thinking and actions toward liberation like no other time in American history. Indeed, a more careful political framing of race in education is necessary today if we are to address the shortfalls and critiques of a previous agenda framed by former supporters of color-blindness and race-neutrality (e.g., Wilson, 2009). The difficulties of implementing this agenda in ways "to generate the broad political support necessary to enact legislation" (Wilson, 2009, p. 11) ultimately seems to have led to Wilson's (2009) unprecedented change in his position on the declining significance of race:

> So now my position has changed: In framing public policy, we should not shy away from an explicit discussion of the specific issues of race and poverty; on the contrary, we should highlight them in our attempt to convince the nation that these problems should be seriously confronted and that there is an urgent need to address them. The issues of race and poverty should be framed in such a way that not only a sense of fairness and justice to combat inequality is generated, but also people are made aware that our country would be better off if these problems were seriously addressed and eradicated. (pp. 10–11)

In line with Wilson (2009), we find the evolving significance of race offering an ever-increasing need for dismantling master narratives (Romeo & Stewart, 1999) and for revising our original conceptualizations of race and its relationship to lived experiences in North America (Aboud & Doyle, 1996; Delpit, 1995; Hughes, 2003a, 2004; Ladson-Billings, 1998; Ladson-Billings & Tate, 1995) and throughout the globe (Hughes, 2003b). The review of scholarship cited earlier recognizes race or, perhaps more accurately, how understandings of race play out as a factor that *does* make a difference in the praxis of educational institutions, preservice teacher education, teachers' lesson and unit implementation, and, perhaps most important, the degree to which varying students representing different racial experiences come to reach their highest potential in particular educational subjects and settings.

In the spirit of critical race pedagogy (Jennings & Lynn, 2005; Lynn, 1999), this book addresses problems and possibilities of living, learning, and teaching about "race" while remaining cognizant of other interlocking systems of inequity (Hill-Collins, 1990; Wing, 1997), such as class, gender, religion, and sexual orientation. *The Evolving Significance of Race: Living, Learning, and Teaching* is a book tapping the expertise of other educators, activists, and researchers within and outside the field of education that will address race and education from multiple perspectives that allow us to center race without the mandate for decentering other forms of oppression (Hill-Collins, 1990). In this volume, race is centered on critiques of how it is used for inferring human group differences largely based on superficial, physically observable differences (e.g., Eberhardt & Fiske, 1998). Although the notion of race as a social construct is necessary, it is insufficient because few scholars (e.g., Gossett, 1997) are explaining how race came to be such a detrimental *living* construct. And "the race is a social construction" statement alone is limited in explanatory strength for answering tougher questions "if race is merely a social construction, why is it so persistent, debilitating, and power-driven in educational settings and in lived experiences?" (Bowers, 1984) and "So what can we do about it?"

The evolving significance of race also involves complicated conversations (Pinar, 2004) around equity that are addressed in this volume. Equity has eluded many of us in the field for reasons that may be just as numerous. Attempts to provide every child and adult learner with what he or she needs to make the most of their educational experiences are still consciously and unconsciously thwarted by fundamental attribution errors evident in our (a) teaching audiences that represent diverse political experiences of race, (b) teaching diverse audiences about the evolving significance of race, and (c) teaching diverse audiences to develop a more critical, reflexive lens focused on the new politics of race. Traditionally, liberals and conservatives alike have public and private transcripts (Scott, 1990) reflecting beliefs that "students of any 'race' should adapt my teaching style because my style is a colorblind, one size fits all approach." The diverse array of authors in this book are finding empowering ways to begin co-constructing and connecting their own experiences of the evolving significance of race and struggle with their experiences of the evolving significance of race and hope. In this way, we acknowledge that race is inextricably tied (Watkins, Lewis, & Chou, 2001) to our living, learning, and teaching experiences. There are at least three interdependent challenges posited here as evidence of an evolving significance of race. These challenges are organized into the following three parts:

I: Living, Learning, and Teaching Youth
II: Living, Learning, and Teaching Teachers
III: Living, Learning, and Teaching for a Political Future

# I: Living, Learning, and Teaching Youth

It is commonly stated that youth are 100% of our future. This section is intended to challenge the ideology that all U.S. Black, White, Asian, and Latino children are separate "races" rather than being separated by historical and new political experiences of race that in tandem comprise intergenerational self versus other identification (i.e., Black, White, Latino, gay, etc.) and drives intergenerational senses of the worth and civility of the self versus others. Authors in this section suggest that we must understand youth perspectives and not ignore evidence arguing that the traditional and prevailing concept of a "natural" racial hierarchy is a misnomer that begins at birth and is salient among elementary- and high school-age kids. They remind us that achievement gaps by "race" are also misleading descriptions of educational outcomes and tendencies, and they confront how an adult stakeholder can continue to cripple youth if he or she denies and devalues sociohistorical, sociocultural influences on lived experiences and educational disparities (Hilliard, 1999; Montagu, 1975; Wells, Holme, Revilla, & Atanda, 2005).

Theodorea Berry begins Part I with a reflective Chapter 1, uncovering how her relationship with her father and with schools helped construct and deconstruct her notions of gender and racial roles in society. Drawing on Adrien Wing's (1997) scholarship, Berry notes when she discovered and engaged critical race feminism while in graduate school. In that space, she was able to finally resolve some of the inherent societal contradictions she faced by living, learning, and teaching through the social constructions of "Black," "female," and "smart" her entire life. Although other theoretical frameworks seek to disassemble identity into Black and female categories, critical race feminism seeks to marry these identities as indivisible, intertwined, and functioning simultaneously, which for Berry provides a powerful starting place to frame her thinking and acting for equity and equality.

In Chapter 2, Brian Schultz confronts the notion of the "White savior" in urban classrooms and discusses the color-blind lens many of these well-meaning teachers use when viewing their roles and positionality in educating Black students. Schultz provides a thoughtful chapter that reveals how his role as a fifth-grade teacher to his Black students at a low-income Chicago school was influenced by his identity as being both White and privileged. Instead of donning color-blind lenses, Schultz, in an effort to build relationships and confront the inherent power dimensions of his role and status in relation to his students, embraced the racial and class-based conflicts inherent in his practice and created a classroom space where issues or race, class and privilege were openly discussed and dissected.

Similarly, in Chapter 3, Sachi Feris discusses a revolutionary program that actively engages racially and ethnically separated students from the second through sixth grade to gather and explore issues inherent in social inequity and discrimination. Founded in 2001 by Feris, Border Crossers (www.border-crossers.org) is a social justice advocacy organization in New York City, whose purpose is to bridge the divide between students who might live relatively close in geographic proximity but are separated racially and demographically. In this chapter, Feris details the theoretical conceptions and curriculum of Border Crossers, the instructional strategies implemented in the program, and its goals and struggles as it provides meaningful leadership education for diverse young students to actively dismantle the borders that separate them.

In Chapter 4, Connie North, who conducted research at a Facing History and Ourselves youth leadership program, examines how an impromptu, yet appropriate, discussion arose on students' beliefs about homosexuality. North discusses how an analogy made by the program director between the civil rights movement and homophobia triggered a dialogue between this diverse group of teenagers, where they were encouraged to openly dialogue about how their sentiments of homosexuality were deeply interconnected, and in many ways disconnected, from their sentiments on prejudice, social justice, and discrimination for oppressed racial groups. North posits the importance of teachers and students to create space for these discussions of difference to avoid silencing those deemed *other* and to nudge students to interrogate oppressive societal constructions such as sexuality.

In Chapter 5, Tara Brown, Summer Clark, and Thurman Bridges discuss an innovative approach to teacher education and professional development to combat the lack of preparation that many new teachers have for teaching students from cultural backgrounds different from their own. Drawn from participatory action research, Action Research Into School Exclusion (ARISE) promotes the betterment of school experiences for students who have been excluded, mostly for disciplinary reasons. The model they propose encourages cross-cultural encounters with youth by bringing K-12 students of color into the teacher education classroom so teachers may learn from students' expertise and to challenge their own perceptions of low-income adolescents of color. This chapter discusses the implementation of this program where adolescent students co-facilitated teacher-training workshops to help bridge the seemingly impossible cultural and racial divides between teachers and students, to improve the culturally relevant teaching practices of new teachers, and to improve the school experiences for students of color.

# II: Living, Learning, and Teaching Teachers

Because we, as teachers, are limited in time and/or dispositions toward critical reflexivity and self-critiques of our own racial perspectives (due partially to constraints from national and state educational structure and standards), we base our expectations for which "race" is and which "race" can be *smart* or *intelligent* (Oakes & Lipton, 2003) in a given learning context without considering the influences of our hidden rules and norms on student success—rules and norms founded on the social factors separating the educational oppressors from the educationally oppressed (Kumashiro, 2001). This history weaves a complex relational web of (a) genotype (human capacities for survival in geographic space), (b) phenotype (degree to which survival and social mobility depend on physical characteristics, observable resemblance, and immediately traceable genetics to claim ancestry with the group in power; if power is multiplicity of force [numerical differences, technology, innovation, natural resources, etc.], and ability to manipulate human relations through that force), and (c) politics (the degree to which human groups have access to power, believe it is inevitable, or aspire for same power that oppresses us). The challenge of Part II is to address the politics of race and possibilities in the classroom from teacher educators' perspectives.

In Chapter 6, Rita Kohli writes about interviews she conducted with nine women of color enrolled in an undergraduate education program in Southern California. After unravelling White cultural dominance in classroom discourse, Kohli provides a biographical account of her experiences with racial discrimination in schools and then provides a brief literature review on Critical Race Theory, which informed her processing of teacher interviews in this study. Underlying much of the teachers' narratives were racial encounters that helped reaffirm societal views of their inferiority in schools. Kohli notes that these experiences of racial discrimination influenced how teachers of color approached their lives and their work with minority students, and thus created a cycle. In an effort to break these cycles of racism, Kohli advocates for the voice of teachers of color to be heard and reflected on, as leaving their voices silenced and their experiences invisible would allow this cycle to continue in teachers' own practices with minority youth.

In Chapter 7, Sherick Hughes discusses how autoethnography and Critical Race Pedagogy (Jennings & Lynn, 2005) can be utilized as effective tools to better investigate how parts of individuals' categorized selves, such as race, class, or gender, impacts researchers' work with others. In this chapter, Hughes contends that any sustainable school reform must begin with critical reflexivity or rather an inquiry stance that admits researcher positionality and considers how researcher involvement could influence results, in addition to subsequent collective action. For his investigation, Hughes writes about his efforts to teach teachers considering his position as a Black, male professor from a working poor background, teaching mostly female, White teachers at a university in the Midwest. Hughes draws from his experiences with one of these students, "Maggie," to illustrate how autoethnography and Critical Race Pedagogy can serve as powerful tools to disrupt assumptions and biases when teaching for social change.

In Chapter 8, Hilton Kelly draws from DuBois' (1903) notion of "double consciousness" and critiques its contemporary implications in current contexts of intersectionality and multiple identity theories. Kelly notes that when "consciousness" is considered in this double consciousness (two souls, two thoughts, and two unreconciled strivings) frame, it again becomes relevant to all people with marginal identities in this society still grappling with "otherness." Kelly draws on narratives from teachers who taught in segregated schools, discussing how these teachers strategically used double consciousness with their students to combat marginalization during segregation. Kelly concludes with investigating how double consciousness can be utilized in a contemporary multicultural classroom and discusses the questions that implementation might raise for teachers and schools.

After receiving his PhD in education, Ben Blaisdell returned to teach English as a second language at a Southern elementary school. In Chapter 9, Blaisdell writes about his autoethnographic study on his experiences at this school, with a focus on his attempts to promote antiracism and racial equity in the classroom. Blaisdell highlights three particular barriers to antiracism that he encountered at the school. The first is standards-based reform, which Blaisdell deems as inhospitable to culturally responsive teaching. The second is the technocratic leadership ideology, whereas a limited outside view of school culture is adopted rather than created in schools. The third is the stringent adherence to a liberal ideology, which masks the social inequities inherent in schooling because of the underlying assumption of schooling being a socially just institution. Blaisdell concludes with discussions of how teacher education can be informed by Critical Race Theory, with the hope being to educate and motivate teachers to work diligently to remove racial and ethnic barriers and locate and resist inequity in schooling.

In Chapter 10, Theodorea Berry poses and investigates the essential questions around how prospective teachers come to understand fairness in the context of the classroom and why fairness is important for them to consider as emerging educators. Berry discusses how she artfully constructed a lesson where students experienced and confronted issues of equity. For her mostly Black pre-service teachers, her pedagogy on the *Brown v. Board of Education* decision focused on highlighting the important distinctions between equality and equity in education. Using critical autoethnography, informed by critical race feminism as a theoretical framework, Berry candidly discusses the lessons she gleaned about power and positionality for herself as a teacher. She concludes by writing about her hope that these lessons will be internalized by her students and transfer from the hearts and lives of the preservice teachers to the hearts and minds of their future students.

In Chapter 11, Josh Diem discusses the current state of the relationship between Jews and Blacks in the United States and indicates why dissecting this relationship might matter for teacher education. Diem begins unpacking some of the shared historical traits between American Jews and Blacks, citing their heterogeneity, their deep ancestral roots, their complex histories with each other, and their shared reality as two historically marginalized groups. Admitting that his understandings are partial but still worth sharing, Diem writes about how interactions with some of his Jewish preservice teachers and personal reflections on them have left him troubled about how current Jewish cultural shifts to the "right" create limited spaces to critically engage with issues of race, class, gender, ethnicity, religion, and sexuality. Diem is also troubled with how these issues are not taken up in teacher education programs and confronted in the deeply meaningful and fruitful ways that promote social change.

## III: Living, Learning, and Teaching for a Political Future

Due to a misrepresentation of historical politics of race, we (as individuals, groups, and institutions) act on racial prejudice in self-justifiable and more incorrigible ways. To become a U.S. racist, one must first and foremost hold a misunderstanding of the myth of "race" as a *real entity influencing human capacities* in education and elsewhere (Hilliard, 1999; Montagu, 1975). The widely cited W. I. Thomas theorem suggests that if a myth, like "race," is socially defined as true, then it is real in its consequences. So the misunderstanding of race can lead some authors to equate IQ and race without deconstructing IQ and without considering sociohistorical forces, which account for 100% of differences in group educational outcomes. Racial prejudice is not a synonym for racist, but certainly at worst it is a key factor in racist acts (Eberhardt & Fiske, 1998), and at best it is a sign of in-group ignorance and/or insensitivity. Arguably, educators throughout the world, at least occasionally, are guilty of one or more of the following offenses: (a) exaggeration of "racial" in-group similarities and between-group differences, (b) exaggeration of "racial" in-group and out-group characteristics rendering human tendencies inevitable and unchanging and subsequently self-fulfilling, and (c) delivery of commentary and other communicative acts consistent with beliefs in "racial" group hierarchy (e.g., Asian students are naturally better at mathematics) (Blum, 2002; Hughes, 1998). Unfortunately, "Americans tend to de-emphasize the structural origins and social significance of poverty . . ." and "explanations focusing on the cultural traits of inner-city [Black and Brown] residents are likely to draw far more attention from policymakers and the general public than structural explanations will" (Wilson, 2009, p. 2).

Without further problematizing and then reframing the U.S. history of political economy in relation to race and education, we will certainly dismiss key issues that influence opportunities to learn. We might do well by seeking accessible praxis that will not only show up in our academic journals but also in the hands of policymakers. Wilson (2009) concurs with our optimism "just because cultural explanations resonate with policymakers and the public today does not mean that structural explanations cannot resonate with them tomorrow" (p. 10). The challenge of Part III is to connect historical federal, state, and local education policies to current political economy issues and possibilities at the intersection of race and education (i.e., Jim Crow, The New Deal, the G.I. Bill, No Child Left Behind [NCLB], Affirmative Action, and *Brown v. Topeka*).

Chapter 12 by Leticia Alvarez and Francisco Rios begins with vivid personal narratives from various Latino high school teens who represent new immigrants in a mostly White community articulates the range of negative interactions these students have with both students and adults in their school communities. Alvarez and Rios discuss the tensions between student groups and between teachers and students in a school setting experiencing a major influx of newcomer students. Situating the school culture in a broader political context, where these new immigrants are valued for their contributions to the economic development of the community, Alvarez and Rios note that these students are also simultaneously resented and discriminated against in the community and school. Alvarez and Rios assert that the interpersonal relations at the school site reside within the sociopolitical context of the school, which resides within the sociopolitical context of the local community. Toward the end, the authors provide specific implications for schools and other communities grappling with similar issues.

In Chapter 13, Dedrick Muhammad and Chuck Collins cite the Black–White racial wealth divide as a primary obstacle to racial reconciliation in the United States. The authors assert that the myth permeating contemporary culture of how private wealth is created through individual effort solely is a tragic misperception because it ignores the various forms of "common wealth" that we have and share all around us. Common wealth can arise not only from nature, such as fisheries, seeds, animals, and from the soil, but also can emerge from social or knowledge wealth, such as libraries, transportation, music, indigenous medicine, or the Internet. What Muhammad and Collins assert is that, although Black labor has added tremendously to the building of common wealth, Whites have had much more access to capitalizing on this wealth in the form of individual, government, and corporate efforts that have systematically and systemically excluded Blacks, indigenous peoples, and other marginalized groups from accessing these resources equally. Citing numerous examples of how Whites have benefited at greater proportions to institutions such as the GI Bill, Social Security, and the Homestead Act of the 1880s, Muhammad and Collins call for a rethinking, reinvestment, and redistribution of common wealth and other civic investments for a broadening of educational access, opportunity, and wealth.

In Chapter 14, Cooper Thompson provides an honest and illuminating account of how he, as a White male, has historically benefited and continues to profit financially and socially from the systematic and systemic forms of racism in America. Thompson provides historical accounts of how, beginning in 17th-century America his paternal and maternal ancestors used their Whiteness and social positioning to acquire land and even slaves to help create wealth and security for the family. In addition to offering detailed histories of decisions and transactions that helped his family build wealth and status in early America, Thompson concurs with Muhammad and Collins by addressing directly the more specific federal policies, housing regulations, restrictions, and financial investments that have all allowed him to create and maintain wealth in ways that may not have been accessible if he were a man of color. Admitting that many Blacks would agree with his assertions, Thompson then addresses the anxiety, especially among Whites, that comes with such a discussion and provides challenges to White political leaders specifically to address the legacy of racism in our nation.

In Chapter 15, Goodwin Liu discusses the commonly held myth that race-conscious affirmative action policies at public universities that benefit minority students in admissions processes for selective colleges and universities make it much more difficult for Whites to gain admission to the same schools. Liu investigates the popular cases of Jennifer Gratz, who was denied admission to the University of Michigan in 1995 (and claimed reverse discrimination), and Allan Bakke, who in 1978 was awarded admission into the University of California at Davis' medical school claiming that reserving 16 of 100 seats in the admitted class for minority students was unconstitutional. While Bakke was a stellar student in his undergraduate program, Liu discusses that other factors, including compassion and communication skills, were traits uncovered in his interview that proved that he was "rather limited in his approach" to medical problems. Using basic arithmetic coupled with statistical probability, Liu discovers that for Bakke, given the 1974 applicant pool of 3,109, the likelihood for admission for regular students was 2.7% (84 divided by 3,109). The likelihood of rejection would have increased from 96.8% to 97.3% given the racial quota. After uncovering numerous other examples of how misunderstood math has led to the myths and misunderstandings surrounding affirmative action, the author provides insights that would lead to what Liu refers to as a rethinking of the race-based admissions policies that seemingly pit Whites against minorities in a zero-sum game. This reprint of Liu's 2002 essay is particularly timely in the wake of the Supreme Court's recent summer 2007 decision against the race-conscious public schooling policies of Louisville and Seattle.

In Chapter 16, Sherick Hughes and Dale Snauwaert address the dangerous assumption that all members of colleges of education understand the importance of implementing policies and procedures that support diversity. Hughes and Snauwaert were charged by a Recruitment and Retention Sub-Committee to respond to a simplistic, yet complex question: "Why is diversity important to the university? In this chapter, Hughes and Snauwaert address more specifically, "Why is it important to work toward an informed and transparent philosophy of racial diversity in colleges of education?" They provide evidence for four tenets that would support such a philosophy: (a) checks and balances of the law, (b) optimal decision making, (c) social justice, and (d) peace.

In Chapter 17, Zeus Leonardo discusses how confronting centuries-old racism in America remains as a paramount political and social agenda, especially regarding high-stakes testing. Leonardo frames NCLB as a racial text that implies an attempt at creating color-blindness in educational policy. Leonardo asserts that NCLB does not implicate a vulgar color-blindness but rather a more sophisticated color-blindness, whereby racial symptoms and not its structural causes are considered. Leonardo sees the "pull yourselves up by your own schoolstraps" mentality as lacking the appreciation for the racial conditions in which schools are nested. He further critiques NCLB as a program that will perpetuate oppressive racial structures. Leonardo connects his work to the scholarship of Eduardo Bonilla-Silva to call for an exchange of color-blind discourse for a more color-conscious one that confronts the evolving significance of race and exposes educational policies that continue to reveal an appreciation of Whiteness at the expense of racially and economically marginalized groups.

Following Chapter 17 is an alternative dialogic counternarrative in the form of an interview. Authors were encouraged to submit alternatives to the traditional book chapter as part of the original call in *Teachers College Record*. The interview details an infamous January 2010 airport security experience of Nadia Hassan and her 5-year-old daughter, Rayanah. Building on the *USA Today* and CNN reports of her experience, Nadia Hassan felt the interview for this book "could add more content, context, clarity, and transparency for anyone willing to hear [her] voice on the matter." Her counternarrative challenges readers to recognize patterns of racialization, misrepresentation, and mistreatment of Muslim women and their families in post-9/11 America and to revisit the ideological connections of Muslims, Jews, and Christians en route to future collaboration, reconciliation, social justice, and peace. The interview is followed by an alternative Afterword. Authors were invited to respond to the prompt, "I hope political leaders of the present and future work toward/advocate for, etc. . . . ." Authors' responses essentially offer recommendations to current and prospective political leaders, voters, and the general public who are living, learning, and teaching at the intersection where the significance of race evolves and the promises of educational theory and practice are challenged.

# References

Aboud, F. E., & Doyle, A. B. (1996, July). Does talk of race foster prejudice or tolerance in children? *Canadian Journal of Behavioural Science, 28*(3), 161–170.

Blum, L. (2002) *"I'm not a racist, but . . .": The moral quandary of race.* Ithaca, NY: Cornell University Press.

Bowers, C. (1984). *The promise of theory.* New York: Longman.

Delpit, L. (1995). *Other people's children: Cultural conflict in the classroom.* New York: New Press.

Du Bois, W. E. B. (1903). *The souls of Black folks.* Chicago: A. C. McClurg & Co.

Eberhardt, J. L., & Fiske, S. T. (Eds.). (1998). *Confronting racism: The problem and the response.* Thousand Oaks, CA: Sage.

Gossett, T. F. (1997). *Race: The history of an idea in America.* Dallas, TX: Southern Methodist University Press.

Hill-Collins, P. (1990). *Black feminist thought in the matrix of domination: Black feminist thought: Knowledge, consciousness, and the politics of empowerment* (pp. 221–238). London: HarperCollins.

Hilliard, A. G. III (1999, Winter). "Race," identity, hegemony, and education: What do we know? *Rethinking Schools,* pp. 4–6.

Hughes, S. A. (1998, October 8). Free speech shouldn't protect hate groups. *Old Goldand Black,* 82(6), A8.

Hughes, S. A. (2003a, December). An early gap in Black-White math achievement:Holding school and home accountable in an affluent city school district. *The Urban Review,* 35(4), 301–330.

Hughes, S. A. (2003b, January). The convenient scapegoating of Blacks in postwarJapan: Shaping the Black experience abroad. *Journal of Black Studies,* 33(3), 335–354.

Hughes, S. A. (2004). Beyond the silenced dialogue: What we tell ourselves when the White academy ain't hearing us. In D. Cleveland (Ed.), *A long way to go: Conversations about "race" by African American faculty and students on the journey to the professoriate* (pp. 58–71). New York: Peter Lang.

Jennings, M., & Lynn, M. (2005, Summer–Fall). The house that race built: Critical pedagogy, African-American education, and the re-conceptualization of a critical race pedagogy. *Educational Foundations,* 19(3–4), 15–32.

Kumashiro, K. K. (2001). "Posts" perspectives on anti-oppressive education in social studies, English, mathematics, and science classrooms. *Educational Researcher,* 30(3), 3–12.

Ladson-Billings, G. (1998). Just what is critical race theory and what's it doing in a nice field like education? *Qualitative Studies in Education,* 11(1), 7–24.

Ladson-Billings, G., & Tate, W. F. (1995). Toward a critical race theory of education. *Teachers College Record,* 97(1), 47–68.

Lynn, M. (1999). Toward a critical race pedagogy: A research note. *Urban Education,* 33, 606–626.

Montagu, A. (1975). *Race and IQ.* New York: Oxford University Press.

Oakes, J., & Lipton, M. (2003). *Teaching to change the world.* New York: McGraw-Hill.

Pinar, W. (2004). *What is curriculum theory?* Mahwah, NJ: Lawrence Erlbaum Associates.

Romeo, M., & Stewart, A. J. (Eds.). (1999). *Women's untold stories: Breaking silence, talking back, voicing complexity.* New York: Routledge.

Scott, J. C. (1990). *Domination and the arts of resistance: Hidden transcripts.* New Haven, CT: Yale University Press.

Watkins, W. H., Lewis, J., & Chou, V. (Eds.). (2001). *Race and education: The roles of history and society in educating African American students.* Boston: Allyn & Bacon.

Wells, A. S., Holme, J. J., Revilla, A. J., & Atanda, A. K. (2005). How society failed school deseg-
    regation policy: Looking past the schools to understand them. *Review of Research in
    Education, 28* (Special Issue for the *Brown* Anniversary), 47–100.
Wilson, W. J. (2009, May/June). More than just race: Being Black and poor in the inner city.
    *Poverty and Race, Poverty & Race Research Action Council, 18*(3), 1, 9–11.
Wing, A. (1997). *Critical race feminism: A reader.* New York: New York UniversityPress.

# PART I

# LIVING, LEARNING, AND TEACHING YOUTH

· 1 ·

# Father, Daughter, and Schooling

## Curriculum Theorizing From a Critical Race Feminist Perspective

THEODOREA REGINA BERRY

Blame it on my dad. It's all his fault. Born of a Bajan man he never knew (and it's not what you think) and raised by a southern, educated, no-nonsense woman, he was a walking contradiction. The man could cook and clean like nobody's business. He taught us all (my siblings and I) how to wash, dry, and iron our clothes to a crisp. He taught us to make our beds so tight that you could toss a quarter on it and it would bounce. And because he was such a math wiz, he was the one who checked over our homework on a daily basis.

However, he divided household chores among my siblings and I by gender: My sister and I did the inside work (washing dishes, dusting, etc.) while my three brothers did the outside work (taking out the trash, shoveling snow, etc.). We were each responsible for the care and cleanliness of our own bedrooms.

As far as school was concerned, however, we were all equal. My father expected each of us to attend school daily, be punctual, mind our teachers, and work hard. He expected all of us to do well in the liberal arts as well as the sciences. My sister and I were expected to perform as well in math and science as my brothers were to perform in English and history. Failure was never an option.

Socially, I was expected to play with dolls, jump rope, wear frilly dresses, and be polite. Wearing sneakers to school was a no-no. "Sneakers are for the gymnasium," I would hear him say. Climbing trees and playing freeze tag or dodge ball was not considered lady-like. And even though I was usually quiet and shy around many adults, when I had something to say it was, usually, definitive and decisive. Hell, I was just downright blunt. Neither one of my parents knew how to handle my unexpected choice of words.

So, as a child of the 1970s, I was expected to be feminist and feminine. I was to be smart, thought-full/thoughtful, and lady-like. I was to be domesticated and opinionated. I just wanted to climb the tree in front of my house and play freeze tag with the fellas. Instead, I could see my father standing on the porch looking at me as if sending a message telepathically. "Stop playing, get out of that bloody tree, come inside, wash the dishes, and do your studies." As the middle child and the firstborn daughter, I was expected to set an example of femininity for my sister (3 years my junior) and my three brothers (two older and one younger) while exhibiting cultural pride and loyalty through my academic prowess. Way too many complex identities for me to possess, process, and operationalize. I mean, really, who was I supposed to be? I couldn't really be expected to be all of these identities all at once.

This chapter is a counternarrative of the influences of fathering to a daughter and the curriculum notions of growing up feminist. In the spirit of currere, past and present educational stories here lead down the road to a theoretical framework I have embraced: critical race feminism.

Fast forward about 30 years. I think of my father now in the past tense, ever thankful for being, for me, a walking contradiction and setting me on a path toward understanding my multiple, intersecting, and complex identities. And I thank my mother, a near memory of recent history, for pushing me to want to know more. It was her example that led me to Adrien Katherine Wing and her work on critical race feminism. Her scholarship on multiplicative praxis (Wing, 1997a), which creates spaces by which scholars can exercise the multiple and intersecting ways of being through their work, has proven pivotal in the merger of my scholarship with my identities.

Before this, I struggled to merge my academic endeavors with my Bajan-American urban sense of femininity: Blackness as strength, femininity as weakness. This became especially problematic in the seventh grade. I was bussed to what was supposed to be one of the better middle schools in the city, but I found myself in classes with what I believed were average students. It's not that I thought I was better than my classmates, but I was very aware that I knew more than they did. The teachers taught for them and rarely pushed any of us to discover more so, naturally, I was bored. In an attempt to "fit in," I tried to "help" one of the only classmates I considered a friend.

Tracey and I were about the same height with about the same build and complexion. This is where the similarities ended. She was the youngest of two children of a single mother living in a neighborhood southwest of the community where I lived. But, more important to this story, Tracey was, at best, a C average student. Our science teacher, Mr. G., was the most challenging of the seventh-grade faculty. Tracey struggled in this class, earning Ds and Fs on her tests. Mr. G. was giving a midterm test that would cover all of the material we had studied thus far. About a week before the test, I asked Tracey how she thought she would do. "I think I'm gonna fail, but I don't care," she replied. I agreed to help her study during the lunch period each day until the test. But no matter what I did to help her, she just didn't seem to understand the information. On test day, I finished first, as usual. But when I looked over to Tracey, who sat directly across from me, I noticed she was still on the first page of an eight-page test. She looked over at me, sadly, then took out a piece of paper, wrote something on it, and passed it to me when Mr. G. wasn't looking. "HELP ME" were the words written on the piece of paper. I balled up the piece of paper and stuck it inside of my shoe. Then I took out another piece of paper and started copying the answers to the test on it. As I attempted to pass my piece of paper to Tracey, Mr. G. walked over to us, took the paper from my hand, and then took our test papers and marked large letter Fs on them in red ink. I was stunned. I had never received an F in my life. Shortly after the test was over, and Mr. G. called Tracey and me to the front of the classroom while he excused the rest of the class. I pleaded with him not to punish Tracey and to allow her to retest, proclaiming that she didn't ask for the answers (I lied). He said he would think about it depending on the outcome of a meeting with my parents.

Parent–teacher meetings were usually laden with complaints of my smart-aleck syndrome from teachers who looked forward to the two days each week I went to another school for an academically talented pullout program. At the time, I didn't realize that their complaints were just masks for the inadequacies as teachers, recognizing that they did not have the professional skills or the cultural capital to teach me, unlike my elementary school teachers, who all lived in or around my home community. Mr. G. was no exception. He explained to my father that I was normally an A student but that my behavior on that occasion warranted an F. My father agreed, not understanding that I was trying to help a friend. My classmates who normally complained about my consistent As and teased me for my skinny frame and braces (for which I got into periodic fights) were elated. I was just trying to be everything I was supposed to be. At the end of the last parent–teacher meeting of the school year, I promised my father that I would figure out how to resolve all of the contradictions. Two years after his death, I was able to keep my promise to him.

Critical race feminism resolves those contradictions for me. I was in graduate school when I came across the work of Adrien Wing (1997b) with the hope of finding a theoretical framework that would embrace my experiences, my stories, and my multiple ways of being into my scholarship and praxis. I desired a framework that would appreciate the fact that I was a different kind of African-American woman and that my difference wasn't good or bad, just different. Critical race feminism not only integrates multiple and varying ways of understanding and being and issues of marginalization based on race but also addresses marginalization through the intersection of race and gender and offers ways to address all of these issues through storytelling as a counternarrative/counterstory to the mainstream and often oppressive ways of being. Counterstory, as described by Delgado (2000), is created by the outgroup, the members of the socially marginalized group, and is aimed to subvert the reality of the dominant group. For socially marginalized groups, this reality centers on a host of presuppositions, commonly held wisdoms, and shared understandings by the dominant group about the outgroup.

You see, this story and the many others in the educational memory of my father does not function, live, or exist, in isolation (Harris, 1997). It is intertwined with others' stories and counterstories that have now become part of my existence as a sister-scholar, researcher, and teacher educator. I share these stories through the multiple roles that I possess. My father emphasized the importance to do what is right and proper for a young girl, whereas the streets and my homies valued loyalty and fidelity. My teachers focused on individual learning and success, whereas my classmates hailed my willingness to help another buck the system. All the while, I just didn't want to see my friend fail. It's not that I believed any one of these people was more important than the others in my life; my life cannot be essentialized in such ways. They were all deeply connected to the person I was at that time. Our life stories were connected. This connectedness makes our stories stronger. What I reveal here is only one story that isn't truly my own. I do not own it because of its connectedness to others. Because I do not accept one prevailing story—the story that says that existing norms and modes of behavior and assessment of value, worth, and contribution are natural, inevitable, fair, and neutral—each story/counterstory bears questions and wonderings I alone cannot completely address.

As an African-American woman, I am more than just the sum of all my separate parts. I am one indivisible being (Wing, 1997b) whose life experiences and multiple identities are intertwined and interconnected, functioning simultaneously. Talking about my multiplicity simply isn't enough. I must act on it in ways that transcend stereotypical and, often, negative perceptions of our people. By doing so, I, as an educator, can attempt to address issues of equity and equality in the spaces I share with my students for the purpose of shared teaching and learning.

# References

Delgado, R. (2000). Storytelling for oppositionists and others: A plea for narrative. In R. Delgado & J. Stefancic (Eds.), Critical race theory: The cutting edge (2nd ed.). Philadelphia: Temple University Press.

Harris, A. P. (1997). Race and essentialism in feminist theory. In A. K. Wing (Ed.), Critical race feminism: A reader (pp. 11–18). New York: New York University Press.

Wing, A. K. (1997a). Brief reflections toward a multiplicative theory and praxis of being. In A. K. Wing (Ed.), Critical race feminism: A reader (pp. 3–7). New York: New York University Press.

Wing, A. K. (Ed.). (1997b). Critical race feminism: A reader. New York: New York University Press.

# · 2 ·

# Two Scoops Vanilla

## Teaching Against the Notion of White Savior

BRIAN D. SCHULTZ

The class thought they could gather more information about getting a new public school in Chicago by interviewing folks that had been around the community for a while. Jaris and Dyneisha arranged for Reverend Tinter—an African-American community member and president of Carr Community Academy's Local School Council—to come to our class for our first interview. We were able to role-play and mock the entire interview before the minister arrived. Everyone paid attention as I modelled with two boys how to set up a real interview and guide the responses. They were all very attentive and interested in the process. Together the class thought the best way to approach the interview would be to have the two students sit in the center of the room with the person being interviewed and the rest of the class assembled around the triad. One student commented appropriately it would be easier to catch everything the person says if one person asked questions and the other took notes. Another student mentioned this approach would be good because if one kid got scared the other could help. Instead of having Dyneisha interview, she decided that she wanted Demetrius to have the opportunity to be the interviewer along with Jaris. As we continued with the practice session, Jaris even took notes during our mock interviews so that he could ask some more probing or pertinent questions of Reverend Tinter. Then, he asked if he could talk about Blackness and that being a reason why they were not getting the school! At first I was taken aback by his question. Other teachers might have thought this topic was taboo or inappropriate. Other White teachers may have felt uncomfortable, but in this case I was so gratified; I had been working hard to have our classroom be a safe place to talk about race and power.

—EXCERPT FROM MY TEACHER REFLECTIVE JOURNAL

Jaris' desire to bring up race as the reason for the school's inequities showed how aware he was of the current disparity in educational resources for poor communities. That this student sought my permission to address such a topic demonstrated Jaris' understanding of power in our classroom. He understood that I served as a gatekeeper of classroom discourse and, as a result, controlled the knowledge permitted. Further, Jaris was keenly aware of how the politics of race and racism in this country positioned me as a White teacher quite differently than the African-American guest interviewee and his fellow fifth-grade peers. As a White teacher—even though I was deeply committed to anti-racist and anti-oppressive teaching—still positioned me as less expert. It was necessary for me to follow this student initiation. Not only did I need to assure the class that this project was being directed by their ideas, I needed to nurture the space to discuss issues related to race, positionality, and power. Thus, as the teacher, I needed to send a strong message that student content authority had a legitimate role in the classroom while also knowing that the complicated nature of race certainly needed to be problematized by me (Schultz & Oyler, 2006).

The short classroom vignette and interpretation introduced here is meant to set the tone for a theoretical and philosophical analysis of my race identity. As a fifth-grade teacher, I constantly worked to better understand the African-American students in my elementary classroom. Through a personal narrative, I examine how my race identity was constructed to reflect conscious and subconscious forms of racial knowledge. Through a journey of texts as well as context, my examined White race identity details how individual, institutional, and cultural racism may be investigated while I seek to find the space, resources, and processes to challenge such racisms. Through my reflections, I contextualize my identity in the classroom as an aspect of my political, professional, and personal development.

By examining the complicated and problematic nature of race in teaching, I attempt to better understand how race complicates my role as a teacher, especially given my inclination to promote a democratic classroom and enact a justice-oriented curriculum relevant to the lives of students in my classroom. As a fifth-grade elementary teacher in a school serving a public housing project in downtown Chicago, issues of positionality are at the forefront of understanding what it meant for me to teach young people in an urban area. I had choices about the environment in which I taught, whereas the African-American students in my classroom did not have the same choices about where they were to be taught. Coming from a White, middle-class, and seemingly comfortable environment (especially in terms of race, socioeconomic class, and gender), in addition to a privileged educational upbringing, my social location is paramount to continuous learning and reflective teaching.

## Modes of Inquiry

This speculative, philosophical text uses the written essay as a form of curriculum inquiry (Schubert, 1991) to examine the complicated and problematic nature of race in teaching. This methodological approach provides me with the opportunity to examine the common and cliché notions of "hero teacher" and "White saviour" through autobiographical inquiry (Pinar, 1994) and currere (Pinar & Grumet, 1976). By examining my teaching with attention to how I struggled with my experiences as a White teacher in a classroom comprised entirely of African-American students in a school that served a large, urban housing project in downtown Chicago, outsidedness (Bakhtin, 1986), perspective, and reflection became critical components of how I interpreted and made sense of culture and my role as a teacher within the classroom. Questions involving dominance, race, power, and the political nature of teaching challenged me to better understand what it means to be a teacher within this context. The complicatedness of teaching, along with my pondering into cultural and racial dynamics in the classroom, led me to wrestle with their implications. How did race impact decisions made with students and the curriculum? How can race complicate a White teacher's role when seeking to promote justice-oriented curricula in a democratic space? What does it look like when a White teacher challenges the common notion of saviour for students of color? As part of the dominant culture in the United States, how could I reconcile my identity as the teacher while connecting with my students and ultimately teaching for social justice?

Examinations of the implications and dimensionality of race helped me interpret the classroom, claim identity, trouble that identity, and ultimately better understand my teaching endeavors. Seeking to contextualize the lived experiences of my students in my writing, I consider what I emphasize or omit and how my personal educational experiences in school growing up contribute to my present interpretation. Further, through this speculative essay, the complexity of my teaching experiences becomes better understood as I work to consider how schooling and society misinforms my understanding and perceptions about the racial and the cultural other.

The complicated nature of race was and continues to be important to the examination of my teaching practice in order to promote, advocate, and facilitate justice (especially in school) for my students. By examining both culturally relevant pedagogy and culturally responsive teaching, coupled with a reflective examination of my experiences while allowing the curriculum to be based on student interest as the curricular starting point, I trouble race not in an effort to arrive at a finite conclusion. I do not intend to implicate whether the problematizing is good or bad or right or wrong. The intention to avoid ascribing to what Dewey (1938) called an either–or dichotomy, but instead to better understand my responsibility as a teacher and what my role was in working to make a difference in the lives and achievement of students in my classroom. Through a better understanding of my own experience and the journey described in this speculative essay, my hope is that other teachers resonate with my reflections and, as a result, may trouble their own positionality, while working to challenge their assumptions and teach against the teacher-hero-savior-narrative commonalities of White teachers in urban classrooms.

## Beginning to Reconcile the "Problem of the Color Line"

The ideas inherent to the progressive classroom that seek to incorporate democratic ideals and promote integrated, emergent curriculum can be seen as problematic, especially when concerned with race or as W. E. B. Dubois (1903) asserted, "the problem of the color-line" (p. vii). Whereas I aspired to having a classroom based on these democratic ideals I read about in the writing of Dewey, Schwab, and Hopkins, I realized that the foundations for such practices emerge from a biased, White-washed perspective. Encouraged by Ladson-Billings and Tate's (1995) call to examine "Critical race theory applied to education," I was forced "to rethink traditional educational scholarship" (p. 60) as it applied to my classroom situation. I wondered whether it was a possibility to do as DuBois (1903) proposed and "lift the Veil" (p. viii) for my students when the theorizers, researchers, and proponents of these progressive educational practices almost all come from a dominant cultural perspective, espousing values associated with privilege, power, and Whiteness.

Historically, progressive educational approaches rarely discuss these inherent power dynamics that exist when working with students of color. The students' communities and schools lack the access and resources that a White, middle-class, male teacher like myself had previously accepted as commonplace. As Carter G. Woodson (1933) stated in the *Mis-education of the Negro*, I was "able to choose [my] course because of the numerous opportunities offered" (p. 39) because of my racial perspective. My thoughtful inquiries into how "power plays a critical role in our society and in our educational system" (Delpit, 1995, p. xv), explicitly issues of race and its implications in education and teaching, needed to be addressed when I attempt to bring in my culture, values, experiences, and overall background into a classroom where I considered myself an outsider. Not only did I need to introspectively examine my "journey into understanding other worlds" (p. xv) as it created a problematic phenomenon, I needed to consciously look at how and why I wanted to tell stories of what occurred in my classroom with an all–African-American group of students. Because of "the haze of my own cultural lenses" (p. xv), my journey into reconciling the color line in my classroom was critical.

## Complicating and Complicated Good Intentions

Although my intentions were good, as are most teachers, I have come to understand that my background and positionality affected the ways in which I interpreted and made sense of the classroom and my students. Even my description of disadvantaged schools comes from my privileged cultural perspective. In an effort to think about and reflect on the way I interpreted the way I made sense of the classroom, I turned to more literature that help me reflect. Particularly, Woodson's (1933) claim affected the way I thought about the classroom and my descriptions of it:

> The same educational process which inspires and stimulates the oppressor with the thought that he is everything and has accomplished everything worthwhile, depresses and crushes at the same time the spark of genius in the Negro by making him feel his race does not account too much and never will measure up to the standards of other peoples. (p. xiii)

This idea raises valid questions that must be addressed: From whose viewpoint are the areas "disadvantaged"? Why are they disadvantaged? Is it my place or is it appropriate for me to want to bring my ideas or, better yet, my ideals of what this group of African-American students should have in their education? Moreover, how could I avoid making sure not to squelch the insight and genius of my students as Woodson (1933) implicates? I understand my students not as a different 'race' than me, but as affected differently by 'race' (Hughes, 2005) in ways similar to what Woodson and others describe and critique.

A reading of Lisa Delpit initially challenged my progressive teaching orientation. Her critique in "The Silenced Dialogue" (1988) of White educators in "the culture of power" thinking they knew best how to educate students of color resonated strongly with me. Delpit's prose more than once made me question my teaching approach. Her almost accusatory style made me realize I had to look at a bigger picture so the students in my classroom could "be taught the codes needed to participate fully in the mainstream of American life…the culture of power" (Delpit, 1995, p. 45). I realized this was important to the underlining processes that my students and I were engaged in throughout our learning.

I believed progressive models would work with my students as a means for progress allowing them to go beyond going "to school to find out what other people have done, and then [you] go out in life to imitate them" (Woodson, 1933, p. 138); I also believed I could not do this alone, heeding Delpit's assertion "that appropriate education for poor children and children of color can only be devised in consultation with adults who share their culture" (p. 45). Further, I learned that by deliberating with my students, I could better understand their culture and be a student of them.

At first offended by what seemingly were attacks on me as a White teacher in Delpit's work, I came to believe that too often teachers (me included) are encouraged to focus on making teaching conform to perceived best practices and miss the opportunity to actually get to know and reach their students. In my desire to teach against the tradition of "Negroes have no control over their education and have little voice in their affairs pertaining thereto" (Woodson, 1933, p. 22), I reflected on what I had read, understanding that some of these progressive tactics alone were not providing the students access to what they really needed. It was imperative for me to teach the codes of power, provide access to Standard English, and clarify the skills that will help the children in the classroom to achieve in their future.

My "good liberal intentions" (Delpit, 1995, p. 45) could have easily been off target if I had not exposed myself to relevant literature that sought out effective ways to teach African-American children. Although initially frustrated by my first reading of Delpit, it prompted me to read further and expose myself to other material dealing with educating African-American students. An assortment of texts on teaching culturally relevant and responsive approaches (e.g., hooks, 1994, 2003; Irvine, 2000, 2002, 2003; Ladson-Billings, 1994; Perry & Delpit, 1998; Perry, Steele, & Hilliard, 2003)pushed me. I needed to study what was considered to be effective by people sharing their culture.

In addition to my exposure through literature, I also sought other means to better understand the students in my classroom. I had to actively listen and consciously learn from and with my students so that together we could find the means necessary to explore the processes in which we were engaged. Beyond this reading, listening, and learning from, I came to understand that I knew very little about the students' culture. I sought out ways to delve deeper into their lived experiences, including visiting students' homes, meeting with parents in and out of school, and becoming active in the community (i.e., local tutoring, spending time with students and their families out of the context of school, etc.).

At the turn of the last century, W. E. B. Dubois (1903) questioned whether the "Negro need separate schools." The reality of the school in which I taught presented an ultimate irony to his query. A century later, this school was completely racially separate. More important questions needing to be addressed were what makes "culturally responsive teaching" (Irvine, 2000, 2002) "culturally relevant pedagogy" (Ladson-Billings, 1994), and what are the "inherent conceptions of the teacher and others; of classroom social interactions . . . and of knowledge itself?" (Ladson-Billings, 1994, p. xii). Without these challenges to the best interest of my students and what may help them learn, my teaching would merely be a series of lessons for their own sake.

As Ladson-Billings (1994) asks in her book, *Dreamkeepers*, "Does culture matter?" A quick answer to her question was an emphatic "yes!" If I accepted that culture mattered, how was I to know about a culture that was not my own? How could I create a classroom that promoted "the development of a 'relevant black personality' that allows African-American students to choose academic excellence and yet still identify with African and African-American culture?" (p. 17). Could I encourage my students to identify with their culture as Booker T. Washington (1901) proudly stated in his autobiography, *Up From Slavery*: "I had rather be what I am, a member of the Negro race, than be able to claim membership with the most favored of any other race" (p. 40)? Would it be possible to use "student culture in order to maintain it and transcend the negative effects of the dominant culture?" (Ladson-Billings, 1994, p. 17).

# Learning From, With, and Alongside My Students

The critical issues of color, power, and identity were a common thread throughout my teaching practice. Literature both informed and challenged the way I taught and learned from my students. Because both the students and I were explicitly aware of racial and class dynamics, together we addressed issues head on through class discussion, journaling, or individual conversations. My exposure to literature promoting cultural relevance in teaching pushed me to develop a classroom forum where I was learning from my students. In many ways, my students became my teacher, exposing me to what their culture encompassed that went beyond the books, as I worked to embrace their individual identities and honor what they offered to me. I recognized that the young children were willing, able, and capable of being contributors to their curriculum and their development and also to teaching me.

Ladson-Billings (1994) describes the culturally relevant teachers practicing an art rather than technical skills. These teachers believe all students can be successful, and they help make connections to students' identities in a community of learners and collaboration. Stressing that knowledge does not come from the outside but is rather "continuously re-created, recycled, and shared by teachers and students alike," Ladson-Billings asserts that these educators seek to teach against "expecting students to demonstrate prior knowledge and skills" but rather "help students develop knowledge by building bridges and scaffolding for learning" (p. 25). Using this framework for what makes teachers who practice culturally relevant methods, I could see how the development of integrated and democratic methods in an all-Black school can be fostered, but at what or whose expense?

# Deliberating About Differences and Understanding the Relevance of Race

Talking with the students about perspective and cultural differences was one of the first steps in connecting with my students. I understood from them that I needed to discuss the distinctions between all of us so that it could be a source of value, topic of conversation, and a dimension of our relationships as well as our curriculum. I also learned that I could and should explicitly confront race and in turn problematize it in our classroom. Initially, I was uncomfortable in these discussions, but working to overcome the awkwardness and reservations I had led to fruitful, deliberate discussions about differences. I recognized that confronting this in the classroom was not only important but also essential for me "getting to know my students" (Ladson-Billings, 1998, p. 18). When I began teaching, I felt uncomfortable pointing out the differences because I felt that by admitting there was a person reflecting the dominant culture coming in to their classroom could have provoked tensions. I believed that talking about it furthered a division and escalated a "me and them" mentality. But I quickly learned from the students that avoiding such deliberations would have been the real culprit. Recalling the attempts at a "race-neutral or color-blind perspective" (Ladson-Billings, 1998, p. 18) that I initially tried, I knew that I felt even more awkward because I was sensing the effort to "erase our racial categories, ignore differences, and thereby achieve an illusionary state of sameness or equality" (Howard, 2006, p. 53). Although I was seeking equality, this was certainly not the way to reach the goal.

A color-blind approach treated "race as irrelevant, invisible and taboo topic" (Schofield, cited in Howard, 2006, p. 53). Instead, I began to value the need to confront race directly. I began to want to discuss our differences in the classroom. By actively listening to my students' experiences and having the opportunity to present mine, I could not only hear the youth in my classroom, we could begin to share experiences. From our shared experiences, I readily saw how I was learning from them but also ways I could help make the classroom curricula relevant to their lives. These initial unsettling emotions began to provide me with an important context, a reminder of who I was and what sorts of impediments I brought with me. As I continued reading accounts of successful ways to teach and reach African-American students, my exposure to the body of literature helped me understand how to revolve curriculum around cultural relevance. It provided me the space to wrestle with the complexities of what Joyce King (1991) refers to as "dysconcious racism" (p. 133) associated with what I was feeling by entering the classroom every day with my current status and identity.

Instead of avoiding the privilege and power in the classroom, I took it up with them to begin reconciling a better way of understanding how "African American students face challenges unique to them as students in American schools at all levels by virtue of their social identity as African American and of the way that identity can be a source of devaluation in contemporary American society" (Perry, Steele, & Hilliard, 2003, p. vii). Simultaneously, I needed to address the achievement gap because, as Perry and her colleagues

(2003) argue, "The task of achievement . . . is distinctive for African Americans because doing school requires that you use your mind, and the ideology of the larger society has always been questioning the mental capacity of African American, about questioning Black intellectual competence" (p. 6). But as Perry et al. (2003) clearly assert, "The conversation about African American achievement is problematic because it fails to begin with a careful examination of all aspects of school, with an eye toward *how* the schools' day-to-day practices participate in the creation of underachievement" and "reproduction of inequality" (p. 6; italics original). Encouraging the reader further, they suggest, "These constraints were tied to social identity and the political location of African Americans *as* African Americans" (p. 49; italics original).

In dialoguing about race, open discussions about our differences evolved. This openness allowed for the students to assert their creativity especially in pursuing their interests regarding problems they felt needed to be solved. Accordingly, the students in my classroom attacked the inequities and power dynamics both inside and outside the school when provided the opportunity. The actions of the collective classroom reflected the sought-after learning that Woodson (1933) described, where, "Every man has two educations 'that which is given to him, and the other that which he gives himself.' Of the two kinds the latter is by far the more desirable" (p. 126). I came to understand that my role and even my purpose in the classroom were to allow the students to learn from themselves while, consequently, I learned with and from them. They were clearly "naming their own realities" (Crenshaw, cited in Delgado, 1989, p. 2437), and I was a learner alongside them. Through the naming, students were able to "challenge a stock story" by telling their "counterstory" (Delgado, 1989, p. 2416) about the severe injustices and shameful inequities they faced daily inside their school. The counternarrative they developed together showed not only their imaginative minds but also their promise.

They readily challenged what Claude Steele (cited in Perry et al., 2003) calls "stereotype threat" (p. 109) in the classroom through their pursuits while I began to understand firsthand the importance of problematizing race when I was in the classroom. I confronted openly with students the notion "that a Black student with a book is acting White" (Obama, 2004), and they readily engaged in dialogue and deliberation about what it meant to them. Challenge the "acting White mantra," their inquiries and discussions were counternarratives in and of themselves. But even amid this hopefulness, I knew that for me to come into the classroom encouraging achievement, among the stereotype threats, was a problematic issue. My push of achievement was for students' self-realization, but I understood that it could have easily been taken the wrong way or out of context. Although I do not believe I was encouraging Whiteness, I saw how my actions and challenging expectations could have been perceived by my students or others in the school or community in this way. This raises the key questions of how and why race was so important to the processes in which my students and I were engaged throughout our journey of teaching and learning together.

In my effort to readily confront and acknowledge White dominance, I turned to Gary Howard's (2006) writing about positionality and issues of social location. Howard, a multicultural educator, has written accounts of his personal and professional journey in terms of understanding racial identity in *We Can't Teach What We Don't Know* (2006). Reading and reflecting on Howard's account forced me to look at "the unexamined nature of White dominance" (p. 26). Because Howard is a White male with a privileged educational upbringing similar to my own, I resonated with his insights while reading his work. His writing provided a means to see a valid critique of my own practices, providing me with an avenue to examine and challenge myself in an introspective manner. Howard says, "If we do not face dominance, we may be predisposed to perpetuate it" (p. 26). I desired "to overcome the effects of dominance" (p. 27) with my students of color, but how was I attempting to make sure I did not continue in such reproductive traditions? By describing the uncomfortable journey he experienced, I was able to relate as well as apply his insight to my teaching and learning situation so that I could "begin to understand the significant and varying impact of dominance in the lives of the students we serve" (p. 47). Howard emphasizes acknowledging that teaching students of color do not all "come to us with the same stuff" (p. 25) (as is the case with any group of students), but he insists that it is up to educators to focus on the individual needs of students to identify the means to inhibit the perpetuation of dominance.

Because I am one of the White teachers who wants "schooling to become more than a mechanism of social control that favors White children" (p. 48), I found Howard's relentless urging a means for me to expose the reality of dominance in my own practice. I was willing "to transform both (myself) and the social arrangements of positionality and dominance that have favored us as White people" (p. 48) so that I could begin to better understand my place within the all-Black school and my ability to embrace the "silenced dialogue" (Delpit, 1995, p. 24) associated with my students color and the power dynamics inherent to them. Avoiding the excuse or even the goal of color-blindness all too common of White teachers educating Black children, I was able to get in touch my own previous, perhaps ignorant, inclinations. I became more aware of how, while discussing these issues and my perspective about them, I could better connect with my students to build the relationships I felt were necessary to our shared learning.

Another avenue that resonated with me was urban classroom teacher Greg Michie's (1999) valuable insight about his outsidedness and otherness. This perspective provided me with another opportunity for my own reflection. Michie's experiences as a White teacher in Chicago schools that predominantly served students of color encouraged me to reexamine my positionality in teaching on an ongoing basis. Michie writes about the relationships and learning he endures with his students while he examines the effects that race has on educators teaching for change (Michie, 1999; 2004). Michie's bold manner of confronting race issues as part of the artistry of teaching provided ways for me to think about what I was and was not doing, what I should do, and what I could do.

In his second book, Michie (2004) reflected on what he learned, especially the mistakes he made in his initial writing about people of color. Michie raises issues about race, class, and outsider status head on. He expresses his concerns about the decisions he made that affect the outcomes of his teaching related to race. His forthrightness about the power dynamics made me want to admit to, confront, and express my concerns, reservations, and apprehensions as well. This notion of getting in touch with this idea was not only limited to discussions with my students in the classroom, but also in the stories I tell and write about our experiences in the classrooms. Although the accusation of being "vanilla" or having the attitude of the "White savior" was far from my mind as I taught and learned with my students, I have emphatically realized the issue of race is inherently part of the story. I need to point them out, trouble them, and also find ways to make sure to keep student voices prominent while I told stories and wrote about the classroom. Abhorring the "saving children" notion was not good enough. I needed to find ways to demonstrate my resistance to the idea in my daily teaching and beyond. Keeping Michie's admission close helped me begin to navigate my situation:

> I understood going in to this project that I would be an outsider, in many respects, to the people and the communities I planned to write about, and that my efforts to convey the meanings of these teachers' experiences would be in certain ways limited and complicated by that reality. I'd learned—the hard way, you might say—that issues of representation are important to keep in mind especially for a person of relative privilege, like me, writing about people of color.

Though the stories I told hoped to counter stereotypical notions both of what it means to teach in an urban school and—through extensive use of my students' own words—what city kids are like. I wanted to portray the struggles of trying to teach with one eye on all the hope and possibility and the other on a school system and larger society that seemed intent on shutting them up, shutting them down, and shutting them out. (Michie, 2004, p. 8)

I knew that I, too, needed to "listen to the criticisms, take everything in, and read and think about the issues involved" (Michie, 2004, p. 9). Race was not something to avoid but was a means to learn about, learn from, and further the educational opportunities for my students. My status as an outsider had the potential of helping all of us learn and grow. In many ways, it allowed me the opportunity to teach against the assumptions about White teachers in classrooms with all students of color. Problematizing, troubling, and challenging the status quo with the students in my classroom and on my own allowed me to become a better teacher. It provided me with the means and sustenance to continue to work against the systemic injustices commonplace to the current educational inequities in this country.

# References

Bakhtin, M. M. (1986). *Speech genres and other late essays* (V. W. McGee, C. Emerson, & M. Holquist, Trans.). Austin: University of Texas Press.

Delgado, R. (1989). Storytelling for oppositionists and others: A plea for narrative. *Michigan Law Review, 87*, 2411–2441.

Delpit, L. (1988). The silenced dialogue: Power and pedagogy in educating other people's children. *Harvard Educational Review, 58*(3), 280–298.

Delpit, L. (1995). *Other people's children: Cultural conflict in the classroom.* New York: The New Press.

Dewey, J. (1938). *Experience and education.* New York: Dell.

Dubois, W. E. B. (1903). *The souls of Black folk: Essays and sketches.* Chicago: C. McClurg.

hooks, b. (1994). *Teaching to transgress: Education as the practice of freedom.* New York: Routledge.

hooks, b. (2003). *Teaching community: A pedagogy of hope.* New York: Routledge.

Howard, G. (2006). *We can't teach what we don't know: White teachers, multiracial schools* (2nd ed.). New York: Teachers College Press.

Hughes, S. (2005). *Black hands in the biscuits not in the classrooms: Unveiling hope in a struggle for Brown's promise.* New York: Peter Lang.

Irvine, J. J. (Ed.). (2000). *Culturally responsive teaching: Lesson planning for elementary and middle grades.* New York: McGraw-Hill.

Irvine, J. J. (Ed.). (2002). *In search of wholeness: African American teachers and their culturally specific classroom practices.* New York: Palgrave Macmillan.

Irvine, J. J. (2003). *Educating teachers for diversity: Seeing with a cultural eye*. New York: Teachers College Press.

King, J. (1991). Dysconscious racism: Ideology, identity, and miseducation of teachers. *Journal of Negro Education, 60*(2), 133–146.

Ladson-Billings, G. (1994). *The dreamkeepers: Successful teachers of African American children*. San Francisco: Jossey-Bass.

Ladson-Billings, G. (1998). Just what is critical race theory and what's it doing in a nice field like education? *Qualitative Studies in Education, 11*(1), 7–24.

Ladson-Billings, G., & Tate, W. F. (1995). Toward a critical race theory of education. *Teachers College Record, 97*(1), 47–68.

Michie, G. (1999). *Holler if you hear me: The education of a teacher and his students*. New York: Teachers College Press.

Michie, G. (2004). *See you when you get there: Teaching for change in urban schools*. New York: Teachers College Press.

Obama, B. (2004). *Keynote address*. 2004 Democratic National Convention, Boston, MA.

Perry, T., & Delpit, L. (1998). *The real Ebonics debate: Power, language, and then education of African-American children*. Boston: Beacon Press.

Perry, T., Steele, C., & Hilliard, A., III, (2003). *Young, gifted and Black: Promoting high achievement among African-American students*. Boston: Beacon Press.

Pinar, W. F. (1994). *Autobiography, politics and sexuality: Essays in curriculum theory, 1972–1992*. New York: Peter Lang.

Pinar, W. F., & Grumet, M. R. (1976). *Toward a poor curriculum*. Dubuque, IA: Kendall/Hunt.

Schubert, W. H. (1991). Philosophical inquiry: The speculative essay. In E. C. Short (Ed.), *Forms of curriculum inquiry* (pp. 61–76). Albany: State University of New York Press.

Schultz, B. D., & Oyler, C. (2006). We make this road as we walk together: Sharing teacher authority in a social action curriculum project. *Curriculum Inquiry, 36*(4), 423–451.

Steele, C. (2003). Stereotype threat and African-American student achievement. In T. Perry, C. Steele, & A. Hilliard III, *Young, gifted, and Black: Promoting high achievement among African-American students* (pp. 109–130). Boston: Beacon Press.

Washington, B. T. (1901). *Up from slavery: An autobiography*. New York: Doubleday, Page.

Woodson, C. G. (1933). *The mis-education of the Negro*. Trenton, NJ: Africa World Press.

## · 3 ·

# Constructing Space for Elementary School Students to Talk About Race and Take Action to Create Change

SACHI FERIS

I have been riding New York City's buses and subways for 30 years. I always appreciate the space provided by the city's public transportation system as a good starting place for a true multicultural America: a contrast of countless cultures crammed in for a collective commute. Yet as the southbound subway crosses the infamous 96th Street border separating Harlem from Park Avenue's doorman buildings, I am suddenly back in a familiar territory where I have spent most of my life—where everyone looks (White) like me. Despite the potential diversity that growing up in New York City supposedly affords, most New Yorkers still live segregated existences. Black students grow up in Harlem, Dominicans in Washington Heights, Whites on the Upper West Side, and Chinese in Chinatown, and these groups of people lack meaningful opportunities to interact with one another.

Within the current policy context of *de facto* school and housing segregation, and the reality that even voluntary school desegregation programs are currently at risk, there is a gap in interracial experiences for young students that are supported by multicultural and social justice pedagogy. According to critical theorist Henry Giroux (1994), "multiculturalism should . . . offer the possibility for schools to become places where students and teachers can become border crossers engaged in critical and ethical reflection about what it means to bring a wider variety of cultures into dialogue with each other" (p. 337). Our current reality, however, generates few schools or other educational spaces that fit this description. In the field of sociology, a border is contextualized as a structure that maintains inequality (Tastsoglou, 1996). By *crossing borders*, then, students and teachers can challenge inequality.

In 2001, Border Crossers, an educational, social justice organization in New York City, began as an attempt to transform Giroux's theory into practice. Border Crossers' mission is to bring together young students from segregated neighborhoods to explore issues of discrimination, inequality, and social justice, and to develop student leadership toward social change. Border Crossers builds Partner School relationships between schools that are geographically close but demographically different. Its programs give students in Grades 2–6 the practical experience in building the skills and inclination to cross borders in their personal and professional lives. Border Crossers' vision is that they will become adults who are able to act as allies across racial borders—and take action to create change when they confront injustice in their lives.

An essential question with regard to living, learning, and teaching race involves exploring what it means to create spaces where students from diverse racial and ethnic backgrounds can be positively impacted by learning about racism, discrimination, and inequality. There is insufficient research that effectively addresses the challenges and practices of confronting these issues with a diverse group of students, specifically students in the late-elementary and middle-school grades. Border Crossers intuitively understands that inter-racial experiences and curriculum that focus on themes of identity, diversity, and discrimination will have different effects on various group members based on group status, prior experience, and personality, and it is committed to the ongoing process of determining how to best create a space in which *all* students are served. In this chapter, lessons learned and practices from Border Crossers' experience working with multiracial groups around social justice themes are shared.

# Pedagogical Background

Border Crossers subscribes to a definition of multicultural education that is both anti-racist and pro-justice (*Rethinking Our Classrooms*, 2001). This level of multicultural education is also called the Multicultural and Social

Reconstructionist Approach (Sleeter & Grant, 1987) or social action approach (Banks & Banks, 1993). This approach examines the root and causes of inequality and paves the way for more just and inclusive classrooms by teaching students how to take action and create change. Moreover, educators pronounce "the ability and willingness to interact with diverse people [as] a central goal of multicultural education" (Ramsey, 1987, p. 124). Border Crossers also incorporates psychologist Gordon Allport's (1954) renown intergroup contact theory, which outlines key components that should drive this interaction process if true integration is to occur. These include (a) interaction among students, (b) cooperative action to achieve common goals, (c) social norms supporting cross-group contact, and (d) equal-status contact.

The Anti-Defamation League (2007) cites a variety of research that suggests anti-bias education is "most beneficial when students are introduced to multicultural education at as young an age as possible." Students in the upper elementary grades are old enough to discuss issues of identity and difference but young enough to do so without inhibitions and to maintain an open mind throughout the learning experience. Despite this, the multicultural education field lacks the resources and programs to support such learning for this age group. Border Crossers' work attempts to help fill this gap, and this is demonstrated through a description of the structure, curriculum, and implementation of its programs. Appropriate theories and strategies are referenced to illustrate how cross-race conversations are supported.

## Program Curriculum

Border Crossers accomplishes its mission through its Partner School model that creates ongoing relationships among schools with distinct demographic compositions. Classrooms in Partner Schools are paired as pen pals and communicate around curriculum themes of identity, community, diversity, justice, and change-making. Students come together for Meet-Ups at each others' schools, park spaces, and an overnight component for fifth- and sixth-grade students, where they gain the tools to cross borders. This is where the magic of Border Crossers comes alive as students interact, build friendships, and teach and learn from each other. Teachers facilitate preparatory and debriefing activities and engage students in social action projects to follow up the Meet-Ups.Border Crossers' curriculum is based on multicultural, social justice education pedagogy and focuses on four program areas: (a) exploring concepts of identity and community, (b) understanding the concept of crossing borders, (c) student leadership, and (d) social action. Border Crossers engages students by incorporating children's literature, poetry, music, writing, drama, and an exploration of primary source documents into the curriculum. Because one of Border Crossers' goals is to encourage cross-group interactions, every face-to-face meeting also integrates team-building and energizer games to foster a group culture and spirit.

The curriculum is organized around the concept of a border, beginning with literal borders by mapping where students live in New York City. Initially, students also look at borders in terms of what makes people within a group different from each other. The curriculum later builds toward issues of inclusion and exclusion on an interpersonal level and, finally, addresses systemic borders in a historical and present-day context with regard to issues of discrimination and inequality.

In Grades 2 to 4, book-based lessons drawing on relevant children's literature are integrated as the centerpiece of the exchange. Students in Grades 2 to 6 take part in a read-aloud and related activities prior to each face-to-face meeting, participate in activities during the face-to-face meetings with their partner class, and debrief with social action prompts following each face-to-face meeting. This enables students to take action on their learning by setting individual, class, and school-based social action goals.

Students in Grades 5 and 6 examine a specific curriculum around the theme of schools and borders, which includes an examination of *Brown v. Board of Education*, and themes of school funding inequity, high-stakes testing, and tracking. This curriculum places students at the center of their daily existence in school by challenging them to critique and question the structure and practices of an institution about which they are, in fact, experts, because students spend much of their time in school! Students take part in a culminating social action project to synthesize their learning around this yearlong curriculum. Past projects have used mural-making, theater, and documentary film as forums for students to take action on their learning.

Students also bring action projects back to their larger school communities. During the schools and borders curriculum unit, students identify areas of change needed in their own schools and work with their classmates to take action. In the past, school-based action projects have included a plan for acquiring new kickballs for the recess yard, a consciousness-raising campaign around the climate of the lunch line, and organizing to improve the availability of supplies in school bathrooms. The goal of these projects is to empower students to create change in their own communities.

mission when the space has been created for students to develop the skills to talk openly and honestly about race in a multiracial setting.

## Making connections across borders: *"It's just like Michelle!"*

Team teaching can also be thought of as a model of "cooperation, democracy, and diversity" for students (Ellis & Llewellyn, 1997, p. 23). The interactions and communication processes between teachers working in interracial teams, if equitable, can serve as a model that has the potential to challenge stereotypes and inequalities (Solomon, 2000). Border Crossers believes it is essential that both the student population and the facilitator group represent the diversity represented in New York City. Border Crossers has worked with schools that are overwhelmingly segregated, including a public school in the Washington Heights/Inwood section of Manhattan that is 99% Dominican, a public school in Chinatown that is 99% Chinese, and a private school on the Upper West Side of Manhattan that is more than 90% white.

On one occasion, a small group of students were discussing the case of *Mendez v. Westminster* (1946), which preceded *Brown v. Board of Education* and ended school segregation in California, and the following interaction occurred. The facilitator was eliciting personal experiences from students regarding immigration to the United States because the protagonists of the case were immigrants. Each student, in turn, shared his or her story, including Michelle, a Chinese student who had immigrated to the United States just 3 years before. A few minutes later, Patricia, a Puerto Rican student, was asked why her parents immigrated to the United States, and she answered, "It's just like Michelle"—making a connection to what Michelle had just shared (personal communication, 2005). It is moments like these that prove what a powerful experience it is to give young people the opportunity to have meaningful interactions with students from different racial and socioeconomic backgrounds. Students benefit from this experience because it provides them with the opportunity to build bridges between similar experiences, develop empathy for those who are "other" to them, and work together as allies in creating future social change.

These interactions are enabled by a teacher training that focuses on building shared understanding and values within the facilitator team with regard to program goals and individual goals for students. As such, facilitator teams have been successful at modeling positive border crossing interactions with each other for students.

## Effectively supporting students as they cross borders: *"Sometimes crossing borders can be hard."*

In anticipating or debriefing Border Crossers, this statement—"Sometimes crossing borders can be hard" (personal communication, 2006)—has been made more than once by a student. Crossing borders can be hard—but Border Crossers does everything possible to structure space so that the burden of participation is not placed on students but rather on the organization of the program and curriculum.

For example, in *Producing Equal-Status Interaction in the Heterogeneous Classroom*, Elizabeth G. Cohen and Rachel Lotan (1995) show that strategies can be used to increase the participation of low-status students without negatively influencing the participation of high-status students. Status is defined based on the specifics of the group by race, class, gender, language, and so on. Among these strategies, multiple ability groupings address the establishment of norms that support a "none of us has all these abilities; each one of us has some of these abilities" spirit (Cohen & Lotan, 1995, p. 102). Teachers may also take a more proactive approach and assign "expert" status to specific students. This strategy, known as expectation training, has been used to equalize status in interracial settings. Expectation training involves the low-status students taking on the role of facilitator or teacher of high-status students (Cohen, 1994, p. 120). These strategies are dependent on the conditions that curriculum tasks "require a broad range of intellectual abilities" and that classroom management "sustains a high rate of interaction between students" (Cohen & Lotan, 1995, p. 105). Cohen and Lotan found that teachers' use of these status treatments or strategies can significantly increase equal-status and positive interactions between high- and low-status students. In Border Crossers, these strategies are utilized with similar success.

Another way that Border Crossers facilitates equal-status interaction is by minimizing the interactions that take place with the whole group. In a whole-group discussion setting, high-status students are more likely to participate or dominate. Therefore, it is necessary to provide various options and modes of communication that do not place the burden of participation on students but rather on the structure of an activity and the facilitators. One of the most important aspects of the Border Crossers Curriculum Guide are the "Discussion Formats," which are used as tools to continuously create and uphold an equal-status space where every voice is heard regardless of power dynamics concerning gender, race, linguistic ability, or social status among peers. Border Crossers utilizes various forms of nonverbal communication, such as drawing and writing, to create a space in which multiple communication styles are honored and more perspectives are shared. These formats range from a simple "Think-Pair-Share" to discussion formats involving silence, writing, or communicating using facial and body expressions.

This highly structured environment is not limited to the formal curriculum. Even "downtime" is structured so as to support friendship-building by limiting the choices for activities by setting up a system that expects students to sign up for activities with a new friend and by giving students the opportunity to set their own friendship goals.

Finally, Border Crossers uses same-school groups to debrief and reflect on the experience of crossing borders in a safe space that complements the work in which students engage in an interracial setting. Multicultural educator and Spelman College President Dr. Beverly Tatum supports the use of affinity groups or "separate 'spaces' that facilitate positive identity exploration, where people can pose questions and process issues. The shared goal in making affinity groups available is to interrupt the cycle of racism . . . they are good for overall community-building" (Tatum, 1997).

## Inspiring students to take action on inequities: "My school is mad poor."

Students had congregated at one of the participating private schools and were in the middle of eating lunch when a visiting student commented to her teacher, "My school is mad poor" (personal communication, 2006). Upon digging deeper as to what motivated this comment, the teacher learned it was a direct response to the private school's recess equipment. Within the context of a curriculum about schools—and a social action continuum—this conversation became the jumping-off point for this student's school action project: a letter-writing campaign to demand new kickballs for the recess yard.

This story might stir questions about the justification for bringing students together across racial borders, specifically for a low-status group. It is implicit to remember, however, that we don't create inequality by bringing these groups together, nor are students' (from both sides of the border) consciousnesses of inequality awakened solely by this experience of crossing borders. In Nathan Glazer's (1997) book, "We Are All Multiculturalists Now," he suggests that there is no benefit in teaching Black students about the legacy and history of slavery in this country—and that omitting such information in the education of Black students is "for their own good" (p. 47). Contrary to Glazer, Border Crossers believes that ignoring these issues or attempting to hide them from students does students a disservice. The Border Crossers experience encourages comments and opinions about inequality to be out in the open, thus empowering students to create change around their observations of inequity and challenge their own daily realities.

In two studies addressing fifth-grade students' responses to curriculum that focused on the issue of racism, the words *anger* and *angry* surfaced as shared student responses. Feelings of shock, sadness, and outrage also emerged as related student responses (words that may be categorized as negative) (Donaldson, 1996; Zack, 1996). Nevertheless, Border Crossers believes that such curricula are both necessary and beneficial not in spite of but because of the previous responses.

Border Crossers integrates social action throughout the curriculum as a tool for students to respond to their learning. One student related the reaction of anger to taking social action: "It makes me angry when bad things are going on but it is good to know it so that you can do something about it. If you just don't know anything about it then you just ignore what you see and you won't know what you think about it. I have learned about how to take action if I don't think something is right" (personal communication, 2006). In Border Crossers, we strongly believe in the benefits of empowerment that can result from providing students with a model for change.

Students in Border Crossers begin to see that they can be change-makers immediately in their own lives and communities. During one meeting regarding their school social action project, students initially looked to their teacher to make a decision for them. Their teacher then turned the decision back to them, saying, "You can make the decision! It's your project!" to which students responded, "We can?!" in an awed realization that the direction and success of their social action project depended solely on their own vision (personal communication, 2006). One student's response highlights the power of social action curriculum: "I like that they teach us what happened in the past and how we can change what's happening and that just by crossing borders we can change people's thoughts and feelings. Because I can go on crossing borders and I could tell other people what they can do to change things and help the community and help the world" (personal communication, 2006).

Border Crossers arms students with tools and experiences that will allow them to envision and implement better solutions to current social problems. As a result of having learned how to successfully dialogue with people who are "other" to them, these students will have an inherent value for diversity. Because these young people will have had practical experiences with how to identify and act on concrete problems, they will see themselves as active members of their community who are capable of creating change.

## Concluding Thoughts

Clearly, there is a great need for further work in the field of crossing borders. Doing this work is not effortless or easy. Despite Border Crossers' intense structure and intricate thought process that supports cross-border experiences, several challenges persist. First, there is a basic inquiry as to the utility of bringing students together across racial borders. Again, a lack of contact between high- and low-status groups will not erase the inequities that exist between them. Only by coming together across borders can people truly challenge systemic inequity. In addition, Linda Tropp and Thomas Pettigrew's research shows differential responses to interracial experiences from people in low- versus high-status groups regarding their desire for future contact. The implications of this research are hugely important to the continuous improvement of programs sich as Border Crossers—including an analysis of these different responses. Finally, the challenge of Tatum's infamous quandary "Why are all the Black kids sitting together in the cafeteria?" is sometimes reaffirmed during program activities. That is why Border Crossers' goal is to become a part of creating authentic Partner School relationships between schools that provide ongoing opportunities for contact.

Border Crossers creates a laboratory for students, teachers, administrators, and parents to become Giroux's (1994) border crossers, "engaged in critical and ethical reflection about what it means to bring a wider variety of cultures into dialogue with each other" (p. 337). Through teacher trainings, parent orientations, and Partner School leadership teams, parents, teachers, and school leaders engage in honest conversations about how to encourage future inquiry about discrimination and inequity in young people. Together, these stakeholders develop tools and strategies for responding to students' questions and observations regarding their cross-border experiences.

As showcased in the aforementioned quotations and anecdotes, these questions and observations are most often related to differences between students in terms of identity, cultural background, and lived experiences. Strategies for responding to students include validating and acknowledging what a student sees, digging deeper to get more information through follow-up questions, exploring students' feelings around their observation, and inspiring students to take action and create change. By engaging students in these conversations, teachers and parents play an important role in living, learning, and teaching race and in supporting young people in a lifelong conversation about the implications of being different. Students must have the tools, inclination, and desire to talk about the implications of being different across borders if they are to become adults who are empowered to shift the balance of power and create innovative and systemic change across borders.

# References

Allport, G. W. (1954). *The nature of prejudice*. Reading, MA: Addison Wesley.

Anti-Defamation League. (2007). *The A WORLD OF DIFFERENCE Institute Philosophical Framework*. Retrieved February 9, 2007, from http://www.adl.org/education/edu_awod/awod_philosophical.asp

Banks, J. A., & Banks, C. A. M. (Eds.). (1993). *Multicultural education: Issues and perspectives*. Boston.

Cohen, E. G. (1994). *Designing groupwork: Strategies for the heterogeneous classroom*. New York: Teachers College Press.

Cohen, E. G., & Lotan, R. A. (1995). Producing equal-status interaction in the heterogeneous classroom. *American Educational Research Journal, 32*(1).

Donaldson, K. B. M. (1996). *Through students' eyes: Combating racism in United States schools*. New York: Praeger Publishers.

Ellis, A., & Llewellyn, M. (1997). *Dealing with differences: Taking action on class, race, gender and disability*. New York: Corwin Press.

Giroux, H. (1994). Insurgent multiculturalism and the promise of pedagogy. In D. T. Goldberg (Ed.), *Multiculturalism: A critical reader* (pp. 326–343). New York: Blackwell Publishers.

Glazer, N. (1997). *We are all multiculturalists now*. Cambridge, MA: Harvard University Press.

Paley, V. (1979). *White teacher*. Cambridge, MA: Harvard University Press.

Ramsey, P. G. (1987). *Teaching and learning in a diverse world: Multicultural education for young children*. New York: Teachers College Press.

*Rethinking Our Classrooms, Volume 2: Teaching for Equity and Justice*. (2001). Milwaukee, WI: Rethinking Schools, Ltd.

Sleeter, C., & Grant, C. (1987). An analysis of multicultural education in the United States. *Harvard Educational Review, 57*(4).

Solomon, P. R. (2000). Exploring cross-race dyad partnerships in learning to teach. *Teachers College Record, 102*(6), 953–979.

Tastsoglou, E. (1996). Mapping the unknowable: The challenges and rewards of cultural, political and pedagogical border crossing. In A. Calliste & G. S. Dei (Eds.), *Power, knowledge, and anti-racism education* (pp. 98–121). Halifax, NS: Fernwood Publishing.

Tatum, B. (1997.) *Why are all the Black kids sitting together in the cafeteria?* New York: Basic Books.

Zack V. (1996). Nightmare issues: Children's responses to racism and genocide in literature. *The New Advocate*, 9(4).

## · 4 ·

# Owning the "Buts"

## High School Students Confront
## History and Heterosexism

CONNIE NORTH

[W]e must learn to practice a systematic form of disloyalty to our own local civilization if we seek either to understand it or to interact equitably with others formed elsewhere.

—PAUL GILROY (2004)

During the fall of 2002, 29 students from eight different high schools left the city and headed for the woods as part of a Facing History and Ourselves (FHAO) leadership program. For 4 days and 3 nights, they engaged in what some would call experiential education, others a camp. Under the careful guidance of five seasoned adult facilitators, this diverse group of students drew on their lived experiences to grapple with various issues of oppression, including racism, poverty, sexism, and homophobia. To demonstrate and inspire student reflection on how the many "isms" in our society are generated, performed, and ultimately reproduced, the facilitators used simulations, roleplays, videocassettes, and, always, dialogue. After the viewing of a film depicting various individual and group struggles for equality in U.S. history, a discussion about homophobia erupted, during which one student asserted, "I don't like gay people," and another said, "I just don't think it's [homosexuality is] right." This chapter examines that conversation and its implications for education aimed at social justice.

Although unplanned, the dialogue on homophobia fit within the camp leaders' intentional instructional approach, an approach that sought to raise and extend students' critical awareness, develop their individual sense of purpose in the world, and inspire them to "stand up" against social injustice. Although the particular context of and participants in the leadership camp make the conversation about homophobia and its consequences unique, student responses to the discussion reveal both the promise and limits of dialogue as an instructional tool to fight injustice in U.S. society. Student interpretations of the program also reveal some of the ways that today's youth construct, resist, and imitate multicultural discourses, especially those focused on diversity and tolerance. This chapter, then, has two primary goals: (a) to locate the discussion about homophobia within a historical moment that attends to complex intersections of oppression—particularly racism and heterosexism, and (b) to examine the potential of dialogue as a tool for social justice by theorizing students' interactions with each other and the facilitators during the dialogue as well as their reflections on it during follow-up interviews several months later.

To contextualize this conversation for the reader, I briefly describe the leadership program and its participants. I also briefly describe the methodology for this research, which analyzed student responses to the leadership program more generally. I next review scholarly conversations and debates about heterosexism in relation to White supremacy, racism, and ideology. This section helps to historicize the students' comments and the facilitators' responses so as to promote continued attention to the broader sociopolitical context in which the dialogue took place and, more important, the implications of that language for queer youth of color. In short, this section strives to deepen understanding about historic patterns of domination so that the process of dismantling insidious forms of oppression and recultivating more humane ways of being and knowing can advance.

After describing the event—the conversation about homophobia—I draw on student interpretations of it to assess the usefulness of the leadership program's intervention into heterosexism. I conclude by asking that educators become aware of our own assumptions about what is "normal" and, in turn, practice a "systemic disloyalty" to those aspects of "our own local civilization" that sustain systems of domination and oppression (Gilroy, 2004, p. 79).

## The FHAO Leadership Program

Established in 1976 by middle-school teachers in Brookline, Massachusetts, FHAO is a renowned classroom-based nonprofit organization dedicated to helping students examine racism, prejudice, and anti-semitism through an analysis of the Holocaust (Fine, 1995). "By studying the historical development and the legacies of the Holocaust and other instances of collective violence," FHAO aims to teach students how "to combat prejudice with compassion, indifference with ethical participation, myth and misinformation with knowledge" (*Facing History*, 2004).[1]

The state FHAO program under study is unusual in that it not only supports the training of educators to teach the FHAO curriculum in high school classrooms but also organizes an "extracurricular" leadership program for students. The 2002–2003 leadership program included a fall camp as well as monthly follow-up activities that sought to raise the students' critical awareness of social inequality and subsequently move them to take action against it. In the director's words, the leadership program sought "to dive deeper into some of the historical material but also just the thematic issues around diversity and social justice."

The fall camp took place at a mountainside facility owned and operated by a major urban public school district. The 29 students who applied to the leadership program participated in FHAO classrooms at their respective schools, and everyone who submitted an application was able to attend the camp. Nineteen of these student volunteers were female (66%), and all students were in Grades 9–11. Ten students self-identified as African American (34.5%), 10 as White (34.5%), 4 as Latino (14%), 3 as multiracial (10%), and 2 as Asian American (7%). Eight participating high schools, all of which were located in a single metropolitan area, were extremely diverse—public and private, suburban and inner city, large and small. The five adult camp facilitators also embodied diverse identity positions and life histories.[2] They agreed that the primary objective of the program, like Paulo Freire's (1970/1994) notion of "conscientização," was to help students learn "to perceive social, political, and economic contradictions, and to take action against the oppressive elements of reality" (p. 17). These adults aimed to transform the students' heightened critical awareness into action by asking them to organize a follow-up school-based project related to the themes addressed during the camp.[3]

# Methodology

Although scholars have theorized several forms of social justice and/or critical multicultural education, few have undertaken classroom intervention research (Bennett, 2001). Therefore, I constructed an "instrumental case study" (Stake, 2000) of student responses to the 2002–2003 FHAO Leadership Program to address that gap. This chapter comprises one section of that larger study.[4]

Given my interest in studying how students interpreted the leadership program curriculum, I used ethnographic methods as investigative tools. Participant observation and semi-structured interviews allowed me entrance to the participants' worldviews, intentions, and behaviors. I also obtained various documents from the director and program coordinator—student and facilitator camp evaluations, educational activity descriptions, and the adult facilitators' résumés—that captured valuable snapshots of the ways in which the facilitators and students conceived of, presented, and assessed the leadership program.

In addition to observing 3 days of the camp, I attended a follow-up "action-planning" meeting in January 2003 and the year-end celebration in June 2003, where 12 students, 10 of whom were female, agreed to be interviewed (41% of the student participants). These interviewees attended seven of the eight participating FHAO schools and reflected the camp participants' diversity of backgrounds, including a wide range of socioeconomic statuses. Among the student interviewees, two self-identified as Asian American, two as Latina, three as multiracial, three as African American, and two as White. The disproportionately small number of male and White student interviewees reflected the student population present at the year-end celebration rather than an intentional sampling choice. I also interviewed all five of the adult camp facilitators. Most of the interviews took place in the interviewees' homes during August 2003, and the interviews lasted between 30 and 90 minutes.

To analyze my data, I transcribed each of the interviews and looked for themes, such as "responsibility-taking," in both the transcripts and my field-notes. I then used NVivo, a type of qualitative research software, to organize these data. Although I have sought to be self-reflexive about the claims I am making, I openly acknowledge "the possibility of alternative accounts" (Williams, 1993) and the power I have had throughout the research process to conduct, write, and present the study as I see fit (Wolf, 1996). In the spirit of more collaborative research, however, I worked with the FHAO leadership program director throughout the course of this project. His perspective, even when not explicitly acknowledged, shaped this entire chapter.

Importantly, I recognize that while undertaking this research, I made "observations within a mediated framework . . . of symbols and cultural meanings" provided by features of my life history (Vidich & Lyman, 2000, p. 39). As a White woman who was raised in an upper middle-class, Christian household and who is committed to working for social justice, I must listen carefully to and *attempt* to understand the perspectives of people who have and have not experienced my multiple, unearned advantages in U.S. society. As a queer woman who spent most of my 32-year-old life accruing the privileges associated with heterosexuality, too, I am committed to working for a world where LGBTQ youth are no longer associated with alarming rates of physical and verbal abuse, homelessness, low academic achievement, substance abuse, self-loathing, and suicide.[5] My responsibilities as an educational researcher include examining critically how my own shifting prejudices and assumptions shape my understanding of the leadership program and the students' vocal and/or silent reactions to it.

# Racialized Conceptualizations of Queerness

During the dialogue about homophobia, a handful of students openly expressed a discomfort with and objection to homosexuality.[6] Their comments inspired the White director to make an analogy between racism during the civil rights era and homophobia as articulated by the students at the dawning of the 21st century, thereby exposing and linking the harmful consequences of both forms of oppression. Before analyzing this conversation and student responses to it, I discuss heterosexism in relation to the politics of race (particularly the races with which students identified) because this complicated relationship influenced the dialogue's enactment. I want to emphasize that a focus on historical and social patterns does not deny the existence of numerous exceptions or the reality that such distinctions fail to capture the complex experiences of multiracial students in contemporary U.S. society. The following work seeks to make sense of—not argue for—the continued existence of essentialist ethnic and racial categories.

## Whiteness and Homosexuality

Various scholars emphasize that in popular culture and multicultural scholarship, homosexuality is often conceived of as a uniquely White identity position even though individuals of different racial and ethnic backgrounds are clearly queer. Kevin Kumashiro (2001), for example, argues that U.S. society and researchers have promoted the association of queerness with whiteness, leading many individuals and groups to think of homosexuality as a "White thing." Tomas Almaguer (1998) attributes the "overwhelmingly White, middle class, and male-centered" (p. 544) gay identity in the United States to historical developments. He contends that while the contemporary gay community is irrefutably diverse, the class, race, and gender privileges of communities that formed in the wake of World War II have enabled White, middle-class gay men to defend more readily and openly a gay identity than low-income and/or queer people of color. Sharing many of these privileges, White, middle-class women also frequently occupy social positions that allow them to self-identify as lesbians more easily than poor women of color. Nevertheless, heterosexism remains prevalent in White cultures, as evidenced by a large-scale study of mostly White high school students in which 33% of students reported, "studented in their school are frequently harassed because of their perceived or actual sexual orientation" (Harris Interactive & GLSEN, 2005, p. 7).

## Asianness and Homosexuality

Outside the familial demand of sexual reproduction, "external sexual expression" is not acceptable in most Asian cultures (Chan, 1997; Okazaki, 2002). In many Asian American homes, a virtuous son should conform to the " 'traditional Asian values' of getting married, having children, and passing down the family name" (Kumashiro, 1999, p. 502). Thus, family and community members may see a gay Asian-American man who "comes out" as selfish, disloyal, and "acting white" (Kumashiro, 1999, 2001). Lesbian Asian-American women also often define themselves through Western cultural constructs to form a homosexual identity because "[w]ithin the Asian part of an Asian American's culture, there is little support for an *individual* public identity of any kind beyond the role one is expected to play within the family" (Chan, 1997, p. 44). As most Asian cultures are both collectivistic and patriarchal, the open expression of sexuality by a woman both challenges the interdependent social order and "proper" moral behavior (Okazaki, 2002). Although these patterns are neither representative of all Asian-American individuals and groups nor stable, LGBTQ Asian Americans frequently have to choose between their racial and sexual identities or risk being ostracized from their communities, from which they draw social support in a society that marginalizes and discriminates against them as racial Others (Chan, 1997; Kumashiro, 1999, 2001; Okazaki, 2002).

## Latinoness and Homosexuality

Like many Asian-American individuals, many Latino individuals depend on families for social support and a sense of social connectedness and thus willingly adhere to strict, patriarchal gender roles and sexual prescriptions (Almaguer, 1998; Diaz, 1998). As Almaguer (1998) writes, "[A]ny deviation from the sacred link binding husband, wife, and child not only threatens the very existence of la familia but also potentially undermines the mainstay of resistance to Anglo racism and class exploitation" (p. 546). Accordingly, la familia often regulates and limits the sexual lives of LGBTQ Latinos and Chicano individuals (Almaguer, 1998; Diaz, 1998). Widespread devotion to Catholicism in many Latino communities—a religion that remains overpoweringly anti-gay—further intensifies this homophobia (Campo, 1999).

Importantly, Latino cultures often do not recognize the Euro-American, "bourgeois" culture's construction of the modern gay man that is dominant in U.S. society (Almaguer, 1998). Rather, such cultures may view sexuality in terms of patriarchal power and dominance, wherein the active sexual partner represents masculinity and the passive sexual partner femininity. Almaguer (1998) argues that the Spanish conquistadors' colonization of Mexico threatened Mexican men's sense of masculinity, leading to a kind of machismo—or "hypermasculinity" (Diaz, 1998)—that celebrates aggressive virility and disdains femininity. For gay Mexican men, then, "it is primarily the passive, effeminate homosexual man who becomes the object of derision and societal contempt" (Almaguer, 1998, p. 541).

This notion of the feminine as weak, submissive, and inferior often translates into traditional gender roles for Latinas that "serve to preserve men's dominant status in all spheres of life" (Hernández-Truyol, 2001, p. 690). Consequently, the lesbian Latina who refuses to maintain the sanctity and solidarity of la familia is frequently seen as immoral, perverse, and unnatural by la cultura Latina (Almaguer, 1998; Hernández-Truyol, 2001). Again, although ruptures in this pervasive homophobia exist in Latina communities, if LGBTQ Latinos want to express openly their sexual identities, they frequently must leave the support and affirmation of their families and neighborhoods and face the racism embedded in mainstream gay communities (Almaguer, 1998; Campo, 1999; Diaz, 1991; Hernández-Truyol, 2001).

to reflect on their claims. First, he situated their comments in a different context, noting that in the Montgomery, Alabama, of 1962, some Whites openly declared, "I don't have a problem with Black people, but I don't want them dating my daughter." He then asked the students to own publicly the "but" in their statements by making revised assertions, such as, "I think I do have a problem with this. I'm wrestling with my problem." After relaying a personal anecdote about facing his own homophobia in college, Mike acknowledged that people of color do not have the option of "staying in the closet" but also emphasized, using the example of Matthew Sheperd, that revealing one's sexuality could be deadly in light of the hostility still openly displayed toward LGBTQ individuals in the United States.[9] He also underscored that the weekend would be lost if people went home saying, "We're all about peace and justice, but I hate gays." As Mike stressed, if the group was going to make claims, "our actions should line up."

After the discussion ended, the facilitators convened to debrief it and ultimately decided to arrange a follow-up activity with a gay/lesbian alliance group. Importantly, several White students and students of color remained silent during this discussion. Given the dominant heterosexism in U.S. society, homophobia was likely more prevalent among the less expressive members of the group than I was able to observe or intuit. As with all accounts, mine is inevitably partial. Moreover, I want to recognize that the students who made heterosexist statements broke the "official silence" (Mayo, 2004) surrounding LGBTQ discrimination and, as a consequence, created the space to confront and challenge it.

## Examining Student Responses to the Facilitator's Intervention

I would describe the previous dialogue as an exemplar of what Ira Shor (1992) calls the "third idiom" and what Walter Parker (2003) calls a "public building activity." According to Shor (1992), unlike traditional classroom discourses, wherein the teacher speaks from a position of "unilateral authority" and the "best" student responds with what he or she thinks the teacher wants to hear, the "third idiom" privileges student expression and encourages the "mutual inquiry" of the teacher and students (p. 255). Ideally, by using the third idiom, the teacher and students will engage in a collaborative teaching and learning process that develops the students' ability to examine critically taken-for-granted assumptions, challenge social injustices, and defend diversity. In alignment with Shor's (1992) vision of "empowering education," Mike started "from inside student life" to help the students become more self-aware and look critically at their own prejudices. He also spoke of his personal experiences, letting students know that he too struggled with homophobia, which made him more human and less "teacherly."

When I asked the interviewees what they remembered about the discussion in my interviews with them 9 months later, some described it vividly. For example, Keeshawn, who expressed discomfort with homosexuality throughout the camp conversation, recalled,

> Everybody was like, "Well, I don't think there's a problem with people being homosexual, but I don't like their lifestyle." . . . Well, if you don't like somebody's lifestyle, then you do have a problem with what they do. . . . So, that activity or little video, we got to see how people really thought about like homosexuality.

Remaining within Shor's (1992) framework, Keeshawn's statement reveals that the dialogue pushed students not only to reveal publicly some of their underlying assumptions about homosexuality but also to reflect on their own beliefs and own up to them. Furthermore, the interviewed students expressed agreement with the director's analogy of homophobia to racism, recognizing both as harmful forms of bigotry. Indeed, when I asked students to respond to the claim that comparing homophobia to racism is like comparing apples and oranges, several students replied that all discrimination is bad. The majority of student responses resembled Keeshawn's: "It's basically all the same." I return to this point later.

The conversation also helped to create the conditions for democratic deliberation via "reversibility." Parker argues that students need to be able to imagine themselves from another standpoint—such as that of a gay man or lesbian—and reflect on what they would desire from that position. Through such perspective-taking, students develop the capacity to understand the privileges and disadvantages associated with their own social positions and membership in various cultural groups and thus move toward a more enlightened vision of democracy. According to several students, the camp discussion successfully used reversibility to build public consciousness. As Lestashia argued, "You've gotta understand them before you say, 'I don't want you hanging out with me because you're gay' . . . you're not walking a mile in their shoes so why would you make an assumption?"

In several respects, then, the students' words and actions at the camp and in their follow-up interviews suggest that the camp dialogue resulted in the critical consciousness and citizenship skill development envisioned by critical multicultural and democratic education advocates such as Shor and Parker. However, several feminist and queer scholars would ask me to consider two additional questions in my analysis: (a) How do "the social demands of being 'normal' . . . help to create queer-based oppression" (Kumashiro, 2002, p. 45)? (b) "[I]n what ways does the world rise or fall in value when a reader or groups of readers perform and let loose in the world [a] particular meaning or reading of a text or event" (Ellsworth, 1997, p. 127)? I thus turn to student responses to see whether the dialogue reinforced rather than destabilized normative queer/straight binaries that serve to alienate and marginalize LGBTQ students of all ethnic and racial groups.

## Re-reading Student Responses Through Feminist, Queer Lenses

The director's refusal to accept homophobia represents a significant step toward interrupting the normal privileging of heterosexuality. By asking students to confront their own prejudices, Mike pushed the students to examine the contradiction inherent in claiming to be innocent of oppressive practices while showing clear intolerance toward sexual difference in their language. As he said about his instructional approach, "You help people reveal assumptions and feel safe about doing it and ask them to . . . publicly weigh them and reclaim them, essentially. And exchange them for ones that are actually more appealing and more convincing."

Mike's intervention broke the common pattern of repetition and comfort, pushing some of the students into the difficult unlearning process (Kumashiro, 2002). As highlighted previously, the interviewed students recognized that "but statements" amounted to a prejudice toward homosexuality. Yet an examination of transcripts from the student interviews 9 months after the dialogue occurred demonstrate how this singular event, although powerful, did not significantly undermine the dominance of a straight/queer binary or the safe distancing of Others. Rather, I found ample examples of what Britzman (1998) calls "the stingy subject positions of the tolerant normal and the tolerated subaltern" (p. 87).

For example, Keeshawn said the following about Mike's comparison of racism to homophobia:

It was basically true, how *people, they're* like, "I don't have a problem with gay people, but I don't have any gay friends." Well, then *you* do have a problem with *them*. So like if *you're* not willing to open up to be friends with somebody, *I* don't think that there's anything wrong with *them* doing whatever *they* want to do. But, I mean it's *their* lifestyle so why does it matter to *you*. It's not hurting *you*, so why should *you* care?

Although Keeshawn's speech reflects an increased tolerance of homosexuality, it does not necessarily represent a transformation of how he views himself or an admission that he was and is implicated in institutionalized oppression (Kumashiro, 2002). Rather, Keeshawn's language suggests a separation from the "people" making homophobic comments—"they" said those things, not him—even though he was especially vocal about his discomfort with homosexuality during the conversation. In the context of the interview, then, Keeshawn did not take responsibility for his own homophobia. Additionally, his language suggests that the issue at hand was no longer one of grappling with difference, as it was framed at the camp; instead, it became one of tolerating the Other. In line with Britzman's (1998) notion of the "tolerant normal," Keeshawn's statement suggests that as long as "they" did not interfere with "him," he could accept—or at least not care—about homosexuality. Accordingly, instead of challenging a conception of self as normal and separate from the abnormal Other, his language repeated, and thereby strengthened, the boundaries of the categories gay and straight.

Among the students who expressed the idea that "people are people" regardless of their differences, there was an underlying seeking of sameness rather than an appreciation of sociocultural differences and/or a desire to learn about the ways in which various political, economic, and social forces have subordinated some groups of people and not others across time (Britzman, 1998). In the following example, although Evelyn, a White female student, did not use us/them language, her description of the camp discussion suggested that the main goal of the leadership program was to "accept" differences rather than question and challenge the association of particular differences with deviance and inferiority (Kumashiro, 2002):

It kind of disappointed me because people really weren't ready to accept that difference . . . even though there's differences in all these different backgrounds, we learn together and we were accepting all these different things and then this homophobia issue came up and a lot of people were homophobic and I really didn't expect that.

Clearly, Evelyn's response signifies more than a trifling tolerance of difference. However, her statement neither acknowledges that the dominant ideal of a heterosexual identity requires the subjection of Others (Britzman, 1998) nor questions the notion of a stable gay identity that remains constant over time (Fraser, 1997).

In addition to upholding dichotomized, fixed notions of sexual identities, most of the student responses did not suggest a recognition that multiple, intersecting oppressions were at work during the dialogue. Instead, their language painted homosexuality as separate from other identity categories through comments such as, "It's the same deal, whether it's race you're talking about *or* preferences, like sexual orientation." Yet as Kumashiro (2002) reminds us, "*difference* always exceeds singular categories since identities are already multiple and intersected" (p. 56). Because single identity positions such as gay or Black remain defined in terms of their opposites—who they are not (i.e., straight or White, respectively)—they perpetuate prescriptive attributes of group members, thereby marginalizing those who do not fit the assumed portrait and doubly oppressing queer youth of color (Kumashiro, 2001, 2002). To interrupt the normalcy of the homo–hetero dichotomy, the leadership program would need to address further the intersections of different "isms" instead of adding them up in a separate but equal framework.

In short, student interpretations of the homophobia dialogue indicate that it did not disrupt students' use of an us/them language or a desire for sameness. Nevertheless, I do not want to understate the influence of this dialogue on several students' perspectives. Jemaar, an African-American male student, reminds us that the camp dialogue about homophobia did "return a difference" (Ellsworth, 1997):

> You think that you don't really have anything about gays . . . but actually you kind of do. You think you might not have a prejudice against another race but, you know, you really kind of do. So it makes you think and then, you know, before you said "but," maybe you thought about it.

## Conclusion: Assessing the Possibilities of Disrupting Othering

This chapter presents two competing conclusions. On the one hand, the dialogue about homophobia led several students to reflect on and confront their own tendencies to discriminate against those with a sexual orientation different from their own. The camp context, instructional strategies employed, and diverse perspectives of the students and facilitators made possible a collective dialogue about a taboo issue during which many students revealed their own prejudices, experiences, and assumptions. On the other hand, several student interpretations of the dialogue during the interviews 9 months later revealed a dichotomous conception of sexuality that was seemingly divorced from racial, ethnic, class, gender, national, and religious affiliations, even though the conversation was clearly shaped by the complicated intersection of these identities. The dialogue did not generally result in students breaking down the gay/straight binary, nor did it ask students to reflect on the historical, political, and cultural discourses that made and continue to make heterosexuality normal and other forms of sexuality deviant.

Although several of the students arrived at the camp feeling like sexual preference was "no big deal," other students had not previously confronted their discomfort with and fear of homosexuality. For them, the dialogue on homophobia disrupted their familiar ways of thinking and challenged their underlying assumptions about "homosexuals." However, the conversation did not necessarily continue when the students left the camp to return to their respective communities and schools. As noted previously, the facilitators intended to organize a follow-up activity with an LGBTQ alliance group, but logistical issues prevented it. Moreover, most of the students I interviewed did not suggest that they had sought out such educational opportunities on their own. The students therefore did not necessarily face situations that demanded further de- and reconstruction of their viewpoints about sexual differences and/or that investigated the specific historical, legal, cultural, and sociological narratives that make meaningful the term heterosexism (Fraser, 1997).

To disrupt the homo–hetero dichotomy that is so prevalent in our society, students need to understand how ideas about homosexuality have been socially constructed and reproduced over time and in different contexts. Foucault (1978/1990) is instructive here for showing how the medicalization of homosexuality in the 19th century shifted the discourse on "peripheral sexualities" from one of "habitual sin" to a "species" (p. 43) or "kind of person" (Hacking, 1986). Foucault's ideas on the "history of sexuality" may be inaccessible to high school students, but the larger point that human beings created (and continue to create) the category of "homosexual" and its attendant policies, practices, and behaviors is not. Students and educators have the responsibility to acknowledge and participate in "the ongoing, never completed historical, social, and political labor of meaning-construction" (Ellsworth, 1997, p. 128).

Educators can draw on other cultures that have constructed alternative, more fruitful conceptions of homosexuality (see, e.g., Roscoe, 1998) or, more ideally, seek out those people and programs in our own local civilization (Gilroy, 2004) who are challenging dominant notions of homosexuality. Byron Hurt (2006), for example, offers us a powerful educational tool with his documentary *Hip-Hop: Beyond Beats and Rhymes*. A self-proclaimed hip-hop head, Hurt interrogates the frequent misogyny, violence, and homophobia in rap and hip-hop culture as well as the profit-making impulse underlying their glorification. In his words, "[W]hat I am trying to do is get us men to take a hard look at ourselves" (Public Broadcasting Service, 2007). Like Hurt, I am calling for a systematic disloyalty to our own local cultural and political affiliations—whether racial, ethnic, class-based, religious, gendered, or otherwise—when they interfere with the realization of justice for all. Coalitions of students and teachers can make urban schools safer and more effective for all students by tackling multiple forms of oppression, including institutionalized racism, poverty, and heterosexism (McCready, 2005). However, such coalitions will not be realized until we name the problem of heterosexism and offer "alternatives to traditional practices with which we have grown too comfortable" (Hirschfeld, 2002, p. 17).

No matter how emancipatory communicative dialogue may appear, we need to question, persistently and repeatedly, our partial understandings of difference so as to avoid using empowerment discourses to dominate, marginalize, or silence Others. Nevertheless, we should not underestimate the power of dialogue to effect long-term changes in how teachers and students view themselves and Others. As Boler (2004) asserts, at times injurious language expressed in educational spaces offer a " 'teachable moment' . . . one of the very few opportunities in which a speaker will be held accountable for the 'legacies of usage' that surround offensive speech and beliefs" (p. 8). I believe Mike showed great courage in challenging high school students to take responsibility for heterosexist legacies of use. May we follow his lead and create more opportunities in our educational spaces to own the "buts."

# Notes

1. For a meaningful portrait and analysis of an FHAO classroom, see Chapter 2, "Facing Ourselves but Not History," in Simone Schweber's (2004) *Making Sense of the Holocaust*.
2. The state FHAO director was a White man pursuing his PhD in theology, philosophy, and cultural studies. He was also a former FHAO teacher. The leadership program coordinator was a White woman with a background in marketing who had previously been a corporate event planner. In addition to working part time for the FHAO program, she was

pursuing a school counseling degree. While both of these educators worked for the state chapter of FHAO year-round, the other three facilitators participated only in the camp component of the leadership program. The female African-American facilitator was a humanities high school teacher who worked at an alternative high school "for kids who don't learn well in traditional settings." The Latino male facilitator participated in various youth seminars as a consultant and was a certified trainer for the National Coalition for Equity in Education. The Asian-American male facilitator was, in his own words, a "cultural competency gadfly" who had also served as a consultant for other youth trainings. At the time of the camp, he was working for a "legal advocacy" group that helped women represent themselves in cases involving domestic violence and attempted to prevent violence through outreach activities with adolescents.

3. At the 2002 leadership camp, the facilitators grouped students from one to three schools together and asked them to organize a "Challenge Day." A Challenge Day is a daylong program in which "youth and adult participants are guided through a series of experiential learning processes" that help "increase personal power and self-esteem, to shift dangerous peer pressure to positive peer support and to eliminate the acceptability of teasing, oppression and all forms of violence" (Challenge Associates, 2002).

4. I became interested in the FHAO Leadership Program while working for the state FHAO chapter during the winter of 2002. In April 2004, I submitted my thesis, "An Instrumental Case Study of Multicultural Democratic Education: The Facing History and Ourselves Leadership Program," for the completion of my master's degree in the Educational Policy Studies department at the University of Wisconsin–Madison.

5. See Earls (2005) for specific statistics and sources.

6. Like Lisa Loutzenheiser (2003), I agree that " '[q]ueer' as a term, as opposed to gay, lesbian, or bisexual, purposefully disrupts the notion that identity is fixed or immutable. . . . It is also a move to highlight the existence of and disrupt a ubiquitous heteronormativity" (p. 167). However, in the context of the camp, the students and facilitators spoke of "gays," "lesbians," "homosexuals," "homosexuality," and "homophobia" rather than "queers," "queerness," "heterosexism," and "heteronormativity." Accordingly, I mostly use the terms articulated by leadership program participants throughout this chapter.

7. The documentary A Place at the Table celebrates the lofty democratic goals on which the United States was founded while simultaneously exposing the many injustices that various minority groups have confronted throughout its history. In the film, eight teenagers from diverse backgrounds discuss their ethnic and religious heritages and the various forms of discrimination that they and their ancestors have faced in the United States. A Place at the Table addresses issues of race, ethnicity, class, religion, and sexuality. This classroom resource, which is a product of the Southern Poverty Law Center, is available to K-12 educators for free. Go to http://www. tolerance.org.teach for further information.

8. All student and facilitator names are pseudonyms.

9. Matthew Sheperd was a gay 21-year-old college student who was brutally murdered outside of Laramie, Wyoming, in October 1998. This hate crime received national media attention and continues to serve as a powerful example of the violence that can result from the intolerance and hatred of Others. Sadly, if the camp conversation were to take place today, Mike could refer to the recent murder of 15-year-old Lawrence King.

# References

Almaguer, T. (1998). Chicano men: A cartography of homosexual identity and behavior. In P. M. Nardi & B. E. Schneider (Eds.), *Social perspectives in lesbian and gay studies: A reader* (pp. 537–552). New York: Routledge.

Bennett, C. (2001). Genres of research in multicultural education. *Review of Educational Research, 71*(2), 171–217.

Boler, M. (2004). All speech is not free: The ethics of "affirmative action pedagogy." In M. Boler (Ed.), *Democratic dialogue in education: Troubling speech, disturbing silence* (pp. 3–13). New York: Peter Lang.

Britzman, D. P. (1998). *Lost subjects, contested objects: Toward a psychoanalytic inquiry of learning.* Albany: State University of New York Press.

Campo, R. (1999). Does silencio = muerte? Notes on translating the AIDS epidemic. *The Progressive, 63*(10), 20–23.

Chan, C. S. (1997). Don't ask, don't tell, don't know: The formation of a homosexual identity and sexual expression among Asian American lesbians. In B. Greene (Ed.), *Ethnic and cultural diversity among lesbians and gay men* (Vol. 3, pp. 240–248). London: Sage.

Diaz, R. M. (1998). *Latino gay men and HIV: Culture, sexuality, and risk behavior.* New York: Routledge.

Earls, M. (2005). *GLBTQ youth.* Retrieved February 2007, from http://www.advocatesforyouth. org/publications/factsheet/fsglbt.pdf

Ellsworth, E. (1997). *Teaching positions: Difference, pedagogy, and the power of address.* New York: Teachers College Press.

*Facing History and Ourselves.* (2004). Available at http://www.facinghistory.org/facing/fha02.nsf /main/mission+statement.

Fine, M. (1995). *Habits of mind: Struggling over values in America's classrooms.* San Francisco, CA: Jossey-Bass.

Foucault, M. (1978/1990). *History of sexuality: Volume 1. An introduction.* New York: Vintage Books.

Fraser, N. (1997). *Justice interruptus: Critical reflections on the "postsocialist" condition.* New York: Routledge.

Freire, P. (1970/1994). *Pedagogy of the oppressed.* New York: Continuum.

Gates, H. L. Jr. (2000). Foreword. In D. Constantine-Simms (Ed.), *The greatest taboo: Homosexuality in Black communities* (pp. xi–xv). Los Angeles: Alyson Publications.

Gilroy, P. (2004). *After empire: Melancholia or convivial culture?* New York: Routledge.

Griffin, H. (2000). Their own received them no: African American lesbians and gays in Black churches. In D. Constantine-Simms (Ed.), *The greatest taboo: Homosexuality in Black communities* (pp. 110–121). Los Angeles: Alyson Publications.

Hacking, I. (1986). Making up people. In T. C. Heller, M. Sosna, & D. E. Wellbery (Eds.), *Reconstructing individualism: Autonomy, individuality, and the self in Western thought* (pp. 222–236). Stanford, CA: Stanford University Press.

Harris Interactive and GLSEN. (2005). *From teasing to torment: School climate in America, a survey of students and teachers.* New York: GLSEN.

Hernandez-Truyol, B. E. (2001). Latina multidimensionality and LatCrit possibilities: Culture, gender, and sex. In T. Davis, K. R. Johnson, & G. A. Martinez (Eds.), *A reader on race, civil rights, and American law: A multiracial approach* (pp. 689–691). Durham, NC: Carolina Academic Press.

Hirschfeld, S. (2002, Fall). What's in a name? Institutionalized heterosexism and everyday forms of anti-LGBT bias in schools. *Respect, 10*, 15–17.

hooks, b. (2000). Homophobia in Black communities. In D. Constantine-Simms (Ed.), *The greatest taboo: Homosexuality in Black communities* (pp. 67–73). Los Angeles: Alyson Publications.

Hurt, B. (2006). *Hip-hop: Beyond beats and rhymes.* San Francisco, CA: Independent Television Service.

Hurt, B. (2006). *Hip-hop: Beyond beats and rhymes.* San Francisco, CA: Independent Television Service.

Hutchinson, E. O. (2000). My gay problem, your Black problem. In D. Constantine-Simms (Ed.), *The greatest taboo: Homosexuality in Black communities* (pp. 2–6). Los Angeles: Alyson Publications.

Kumashiro, K. K. (1999). Supplementing normalcy and otherness: Queer Asian American men reflect on stereotypes, identity, and oppression. *Qualitative Studies in Education, 12*(5), 491–508.

Kumashiro, K. K. (2001). Queers students of color and antiracist, antiheterosexist education: Paradoxes of identity and activism. In K. K. Kumashiro (Ed.), *Troubling intersections of race and sexuality: Queer students of color and anti-oppressive education* (pp. 1–25). Lanham, MD: Rowman & Littlefield.

Kumashiro, K. K. (2002). *Troubling education: Queer activism and anti-oppressive pedagogy.* New York: RoutledgeFalmer.

Loutzenheiser, L. W. (2003). Uneasy similarities, uneven parallels: Race, sexuality and civil rights discourse. In G. Ladson-Billings (Ed.), *Critical race theory perspectives on social studies: The profession, policies, and curriculum* (pp. 149–170). Greenwich, CT: Information Age Publishing.

Mayo, C. (2004). The tolerance that dare not speak its name. In M. Boler's (Ed.), *Democratic dialogue in education: Troubling speech, disturbing silence* (pp. 33–47). New York: Peter Lang.

McBride, D. A. (2000). Can the queen speak? Racial essentialism, sexuality, and the problem of authority. In D. Constantine-Simms (Ed.), *The greatest taboo: Homosexuality in Black communities* (pp. 24–43). Los Angeles: Alyson Publications.

McCready, L. T. (2005). Some challenges facing queer youth programs in urban high schools: Racial segregation and denormalizing whiteness. In J. T. Sears (Ed.), *Gay, lesbian, and transgender issues in education: Programs, policies, and practices* (pp. 185–197). New York: Harrington Park Press.

Okazaki, S. (2002). Influences of culture on Asian Americans' sexuality. *Journal of Sex Research, 39*(1), 34–41.

Parker, W. C. (2003). *Teaching democracy: Unity and diversity in public life.* New York: Teachers College Press.

Public Broadcasting Service (PBS). (2007). *Hip-hop: Beyond beats and rhymes: The film.* Retrieved February 2007, from http://www.pbs.org/independentlens/hiphop/statement.htm

Roscoe, W. (1998). *Changing ones: Third and fourth genders in Native North America.* New York: St. Martin's Press.

Schweber, S. A. (2004). *Making sense of the Holocaust: Lessons from classroom practice*. New York: Teachers College Press.

Shor, I. (1992). *Empowering education: Critical teaching for social change*. Chicago: The University of Chicago Press.

Stake, R. E. (2000). A brief history and some advice. In N. K. Denzin & Y. S. Lincoln (Eds.), *Handbook of qualitative research*, (2nd ed., pp. 257–278). Thousand Oaks, CA: Sage Publications.

Vidich, A. J., & Lyman, S. M. (2000). Qualitative methods: Their history in sociology and anthropology. In N. K. Denzin & Y. S. Lincoln (Eds.), *Handbook of qualitative research* (2nd ed., pp. 37–84). Thousand Oaks, CA: Sage Publications.

Williams, A. (1993). Diversity and agreement in feminist ethnography. *Sociology, 27*(4), 575–589.

Wolf, D. L. (1996). Situating feminist dilemmas in fieldwork. In D. L. Wolf (Ed.), *Feminist dilemmas in fieldwork* (pp. 1–55). Boulder, CO: Westview Press.

## · 5 ·

# Youth Teaching Teachers

## Bridging Racial and Cultural Divides Between Teachers and Students

TARA M. BROWN, SUMMER CLARK, & THURMAN BRIDGES

Research shows that many of the predominantly White, middle-class teachers in the United States are unprepared to effectively teach an increasingly racially and culturally diverse K-12 school population. Lack of cultural and linguistic competencies (Bollin, 2007; Ladson-Billings, 2005), low expectations of and lack of caring for students (Conchas & Rodriguez, 2007; Nieto, 1999), as well as racial/ethnic, cultural, and linguistic biases (Brown, 2007; Fine, Roberts, & Torre, 2004) have all been cited as significant barriers for these teachers. As such, teacher education programs have been charged with fostering cultural competency among preservice teachers. Cultural competency, as defined by Trumball and Pacheo (2005), is "the ability to recognize differences based on culture, language, race, ethnicity, and other aspects of individual identity and to respond to those differences positively and constructively" (p. 4).

Unfortunately, many traditional teacher education programs do not provide new teachers with the skills and understandings they need to be successful—both academically and socially—with students from cultural backgrounds that are different from their own (Ladson-Billings, 2001; Lynn, 2007; Owens & Konkol, 2004; Webster Brandon, 2003). As teacher educators, we see this reflected in the traditional model of teacher preparation, which provides for little meaningful interaction between preservice teachers and the young people they will teach.

In this chapter, we describe an innovative approach to involving K-12 students in university teacher training that seeks to provide preservice teachers with meaningful cross-racial and cross-cultural encounters with youth. By bringing K-12 students of color into the teacher education classroom, as experts of their own experiences and active agents in the educational process, teachers-in-training have the opportunity to learn about young people's perspectives on schooling and to challenge their own assumptions about, particularly, low-income adolescents of color. We describe how we, as teacher educators and researchers, have facilitated this experience through a teacher preparation model that significantly differs from and enriches the traditional university teacher education program. We show this model in action by describing a workshop for preservice teachers, co-conducted with the adolescents with whom we work. We explicate how the model can help to bridge racial and cultural divides between teachers and K-12 students, foster personal growth and critical literacy among youth, and help teacher educators to better understand the educational needs of preservice teachers and K-12 students.

# Project ARISE

This chapter is drawn from a participatory action research (PAR) project, Action Research into School Exclusion (ARISE), aimed at understanding and improving the schooling experiences of youth excluded from school for disciplinary reasons. In addition to the authors, the research team included eight Black and Latina/o high school students attending an urban, special education alternative school in the Mid-Atlantic region. ARISE activities included analyzing educational literature, conducting and analyzing interviews with students and teachers, presenting research findings, and designing and conducting teacher preparation workshops.

ARISE reflects the principles of PAR, described by Minkler (2000) as "systematic inquiry, with the collaboration of those affected by the issue being studied, for purposes of education and taking action or effecting social change" (p. 192). In PAR, local knowledge is essential to understanding and addressing problems (Córdova, 2004; Gaventa, 1993), and local informants are not merely study "subjects" but co-researchers actively engaged in all stages of research with the explicit aim of "action" or intervention into the problem(s) under study. Consistent with this methodology, the concerns and interests of the youth who collaborated in study design, data collection, and analysis and the representation and use of study findings drove the work of ARISE. To train and support the young people in the work of the project, we (the authors) taught a for-credit *Research Seminar* twice a week at their school. The teacher preparation model described in this chapter is part of the "action" component of ARISE, through which the research team sought to prepare preservice teachers to work effectively with, particularly, "at-risk" students from cultural backgrounds that are different from their own.

## Models for Teacher Preparation

Our framing of teacher preparation focuses on three constituents: K-12 students, teacher educators, and preservice teachers. They are represented by the three circles in Figures 5.1 and 5.2 below. The overlapping areas represent the spaces in which these constituents interact.

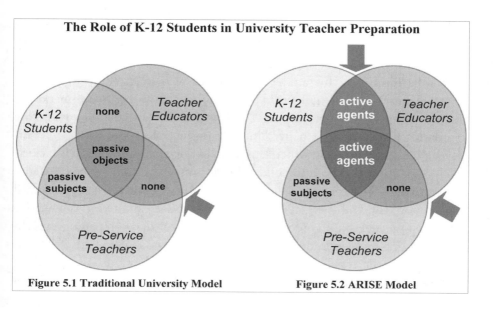

**Figure 5.1 Traditional University Model**       **Figure 5.2 ARISE Model**

We believe that the role of K-12 students—as passive subjects, active agents, or altogether absent—and the activities that take place in those interactions significantly impact the degree to which teacher preparation programs can promote cross-racial and cultural competence. Following, we examine these roles and activities in the traditional university and ARISE models of teacher preparation. Through one example of the work of ARISE, we show how the active and deliberate participation of K-12 students in teacher preparation helps us, as teacher educators, to better prepare preservice teachers to work effectively with students from racial and cultural backgrounds that are different from their own.

## The Traditional Model

As reflected in Figure 5.1, direct interaction between university faculty and K-12 students is not built into the traditional university teacher preparation model, and K-12 students have minimal involvement in teacher preparation. Faculty may conduct research on K-12 students, which informs their university teaching practice, but students usually play a passive role as study subjects. In their interactions with preservice teachers, K-12 students are also relatively passive subjects to be observed or on whom to practice teaching skills. In the traditional university model, all three constituents usually only come together during clinical supervision where, again, K-12 students play a passive role and do not intentionally and deliberately participate in the learning of the teachers-in-training. This lack of participation is reflected in the fact that the primary relationship in this model is between the teacher educator and the preservice teacher. The interaction between these two constituents marks the entry point into teacher preparation (indicated by the arrow) and provides the foundation for preservice teachers' interactions with K-12 students.

We see several ways in which this model of teacher preparation is lacking as a process through which to build cultural competency among teacher education students. First, preservice teachers often do not enter the classroom until their junior year, and their student teaching is usually limited to one or two semesters. We feel that in order to build effective cultural competency, teachers-in-training need sustained cross-racial/cultural encounters with K-12 students that occur regularly from the outset of teacher preparation. Also important is the nature of these encounters, and here we feel the passivity of K-12 students is extremely problematic.

K-12 students hold unique knowledge about what teachers must know, understand, and be able to do to work effectively with students from diverse racial and cultural backgrounds. In relegating them to the role of objects to be observed or to be practiced on, we neglect a vital resource in preparing culturally competent teachers. We believe that K-12 students, particularly students of color, must have an active and intentional role in teacher preparation, and their expertise must be valued and respected. This requires spaces—unlike in traditional observational, student teaching, and clinical supervision settings—in which K-12 students are experts in their own right and have real input into the nature of teacher preparation through meaningful interactions with both preservice teachers and teacher educators.

Last, the traditional model of teacher preparation does not cultivate ongoing interactions between teacher educators and K-12 students. There has been a rapid increase in racial/ethnic, cultural, and linguistic diversity in K-12 schools, and most university instructors have left the K-12 classroom and have since had only tangential experiences with K-12 students. This can impede their understanding of the everyday challenges of teaching in diverse classrooms and the problems that arise due to racial and cultural difference. Sustained interactions between faculty and, particularly, K-12 students of color should be incorporated into the teacher preparation process to help teacher educators better understand what is needed to build cultural competence among teacher education students.

## The ARISE Model

In the ARISE model of teacher preparation, which we use to supplement the traditional university model, the relationship between teacher educators and K-12 students (as between teacher educators and preservice teachers) is also primary. It marks a vital entry point into the teacher preparation process and provides an important model for *how* preservice teachers should interact with K-12 students. This model is based on authentic collaboration with youth as active agents in intellectual work and the design of activities that help preservice teacher to build cross-cultural understanding. In the ARISE model, K-12 students, preservice teachers, and teacher educators come together around these activities in workshops for teacher education students. In the workshops, youth take on the active role of educator, sharing their expertise on what teachers need to know and understand to work effectively with students who are racially and culturally different from them. Drawing on principles of liberatory education (Freire, 1973), this includes critical dialogue among all three constituents about racial and cultural bias and how it impacts teachers' beliefs and practices and the schooling experiences of youth.

In the ARISE model, all three constituents are teachers and learners.

Through PAR and the design and implementation of workshops, youth learn valuable research, teaching, and presentation skills. They become active agents in transforming teacher preparation and deepen their own understanding of schooling processes through the sharing and building of knowledge and expertise. Built into the ARISE model are rare opportunities for preservice teachers to learn from K-12 students, to talk explicitly about issues of race and culture, and to learn about young people's perspectives on and experiences with these issues. It is doubtful that many traditional teacher education programs offer such opportunities, which are vital to building cultural competence. Further, observing their interactions with youth of color around issues of race and culture has given us, as teacher educators, valuable insights into preservice teachers' potential challenges in understanding and valuing youth of color and their perspectives and experiences.

The preservice teacher workshops, one of which is described later, are part of the ARISE's cyclical knowledge-building process, into which we integrate data from the workshops—video footage, our own reflections, and preservices teachers' written feedback. This helps us to deepen our understanding of the nature of racial and cultural conflict in the classroom and identify topics for further investigation. In turn, we increase our capacity to design learning experiences that help preservice teachers to understand K-12 students' and their own cultural and racialized experiences and their significance to classroom teaching and learning.

## Youth Teaching Teachers: The ARISE Model in Action

In April 2007, the ARISE research team conducted a workshop for preservice teachers in a social foundations of education course at the University of Maryland after several weeks of planning. The youth identified what they felt were important themes that emerged from our research data, given our target audience. Among the 31 preservice teachers in the workshop, there were 3 Asian Americans, 2 African Americans, 1 Latina, and 25 Whites. According to the course instructor, most were middle class, few had had meaningful interactions with Black or Latina/o youth before the workshop, and none had student teaching experience. The youth identified several themes, including racial/ethnic, cultural, and linguistic bias. We organized the workshop around those themes and selected the research data to present—excerpts from videotaped interviews conducted with other youth. We agreed that after we (the authors) briefly introduced and described the work of Project ARISE, one youth researcher would take responsibility for each theme and present findings, share a personal experience, and facilitate dialogue on that topic. The workshop was videotaped for later critical self-reflection and analysis.

The themes of respect and disrespect were particularly evocative topics that the students addressed in their presentations. Throughout the workshop, the ARISE youth researchers stressed that respect for students is foundational to teachers' abilities to bridge racial and cultural divides. As stated by Bruce, a youth researcher, the essential point across all topics presented was that "It's all about respect." The youth described respect as unconditional and encompassing concern about and positive action to promote students' emotional and academic well-being, appreciating students' knowledge, and valuing students' cultures and cultural expressions.

Christina, a youth researcher, described being punished by a teacher for speaking Spanish in class as one example of *disrespect*. She and another researcher, José Angel, eloquently highlighted the significance of their home language to their racial/ethnic and cultural identities as Salvadoran Latina/os. One preservice teacher in the class, June, an Asian-American woman, challenged the research team on this issue, stating,

> Like, if I'm giving a lesson speaking another language is just a very big distraction....The problem is that a student is disrupting the class lesson. I would not allow any student to speak their language when others are trying to learn because it's a huge distraction.

In such an exchange, it was our role, as teacher educators and youth allies, to model the valuing of young people's perspectives and support the youth in helping preservice teachers understand how depicting a student's home language as antithetical to learning and prohibiting cultural expression can impact their students and their effectiveness as teachers. Through open dialogue, the preservice teachers and research team together examined strategies for using students' home languages to support teaching and learning in the classroom, including one suggestion from Mike, a youth researcher, that teachers try to learn other languages.

Like June, other preservice teachers struggled with the research team's perspectives on, particularly, unconditional respect. For example, one White man, Steve, responded,

> You talk about respect and it's easy to put it on the teacher but it also has to come back to the students. They have to want to learn. They have to be open to showing respect

> to the teacher. From your point of view it's the teachers that don't understand you but from the teacher's point of view it's the kids that don't want to learn. It's the kids that are trouble-makers. It's the kids that are loud and disruptive. . . . So all of you seem intelligent enough and you seem like great students but it's the other kids. Like how can you get the other kids to be really willing to listen to the teacher and to follow their instruction?

For us, as teacher educators, understanding Steve's perspective that teachers and students have equal responsibility for K-12 classroom relations was both troubling and instructive. His insinuation that students who are loud and resistant do not deserve respect and must first meet particular conditions such as wanting to learn and obeying the teacher was also enlightening. The youth researchers countered this by focusing on the responsibilities of teachers, as paid adult professionals, to respect and invest in the success of all students regardless of the troubles they may have or may have caused. This prompted instructive dialogue around Steve's question about how to foster student cooperation and mutual respect in the classroom.

Also educative was Steve's apparent willingness to give respect to the youth researchers who "seem[ed] intelligent enough" and "seem[ed] like great students" but not to "the other kids" he described. For us, this signaled a disturbing, underlying perception about youth of color in urban schools—that some were neither intelligent enough nor great students. Other preservice teachers, by focusing on imagined and troublesome "other kids," also suggested that the youth researchers, who were engaged in high-level intellectual work, were fundamentally different from their peers. For example, two White women asked the youth researchers,

> Do you guys think you can go into some of those public schools and maybe do talks with some of them to help motivate those students?

> Is there anything that you can do to help influence those students, students who might not want to graduate, students in your own school?

Such comments took focus away from the responsibilities of teachers. Further, in posing the youth researchers as different from their peers, the preservice teachers did not have to challenge negative assumptions about the capabilities of urban students of color when confronted with contradictory evidence. The team continually redirected attention to the role of teachers, but the dialogue often drifted back to problem students. At one point, one of the adult researchers interjected,

You need to understand that these students are exceptional but they are not exceptions. They are representative of the whole school. I don't want you to leave thinking that we hand-picked the best of the best. They represent the general population.

What some preservice teachers failed to understand was that the ARISE youth *were* those "other kids." They all had troubled schooling histories, including multiple suspensions and expulsions. Importantly, they attributed their current school successes to respect, caring, and support from school adults. This was a vital lesson for the preservice teachers—understanding how interpersonal interactions can determine student success and failure. In university teacher education programs, preservice teachers typically do not have such opportunities to face their own assumptions and misunderstandings of K-12 students.

This experience gave us, as teacher educators, a more sophisticated understanding of how to help preservice teachers understand the role of teachers in classroom disruption and to examine assumed links among "disruptive" behavior, intelligence, and aspirations. In traditional teacher preparation, teacher educators rarely have opportunities to observe such interactions that can help them to provide the appropriate support and instruction to challenge preservice teachers' deficit thinking. Without transforming the current teacher education model to incorporate the voices and deliberate participation of K-12 students, teacher educators and preservice teachers miss crucial opportunities to build their understanding of the cultural competencies needed in working with an increasingly diverse K-12 student population.

## Beyond Traditional Models: Enriching All Three Constituents

The ARISE model of teacher preparation has tremendous potential for bridging racial divides and building cultural competence and understandings that benefit all three constituents highlighted in this chapter: K-12 students, preservice teachers, and teacher educators. Whereas preservice teachers develop competencies for working with youth from diverse racial and ethnic backgrounds, K-12 students develop critical literacy skills by taking action on issues that concern them. Finally, teacher educators gain deeper understandings of the issues involved in interactions between the mainly White teacher workforce and students of color.

## What Preservice Teachers Learn

Preservice teachers learn cultural competencies that enable them to teach K-12 students with greater sensitivity and understanding through the ARISE model. Many preservice teachers enter teacher education programs without the concrete experiences necessary for understanding their students; traditional teacher education often fails to provide opportunities for preservice teachers to interact with students and apply the principles they study. However, as preservice teachers take part in these workshops, they can work through several important aspects of cultural competency. As they encounter K-12 students of color, they must face their assumptions and can raise their awareness of issues related to culture and race in society today, as the following student comment on the workshop captures:

> Many people, including myself, think about race issues in schools as a huge part of the history of the 50s and 60s, not necessarily an issue of today. What came as a shock to me [as a result of the workshop] was how frequently these issues still arise.

Such encounters with issues of culture and race can help to expose preservice teachers' deficit models of students. For example, in a written reflection on the workshop, one White preservice teacher commented on a particular K-12 student presenter, saying,

> I feel like he judged us, in our lack of knowledge of what a student feels like in the classroom. . . . Some teachers may not care to form a relationship if students are unwilling.

Such deficit thinking that harms so many students of color can remain undetected and unaddressed particularly when traditional teacher education programs fail to create opportunities for preservice teachers to interact with and learn from K-12 students. When these interactions occur, teacher educators can assist students to work through harmful assumptions about youth of color and develop the higher degree of cultural awareness necessary for cultural competence.

Preservice teachers' reflections attested to the power of the ARISE model in demonstrating what cultural competence means for teacher practice. Before the workshop, preservice teachers had abstractly explored the meaning of affirming student diversity. However, during the workshop, in actually interacting with Latino/a and Black youth in a classroom setting, they gain a more concrete understanding of what culturally competent teaching might look like. How we, as teacher educators, model cultural competence in our own interactions with the youth is vital to this understanding. The power of such experiences in teacher education programs cannot be overstated. For example, we found that, for several preservice teachers, the ARISE workshops raised vital questions about their own commitment to and/or capacity for teaching in public K-12 education, particularly in urban schools. Rather than assuming that we can remake all preservice teachers into models of cultural competency, we should consider the benefit of experiences like those cultivated by ARISE, which can prompt preservice teachers to consider the seriousness of their commitment to students.

## What K-12 Students Learn

The ARISE model benefits K-12 student participants in many invaluable ways. The project provides an authentic inquiry experience built on students' everyday concerns. It also develops students' multiple literacies by providing them with spaces to use their unique "funds of knowledge" (Moll, 1992) to accomplish real-life purposes—better understanding of their own schooling conditions to transform them. Unlike the traditional literacy model in which students are passive receivers of static, fragmented literacy curriculum, in ARISE, young people are actively engaged in deeply personal and transformative literacy practices (Freire, 1973). As students research, design, and implement teacher education workshops, they develop literacy competencies, confidence, and skill in public speaking as well as practical cultural competencies that will help them to navigate future interactions with dominant U.S. culture.

Finally, students gain a heightened sense of self-worth and pride in taking transformational action. For many it provided a vital sense of purpose to their schooling experience, as evidenced in the following reflections by ARISE youth researchers:

> This group ARISE helped me a lot 'cause if my school did not have it then I probably wouldn't be at school till this day.

> [ARISE] helped me in so many ways that the schools haven't . . . we do things that other schools don't like talk about the schools we come from and how we think a teacher should act when working in a school like I am at.

> I have been able to hopefully help teachers teach kids like me more effectively.

## What Teacher Educators Learn

Finally, this experience can be transformative for teacher educators at the university level. In working with K-12 students and their schools, teacher educators gain a clearer understanding of the nature of everyday life in schools and the unique realities of students' lives today. Teacher educators' work in the university gains legitimacy and relevancy as they co-construct knowledge with K-12 students and bridge the disconnect between theory and practice so prevalent in education programs throughout the country. Through this work, they can gain a substantially better understanding of how theory and research produced in academia, particularly concerning race and ethnicity, does (or does not) intersect with the real lives of students.

Teacher educators gain valuable understandings of K-12 students from these interactions, and they also gain clarified understandings of the preservice teachers they teach. They are able to assess preservice teachers' cultural competencies in theory as well as practice to understand strengths and weaknesses in their attitudes, expectations, and interactional patterns with youth from different cultural and racial/ethnic backgrounds. With this understanding, teacher educators can devise more effective plans for addressing areas preservice teachers need to develop more fully in relation to cultural competence.

# Conclusion

The ARISE teacher preparation model is situated within the broader ARISE PAR project. As PAR researchers, we strongly advocate for this method of research but realize that not all teacher educators have the interest in and/or capacity for conducting this type of work. However, one vital aspect of the ARISE model that we believe all teacher education programs can and should incorporate is the facilitation of sustained cross-racial/cultural encounters between preservice teachers and K-12 students, who are deliberate, active agents in the teacher education process. This requires universities and professors to cultivate relationships with K-12 schools and students and to invite young people into the university, to share their experiences, in either a formal or informal manner. It also requires teacher educators to increase their own cultural competency so that they can model and facilitate interactions in which youth and their perspectives and experiences are valued and respected. In our vision of "scaling up" we would require *every* teacher education course to include at least one K-12 student presentation or panel that included young people of diverse racial/ethnic and cultural backgrounds.

As Alvermann (2002) explains, schools today are in dire need of teachers who understand culture. Unfortunately, the current model of teacher induction tends to ignore issues of culture in favor of technical, disciplinary skills—skills that may be ineffective if teachers are not able to culturally connect with their students. Incorporating K-12 students as active agents in teacher preparation, as in the ARISE model, can increase preservice teachers' understandings of culture within a teacher education framework, as part of an effort to bridge existing gulfs between teachers and students of color. In our experience, this approach has been extremely valuable for preservice teachers, K-12 students, and for us, as teacher educators. It has been essential to developing the cultural competencies needed to bridge the racial, ethnic, and cultural divides that are too often left uncrossed in the traditional university model of teacher preparation.

# References

Alvermann (2002). Effective literacy instruction for adolescents. *Journal of Literacy Education*, 34(2), 189–208.

Bollin, G. G. (2007). Preparing teachers for Hispanic immigrant children: A service learning approach. *Journal of Latinos & Education*, 6(2), 177–189.

Brown, T. M. (2007). Lost and turned out: Academic, social and emotional experiences of students excluded from school. *Urban Education*.

Conchas, G. Q., & Rodriguez, L. F. (2007). *Small schools and urban youth: Using the power of school culture to engage students*. Thousand Oaks, CA: Corwin Press.

Córdova, T. (2004). Plugging the brain drain: Bringing our education back home. In J. Mora & D. R. Diaz (Eds.), *Latino social policy: A participatory research model* (pp. 25–53). New York: The Haworth Press.

Fine, M., Roberts, R. A., & Torre, M. E. (2004). *Echoes of brown* [DVD]. New York: The Graduate Center, City University of New York.

Freire, P. (1973). *Education for critical consciousness*. New York: The Seabury Press.

Gaventa, J. (1993). The powerful, the powerless, and the experts: Knowledge struggles in an information age. In P. Park, M. Brydon-Miller, B. Hall, & T. Jackson (Eds.), *Voices of change* (pp. 21–40). Westport, CT: Greenwood Publishing.

Ladson-Billings, G. (2001). *Crossing over to Canaan: The journey of new teachers in diverse classrooms*. San Francisco: Jossey-Bass.

Ladson-Billings, G. (2005). Is the team all right? Diversity and teacher education. *Journal of Teacher Education*, 56(3), 229–234.

Lynn, M. (2007). Pre-service teacher inquiry: Creating a space to dialogue about becoming a social justice educator. *Teaching and Teacher Education, 23*(1), 94–105.

Minkler, M. (2000). Using participatory action research to build healthy communities. *Public Health Reports, 115*, 191–197.

Moll, L. (1992). Funds of knowledge for teaching: Using a qualitative approach to connect home and classrooms. *Theory in Practice, 31*(1), 132–141.

Nieto, S. (1999). *The light in their eyes: Creating multicultural learning communities*. New York: Teachers College Press.

Owens, L., & Konkol, L. (2004). Traditioning from alternative to traditional school settings: A student perspective. *Reclaiming Youth and Children, 13*(3), 173–176.

Trumball & Pacheo. (2005). *Leading with diversity: Cultural competencies for teacher preparation and professional education*. Providence, RI: The Education Alliance at Brown University and Pacific Resources for Education and Learning.

Villegas & Lucas. (2002). *Educating culturally responsive teachers: A coherent approach*. New York: State University of New York Press.

Webster Brandon, W. (2003). Toward a white teachers' guide to playing fair: Exploring the cultural politics of multicultural teaching. *Qualitative Studies in Education, 16*(1), 31–50.

# PART II

# LIVING, LEARNING, AND TEACHING TEACHERS

· 6 ·

# Breaking the Cycle of Racism in the Classroom

## Critical Race Reflections From Future Teachers of Color

RITA KOHLI

As a resource specialist in a middle school in Oakland, California, I worked with many students who were labeled "learning disabled." Contrary to the label, these students were critical of the world and challenged it in brilliant ways that have forever changed my life perspective. During my first year of teaching, I had an African-American student named Eddie[1]; he was a talkative and confident sixth grader who struggled in math. Learning how this young man saw the world pushed me, more than anyone had to that point, to reflect on cultural biases within education. Since then, I have learned a lot about this subject, but I also realize how invisibly the dominant culture can penetrate the way we see ourselves and the world around us.

To highlight the impact that cultural bias in schools can have on Students of Color, this chapter articulates themes that emerge from the personal narratives of nine Women of Color[2] enrolled in an undergraduate education program in Southern California. Through qualitative interviews, these future Teachers of Color reveal discriminatory experiences in their own education, as well as convey advice on how to prevent and break cycles of racism in classrooms of today's youth. The voices of Teachers of Color are often invisible from education discourse; however, this study adds a much-needed perspective to teacher education and can provide a model of pedagogical reflection that, I believe, should be replicated in programs serving prospective Teachers of Color.

## Whose Standards Are the Standards?

One day, a few months into my first school year as a teacher, I was in the hallway during lunch talking with the English teacher, Ms. Wright. Eddie came up to us and asked, "Ms. Wright, I don't got no lunch money, can I sit in your room and use the computer?" Ms. Wright was a seventh-year White teacher who received a lot of respect for the high academic standards that she held students to at this underperforming school. Ms. Wright immediately responded, "I am not going to answer that question until you speak correctly. How can we say that in proper English?" We both looked at Eddie, waiting for him to rephrase his words, but instead he calmly replied, "Maybe not in your house, but in my house that *is* how we speak correctly." Ms. Wright and I were both caught off guard and a little speechless, and Eddie just stood there unphased, waiting for us to let him use the computer.

That incident stuck in my head for the next few days. Eddie, with his direct comment, had pointed out something that I had been taking for granted as a teacher. I knew that Oakland was the center of the "Ebonics" debate. I was also aware that there is controversy over how to address differences that exist between the language that students come to school with and what they need to know for most U.S. colleges and professional jobs. But what I was not conscious of, until Eddie so confidently pointed it out, was that although differences exist in the structure of African American Language (AAL) and Standard American English (SAE), at this school, we were actually teaching a hierarchy of those differences (Faires Conklin & Lourie, 1983).[3] I began to reflect on how many classrooms I had walked into where daily oral language, an exercise for students to work on SAE grammar, involved a teacher asking a class of predominantly Black students to "correct" a sentence that was written in AAL. I began to think of all the times in which I had "corrected" students' speech and writing from AAL to SAE without thinking twice. Rather than teaching youth that languages and dialects have *differences*, and that SAE is something that we often have to know in order to access academic and economic mobility, I was teaching children that SAE was *correct* and AAL was *incorrect*.

Soon after Eddie's comment in the hallway, I began to read about teaching cultural differences, and my pedagogy began to reflect my newfound awareness (Perry & Delpit, 1998; Yosso, 2005). This was a huge lesson that I learned from my 11-year-old student, but I was still not settled around this issue. What I continued to struggle with was the fact that, like Eddie, SAE was not the primary language in my own home growing up.

My family is from India, and Hindi is my parents' first language. In my house, my parents speak what I like to call *Hinglish*—a fluid blend of Hindi and English. So I was perplexed: Why was someone like me, someone who comes from a non-SAE home, so quick to uphold the standards of the English language? Why did I assume that SAE was the best way to express things? What happened in my life that led me to, consciously or not, hold dominant White culture superior while teaching Youth of Color?

Growing up, I lived in several cities and small towns around the country. Although my parents spoke Hindi around us all the time, I could understand it but never was able to speak it. A rare privilege, in college I was able to study the language, but it was not until studying abroad in India that I finally felt fluent. When I have asked my parents why my brother and I never learned Hindi as children, one story they tell makes me reflect on how much power teachers have in reinforcing cultural hierarchies.

I was born in Dayton, Ohio, in the late 1970s. At that time, our family was one of a few immigrant families in this Midwestern city. As my brother was beginning preschool and I was just a baby, a teacher told my mother that she had two Persian children in her class the previous year that spoke Farsi. Her analysis was that, because their primary language was not English, these children had trouble making friends and were often confused at school. This White teacher emphasized that my mom should make sure to teach her kids (my brother and me) only English so that *we* would not feel excluded or confused. As a new mother and recent immigrant, my mom listened to this Ohioan teacher, and she and my father began to censor their Hindi around us. Because language acquisition happens most easily at young ages (Carroll, 1999), this Ohioan teacher's advice was a large reason that I was unable to speak Hindi for most of my life.

## White Cultural Dominance in Schools

Unfortunately, what Eddie and I have experienced is not unique or new. For years, theorists have argued that education has been used as a tool of oppression to teach People of Color that their culture is inferior to the dominant White culture (Freire, 1970; hooks, 2001; Woodson, 1933). In 1933, Carter G. Woodson wrote *The Mis-Education of the Negro* to argue that schools miseducate Blacks (and Whites) to believe that Blacks are of less value than Whites. He claimed that education was used to maintain White dominance by socializing Whites to believe they are superior while internalizing a self-hatred within Black students.

In 1947, Kenneth and Mammie Clarke conducted a study on racial preferences of African-American children to test the notion described previously. Placing both Black and White dolls in front of Black youth and asking them to choose the one they liked the best, the researchers found that the children consistently chose White dolls. Clarke and Clarke's (1947) research proved that many Black children have a racial inferiority complex regarding Whiteness. The scholars claimed that the self-hatred of African-American youth was learned from the conditions of schools during racial segregation. This study was used as a key piece of research in the case of *Brown v. Board of Topeka* (1954) as evidence for the need to desegregate.

In the United States, Woodson's and Clarke and Clarke's discussions may seem out of date because, since 1933, race relations have improved, and schools have legally been desegregated. Although *Brown v. Board* has proved significant for People of Color to access certain educational opportunities, including higher education (Hunter-Gault, 1992), what also resulted was the closure of non-White schools. Districts fired Teachers of Color because it was deemed socially unacceptable for them to teach White children. Mostly White teachers were left educating Youth of Color often not because they wanted to but because they had to (Bell, 1983, 2004). Transitioning to a predominantly White teaching force often had a negative impact on the psyche and/or educational attainment of non-White youth (Bell, 2004; hooks, 2001).

Research by Oakes, Rogers, and Silver (2004) reveals continued segregation today. As of 2004, 41% of public schools are predominantly non-White, including students of African, Asian Pacific Islander, and Latina/o descent. This research also reports that majority non-White schools have poorer conditions, fewer resources, and higher rates of unqualified teachers than schools that are predominantly White (Oakes, Rogers, & Silver, 2004). Other studies also show that much of the curriculum and teaching styles in public schools are not culturally relevant to Students of Color (Delpit, 1995; Menchaca, 2001). The continual segregation of White and non-White children in schools, the conditions in which Students of Color are forced to go to school, and the curriculum used to teach them are all components of an education system that privileges both White students and White culture.

## Breaking the Cycle

Reflecting back on my own education, there have been numerous moments when teachers made comments or acted in ways that prioritized White cultural values over my own. Whether in regard to my language, my religion, or my traditions, I have been taught in both subtle and blatant ways that the cultural knowledge of my family has less worth than that of the dominant White culture. What is even worse is that, as a teacher, I carried this learned perspective with me into the classroom and was instilling a hierarchy of White cultural superiority into the minds of my young students.

I strongly believe that for Black, Latina/o, Asian-American, and Native-American youth to succeed in this nation, we must have strong Black, Latina/o, Asian-American, and Native-American teachers. I also know, however, that many of us have been socialized through racially biased educational systems and carry skewed perceptions of ourselves, our communities, and other non-White racial or ethnic groups. When we talk about increasing the numbers of Teachers of Color, it becomes important that teacher education programs begin to encourage these teachers to reflect on their own educational experiences and how the belief in White cultural superiority may have penetrated their values or worldviews.

Recognizing what I experienced as an injustice, but also as *racism*, has been an important healing process for me. It has also helped me to consciously work with Youth of Color to resist feelings of inferiority. As I enter the field of teacher education, I find it imperative that teacher education programs provide the space for Teachers of Color to reflect, as I did, on racism within their own educational experiences before they enter the classroom. To move in this direction, I used Critical Race Theory (CRT) as a framework to conduct qualitative interviews with Women of Color enrolled in an undergraduate education program in Southern California. With their narratives, I hope to highlight the cultural biases and racism that many Students of Color face in K-12 and the impact that this can have on them as people and teachers. By reflecting on these issues, I also hope that teacher education can begin to adopt practices similar to those in this study in order to push educators of today's youth to become more conscious in identifying and fighting against racism.

# Race, Racism, and CRT

Race, racism, and CRT are central to the analysis of this study; thus, it is important to provide clear definitions of these terms. Race is a social construct that changes over time. For example, individuals who were once considered Jewish or Italian are now viewed as White, and Arabs, who might identify themselves as White on the census, could simultaneously be racially categorized as non-White Middle Eastern when getting on a plane or applying for a job. Although it is often thought of as a simple social category, race is most often used to create hierarchies of power and dominance (Omi & Winant, 1994). In the United States, race has consistently been used to include and exclude certain groups from equal participation, resources, and human rights.

Solórzano, Allen, and Carroll (2002) argue that racism exists when one group believes itself to be superior and has power to carry out racist behavior. These authors also assert that racism affects multiple racial/ethnic groups. Although the power of certain racial/ethnic groups has fluctuated over time, People of Color have never consistently or significantly possessed power in this country and thus are often targets of racism. Although it is tied to race, this racism is not always acted out based on racial categories. It can also manifest against factors affiliated with race or ethnicity such as language, religion, and culture.

CRT was developed in the 1970s among legal scholars such as Derrick Bell, Kimberley Crenshaw, and Richard Delgado. The framework was constructed to acknowledge race and its intersections with racism as a first step to combating the daily oppression of racial injustice. Over the last 10 years, CRT has started to extend into many disciplines, including education. It is used within this field to heighten awareness about racism and educational inequity.

Guided by five principles, research in CRT in education (a) centralizes race and racism and its intersections with other forms of oppression (e.g., gender, class), (b) challenges dominant ideology, (c) represents a commitment to social justice, (d) values lived experience, and (e) uses interdisciplinary perspectives, including education, sociology, and psychology (Solórzano & Delgado-Bernal, 2001). These elements provide an important framework to engage minority voices in identifying as well as challenging racism. I utilized all five of the tenets to develop and guide the research questions, design, and analysis.

# Methods

Data for this chapter were collected as part of a study of the role of race and racism in the educational experiences and perspectives of Women of Color Educators. Participants were selected from an undergraduate education program in a public university in Southern California. Soliciting students in an education course that focuses on inequality, I recruited nine Women of Color who had the goal of becoming a teacher for interviews: three African Americans, three Latinas, and three Asian/Pacific Islanders. Through approximately hour-long individual interviews, this self-selected sample of future teachers were asked to discuss (a) whether they had experienced or witnessed racial, cultural, or linguistic discrimination in their elementary, middle, and high school education; (b) how these experiences might have impacted their cultural perspective, including their relationship to school and their family and their self-perception; and (c) what they might do to prevent those moments from occurring in their own future classrooms. In addition, for the education course from which they were recruited, each student had to write an education autobiography where they were asked to examine their educational experiences through the lens of race, class, and gender. Excerpts from these written autobiographical narratives were used to supplement the data.

The interviews were transcribed and, along with the written narratives, were coded for reoccurring themes. Through this process, three major themes emerged: (a) Whether subtle or overt, all the women in this study unfortunately had a story where they experienced racial, cultural, or linguistic discrimination in their K-12 education; (b) almost all participants revealed that those experiences with racism led them to internalize a racial, cultural, or linguistic inferiority to White culture or English; and (c) these young women had powerful ideas of how to structure classrooms that validate student cultures.

The voices of these future Teachers of Color can shed some light on what Students of Color have gone through and continue to go through in U.S. public schools. Select quotes have been drawn from the data to represent a multiracial perspective of these topics. These quotes have been framed and analyzed to highlight both individual and institutional forms of racism. Additionally, the important stories and ideas revealed through the process of this research draw attention to a pedagogical model that teacher education programs can use to better address the needs of Teachers of Color.

# Critical Race Reflections

## Student Experiences With Racism

I want to believe that when youth enter classrooms, educators will nurture and teach them. This is not always the case; unfortunately, there are teachers who act irresponsibly with the authority and influence they have over young minds. A Chicana[4] from the Los Angeles area described an experience she had in her high school chemistry course. Her White male teacher outwardly made racist comments that revealed low expectations and a lack of respect for his students and Latinas/os generally. She explained,

> It was my first day in Chemistry class in 10th grade. The teacher, the first thing that came out of his mouth was, . . ."Not many of you will be able to pass, because the trends are that mostly." I don't remember the exact words, but it was like, "Your type of people don't do well." And when someone wouldn't get the stuff or understand, he'd be like, "What are you, burros [donkeys], or something?" He'd use, kind of, our own language against us." (Interview, 2005)

The teacher who this Chicana describes began the school year setting up an expectation of failure for many of his students. In addition, his blatant disrespect across racial/ethnic and linguistic lines conveyed a message of cultural and intellectual inferiority to his Latina/o students. This young woman remembered the first day of 10th-grade chemistry well into college not because it was a positive day but rather because of her teacher's racist actions.

Racism, however, is not always consciously conveyed. A Pakistani woman from Southern California, although born in this country and a native English speaker, revealed that teachers made many assumptions about her language skills because she did not fit their perception of what an English speaker looks like. She described the day in high school when she was taken out of class to be tested for the English as a Second Language (ESL) program.

> "Please describe the picture using complete sentences," the lady asked as she pointed to a picture of a dolphin playing with a beach ball. After being summoned out of my history class, I sat in confusion as to why I was in the ESL room. The lady explained that since I was of South Asian background, I needed to pass the ESL test to continue taking regular classes. The fact that I was born and raised in California, and currently had the highest grade in my *honors* English class obviously did not make a difference." (Written narrative, 2005)

Although this action was not malicious like the previous example, this South Asian student was still a subject of racial assumptions. Based on factors as basic as her appearance and name, she was being forced to prove her place in honor's classes—a college-bound track typically closed to ESL students. Unfortunately, racialized messages like these are often sent to Students of Color about where they belong in school.

## Student Internalization of Racism

Racism can hurt and feel disempowering in the moment. However, its impact is rarely isolated to that moment. It can have a lasting effect on the self-perception and worldviews of its victims, especially when those victims are youth (Cross, 1971, 1995; Perez Huber, Johnson, & Kohli, 2006). In this study, I asked the future teachers to discuss how they felt after the incidents they described and whether the racism they witnessed or endured had an effect on the way they or their peers saw themselves or the world around them. Unfortunately, many of them were able to make connections between experiencing racism and beginning to view one's self as inferior and/or culturally subordinate to White cultural values.

One African-American future teacher expressed that many of her teachers, fueled by racist stereotypes, had low expectations of the Black male students at her predominantly Black, overcrowded public high school. She spoke passionately about how her teachers' perspectives had a negative influence on the way many students felt about their abilities as well as their post-high-school aspirations. She gave the example,

> My 11th grade shop teacher used to tell me about the Black male students in the class "They better learn this material, you know, better learn how to do this 'cause otherwise they are not going to have anything to do with their lives. And how they'll be on the street, selling drugs or be in jail and this was the only thing that anyone will ever teach them to do right, so they better learn it now." (Interview, 2005)

The teacher in this example believed the future of his own students was limited to jail, selling drugs, or car repairs, and that they did not have options beyond that. This young future teacher revealed that, unfortunately, this experience was not an isolated one. She felt strongly that there was a connection between the lack of academic engagement of her male counterparts and the racist stereotypes teachers had about Black males as students. Additionally, she argued that the internalization of racism of many of her peers greatly limited their academic and career aspirations and trajectories.

The racism that students endure and internalize does not always occur by individuals or in overt ways. Resource inequalities tend to exist between mostly White schools and schools serving Students of Color (Oakes, Roger, & Silver, 2004). This reality is a manifestation of structural racism and can have an extremely negative effect on the educational opportunities of non-White youth (e.g., access to libraries, Advanced Placement courses, and even college) but also in the way they learn to see themselves. A Mexican-American woman from the Central Valley, California, explained that there were no Honor's classes in her predominantly Mexican town. She remembers how she felt when she was bussed into the predominantly White middle school in the next town over. She commented,

> I always felt that if I raised my hand to voice my opinion about something, or even responded to a question about the material I would say something wrong, and the White students would say "Oh, it's the Mexican girl." Although I was aware that I was in an honors course because I was academically advanced, I still assumed that just because I was Mexican and lived on the poor side of town I was not as smart as them....There was always a feeling of inferiority when I was around White students during my schooling experience." (Written narrative, 2005)

The structural racism of this student's schooling had a negative impact on the way she saw herself. With no Honor's classes in her neighborhood school, a school serving mostly Latina/o children, and by having to enter a White community to gain access a rigorous education, she internalized the message that Whites were intellectually superior to her (and other Mexicans), and she began to doubt her own abilities.

Similar to this young Woman of Color, I too internalized the racism in my education. From the hierarchy of value placed on English and Hindi, to the neglect of my cultural or religious practices in school, by middle school—I hate to think it now—but I was embarrassed to be Indian. I cringed when India came up in class, and I was used as a resource because I wanted to blend in. I knew it saddened my parents when I would try to wipe my forehead if I had to wear tikka [a red mark placed on the forehead in Hindu religious ceremonies] on Hindu holidays, but I did not want to get questions or look "weird" at school. I even stayed up late one night in elementary school memorizing Christmas carols, so when we sang them in music class I would not look like an outsider. As I look back at the cultural biases in my K-12 schooling, and the schooling of these young women, I firmly believe that when we prioritize White culture above others, we are being racist. Whether conscious or unconscious, when we teach dominant cultural norms, we are often teaching students to think less of themselves, their culture, or their people.

## Strategies Against Racism

Teachers of Color are a small minority of the population of educators in the United States. The National Collaborative on Diversity in the Teaching Force (2004) collected statistics on the racial demographics of teachers and found that 90% of all public school teachers are White and more than 40% of schools do not even employ one Teacher of Color. As we increase the diversity of the teaching force, we are helping to validate the various rich cultures of youth in this country. But is it enough to just put Teachers of Color in front of Students of Color? As revealed in this research, through racism, many non-White students have been taught to perceive the dominant culture as better than their own. If we want effective socially and racially conscious Teachers of Color, it is fundamental to provide spaces for them to reflect and heal from the racism they have endured. In addition, we must also give them the room to develop strategies to consciously interrupt racism.

To just begin scratching the surface of this problem, in the last section of the interviews, I urged future teachers to speak on what they will do in their own classrooms to combat and/or prevent the impact of racism on Youth of Color. One African-American participant revealed that many of her teachers throughout K-12 had misconceptions and stereotypes about the Black and Brown students with whom she went to school. She felt that many of the teachers' negative perceptions were developed through ignorance and a lack of interaction with the actual communities in which they were teaching. To break this cycle, she advised, "It's always good to be able to connect with different people in different communities and get different perspectives. I think once you do that you are able to change your perspective, and then you are able to teach that to others" (Interview, 2005). This young woman had made a commitment to break out of her comfort zone to connect with and learn from diverse groups of people. By doing this, she believed that she would broaden her outlook and, in turn, would be better prepared to affirm her students' identity within our extremely multicultural society and schools.

A Latina student remembered a White teacher in her elementary school who she felt was Americanizing her predominantly Latina/o class. Through music, dance, and a celebration of culturally White holidays, she felt forced to choose between her home culture and success in school. She also shared an instance where her non–English-speaking friend asked her a question in Spanish and they got in trouble. After that, she felt pressure to not speak in Spanish and to no longer speak to her friend. These experiences, she commented, made her feel uncomfortable and disconnected from others in the class and from her culture. When asked what she would do in her own classroom, she responded,

> Looking back, or in current experiences, there is no real sense of community in most classrooms; I always felt that I was really uncomfortable in the classroom. I will try to make a community in which students feel comfortable. . . . I feel like that is one of the most important things—that a student could feel comfortable in where he or she is learning. (Interview, 2005)

Reflecting on discomfort within her own education and its impact on her learning and her identity, this student was committed to making her classroom a safe space for students. She saw community building as a means to create an atmosphere of unity, trust, and respect.

## Conclusion

Racism is not uncommon in schools. Every day, Youth of Color are subjected to indignities, including low expectations, stereotypes, inadequate resources, and a curriculum that privileges White cultural values (Johnson, manuscript submitted; Perez Huber, Johnson, & Kohli, 2007). Within these educational conditions, many of these youth internalize negative messages about their own culture. All the women in this study had a story to tell about the racism they went through in their own education, but many of them expressed that they had not thought about these things since they happened. Only now, as adults, had they begun to realize how deeply it affected them. Although barely scratching the surface in the process of healing, these interviews functioned to bring voice to oft-unheard stories of Women of Color within education. They are also a way for the participants to try and turn their experiences with racism into proactive means to think about culturally relevant, racially conscious teaching strategies. Teacher education programs often lack strategies and curriculum that speak to the needs of Teachers of Color. The process that future Teachers of Color underwent within this study proved important and should be viewed as a possible model to be incorporated into teacher education.

It takes great strength to have pride in our culture when degraded and to stand up against cultural biases and racism. We must encourage our students to, like Eddie, resist believing the message that People of Color are inferior. To do so, however, we must also heal from the wounds of our own education. Fighting racism is a difficult and uphill battle, but the more we believe in the immense value of diverse cultural knowledge, language, and rich traditions, the more equipped we are to create spaces that educate and empower our children.

## Notes

*Reprinted with permission. Originally published as: Kohli, R. (2008, Fall). Breaking the cycle of racism: Critical race reflections of Women of Color educators. *Teacher Education Quarterly, 35*(4).

1. All names used in this chapter are actually pseudonyms used to protect privacy and identity.
2. "Women of Color" references individuals of indigenous, African, Latina/o, Asian/Pacific Islander descent. It is intentionally capitalized to reject the standard grammatical norm. Capitalization is used as a means to empower this group and represents a grammatical move toward social and racial justice. This rule also applies to the terms "Teachers of Color," "People of Color," and "Students of Color," used throughout this chapter.
3. It is important that we recognize why SAE has become the *standard*. Faires Conklin and Lourie (1983) argue that SAE is not the standard because it is correct or more useful than any other language or dialect. Instead, it is the standard because it is the language of the powerful, and those who wish to be part of upper and professional classes must speak like the powerful. They argue that because those with socioeconomic power speak SAE, SAE is seen as grammatically and aesthetically superior to all other languages and dialects.
4. Ethnic labels are self-identified by participants in the study.

## References

Bell, D. (1983, Summer). Time for the teachers: Putting educators back into the *Brown* remedy. *The Journal of Negro Education, 52*(3), 290–301.

Bell, D. (2004). *Silent covenants:* Brown V. Board of Education *and the unfulfilled hopes for racial reform.* New York: Oxford University Press.

*Brown v. Board of Education of Topeka*, 347 U.S. 483 (1954).

Carroll, D. (1999). *Psychology of language.* Pacific Grove, CA: Brooks/Cole Publishing.

Clark, K. B., & Clark, M. P. (1947). Racial identification and preference in Negro children. In M. Newcomb & E. L Hartley (Eds.), *Readings in social psychology* (pp. 169–178). New York: Holt.

Cross, W. E. (1971). The Negro-to-Black conversion experience. *Black World, 20*, 13–42.

Cross, W. E. (1995). The psychology of Nigrescence: Revising the Cross model. In J. G. Ponterotto, J. M. Casas, L. A. Suzuki, & C. M. Alexander (Eds.), *Handbook of multicultural counseling.* Thousand Oaks, CA: Sage.

Fanon, F. (1963). *Wretched of the Earth*. New York: Grove Press.

Delpit, L. (1995). *Other people's children: Cultural conflict in the classroom*. New York: New Press.

Faires Conklin, N., & Lourie, M. (1983). *A host of tongues: Language communities in the United States*. New York: Free Press.

Freire, P. (1970). *Pedagogy of the oppressed*. New York: Continuum.

hooks, b. (2001). *Salvation: Black people and love*. New York: HarperCollins.

Hunter-Gault, C. (1992). *In my place*. New York: Vintage Books.

Johnson, R. (submittted). Internalized racism and California US history state standards: Racism, curriculum, and African American identity. Unpublished manuscript, University of California, Los Angeles.

Menchaca, V. D. (2001). Providing a culturally relevant curriculum for Hispanic children. *Multicultural Education, 8*(3), 18–20.

National Collaborative on Diversity in the Teaching Force. (2004). *Assessment of diversity in America's teaching force: A call to action*. Washington, DC: Author.

Oakes, J., Rogers, J., & Silver, D. (2004). *Separate and unequal 50 years after* Brown: *California's racial "opportunity gap."* Report published by UCLA/IDEA Institute for Democracy, Education and Access.

Omi, M., & Winant, H. (1994). *Racial formation in the United States* (2nd ed.). New York: Routledge.

Perez Huber, L., Johnson, R., & Kohli, R. (2007). Naming racism: A conceptual look at racism in US schools. *Chicana/o-Latina/o Law Review, 26*.

Perry, T., & Delpit, L. (1998). *The real Ebonics debate: Power, language, and the education of African-American children*. Boston: Beacon Press.

Solórzano, D., Allen, W. R., & Carroll, G. (2002, Spring). Keeping race in place: Racial microaggressions and campus racial climate at the University of California, Berkeley. *Chicana/o-Latina/o Law Review, 23*(15), 15–112.

Solórzano, D., & Delgado-Bernal, D. (2001). Examining transfomational resistance through a critical race and LatCrit framework: Chicana and Chicano students in an urban context. *Urban Education, 36*(3), 308–342.

Woodson, C. (1933). *MisEducation of the Negro*. Trenton, NJ: Africa World Press.

Yosso, T. (March, 2005). Whose culture has capital? A critical race theory discussion of community cultural wealth. *Race Ethnicity and Education, 8*(1), 69–91.

## · 7 ·

# Maggie and Me

## A Black Professor and a White Urban School Teacher Connect Autoethnography to Critical Race Pedagogy

Sherick Hughes

There are at least two current challenges arising for urban schools, teaching, and teacher education. First, many urban public school teachers and urban teacher educators with whom I have made acquaintances, colleagues, or friends are challenged to explore further how to "care" for students while also resisting oppressive responses. Second, many of us are challenged each year by racial/ethnic/cultural mismatches while attempting to remain "intimately cognizant of the necessary intersection of other oppressive constructs such as class, gender and sexual orientation" (Jennings & Lynn, 2005, p. 26). From June 2003 to June 2007, I worked in the University of Toledo's urban, Midwestern setting. Like most of its counterparts nationwide, Toledo is replete with waning support for inner-city public schools, resegregation, and a growing tension arising from a teacher-to-student mismatch in relation to "personal biography and group or community experiences created by race, class, and gender" (pp. 226–227). Many of my graduate students were self-identified White female, graduate-level teachers responsible for educating large numbers of children of color. This graduate student population also represented the working poor as well as the struggling middle class.

Upon taking a course from me, a Black male, tenure-track assistant professor, these students found themselves in the unusual position of being challenged to both teach and learn daily from Blacks. During the day, they were teaching predominantly Black urban students, and in the evening they were in a course taught by a Black professor that, in part, centers White privilege. It was seemingly the closest these White teachers had come to experiencing life as a minority, albeit temporal and context-specific. Like other scholars of color (e.g., Berry & Mizelle, 2006; and Cleveland, 2005), I sensed the tension of White students seeing me as a Black "other." However, the unequal power dynamics inherent in the professor/researcher–student relationship were also present in this urban setting (Villenas, 1996). Jennings and Lynn (2005) support this notion of a power differential even in Black professor–White student situations. Although they contend and I agree that, due to the overwhelming nature of White privilege in the United States, "scholars of color cannot be easily described in terms of being 'privileged' in the same way that white scholars define their role as privileged" (Jennings & Lynn, 2005, p. 27).

Some education practitioners and researchers alike continue to narrow the race, class, gender nexus by focusing on binary race versus class or race versus gender inquiries (Hill-Collins, 1990). Other educators contend that teachers and learners can overcome oppression at school by centering social justice movements with *race* or *political race* (e.g., Guinier & Torres, 2002). Still other educators center social class/socioeconomic status (SES) above and beyond "race" to expose barriers to the potentially liberatory forms of schooling (e.g., Darder & Torres, 2004; Van Galen, 2004; Wilson, 1980; and Wilson, 1987). Noticeably fewer publications of educational research (Cleveland, 2005; Hill-Collins, 1990; Hughes, 2006a; and Jennings & Lynn, 2005; Van Galen, 2006) seem to center either race, class, or gender as interlocking systems of oppression, whereby each system should be "centered, validated and judged by its own measure without de-centering any other forms of oppression" (e.g., Hill-Collins, 1990, p. 237).

The vision of my former College of Education encouraged faculty to implement pedagogy that responds fully to the needs of citizens in diverse situations, including the urban, metropolitan community we served. Such a vision requires, by default, a sincere effort to change or "reform" schools. Research endeavors involving the social and historical contexts of education (e.g., Hughes, 2006a; Milner, 2003; Noblit & Dempsey, 1996; Valenzuela, 1999) suggest that any sincere and sustainable school reform effort must necessarily begin with critical reflexivity and subsequent individual and collective action. Results of this research also suggest that such an effort must involve a transformative caring agent to disrupt oppressive experiences and narratives of race while remaining "intimately cognizant of the necessary intersection of . . . class and gender" (Jennings & Lynn, 2005, p. 26).

This chapter addresses how autoethnography may contribute to this effort by illustrating a promising connection of autoethnography to Critical Race Pedagogy (CRP) (Jennings & Lynn, 2005) in graduate teacher education. The remaining text discusses the (a) theoretical framework of CRP and its challenges for traditional caring, (b) autoethnography and its extant connection to pedagogy, and (c) evidence and concluding thoughts regarding how I, one Black male professor from a working poor background, connect autoethnography to CRP along with a graduate-level, high school English teacher named "Maggie" (pseudonym). The connection of autoethnography to CRP is illustrated through interwoven narratives of race-, class-, and gender-related struggles and hopes voiced by Maggie and me.

## CRP

Jennings and Lynn (2005) recently presented their revised conceptualization of CRP as another promising route to confront educators' taken-for-granted knowledge about living, learning, and teaching race (Hughes, 2005) without further marginalizing other related forms of oppression in schools. In fact, Jennings and Lynn (2005) stand by CRP as a "theoretical construct that addresses the complexity of race and education" (p. 24). The researchers further describe the roots of CRP as growing upon a set of "very broad yet closely interwoven characteristics that form the basis for this continually evolving construct" (p. 25). Additional strengths of Jennings and Lynn's (2005) CRP are highlighted in the following five tenets:

1. CRP must be intimately cognizant of the necessary intersection of other oppressive constructs such as class, gender, and sexual orientation (Jennings & Lynn, 2005, p. 26).
2. CRP must recognize and understand the endemic nature of racism (Jennings & Lynn, 2005, p. 25).
3. CRP must recognize the importance of understanding the power dynamics inherent in schooling (Jennings & Lynn, 2005, p. 26).
4. CRP must emphasize the importance of . . . reflexivity . . . [and how

the] exploration of one's "place" within a stratified society has
power to illuminate oppressive structures in society (Jennings &
Lynn, 2005, p. 27).

5. CRP must encourage the practice of an explicitly liberatory form
   of both teaching and learning . . . advocating for justice and equity in both schooling and education as a necessity if there is to be
   justice and equity in the broader society (Jennings & Lynn, 2005,
   pp. 27–28).

Moreover, CRP provides tools to challenge the dominant, oppressive, and
oftentimes inadvertently complicit (Gordon, 2005) ideology of caring White
folks (Anders, Bryan, & Noblit, 2005; Delpit, 1988, 1995). It seems to be an
unfortunate and often short-sighted ideal of caring that seems replete in today's
K-12 schools, which comprise teachers who are primarily, white, female, married, religious, and on average 43-years-old (Campos, 2006). Qualitative
researchers (e.g., Delpit, 1995; Hughes, 2006b; Tozer, Senese, & Violas, 2006)
allude to the shared values, attitudes, beliefs, and habits of thought regarding
this limited ideal of caring (Valenzuela, 1999) as including but not limited to:

1. Caring as color-race-gender-class blindness above caring as cele-
   brating difference by building on the funds of knowledge (Moll,
   Amanti, Neff, & Gonzalez, 1992) that each student brings to the
   classroom;

2. Caring as nurturing the cultural rules and norms of Whiteness
   only and the "myth of merit" (Oakes & Lipton, 2006) above "critical consciousness" (Freire, 1970);

3. Caring as modeling "assimilation" only (Valenzuela, 1999) above
   engaging "transformative resistance" (Solórzano & Bernal, 2001);
   and

4. Caring as inculcating complacency regarding systemic race, class,
   and gender oppression above caring as exposing dominant and
   oppressive "codes of power" (Delpit, 1995).

Similar to the vision and mission of which I was to adhere from June 2003 to
May 2007, contemporary urban education research describes caring as a search
for competent professional educators (e.g., Noblit, 1995; Noddings, 1992). In
the Noddings (1992) scenario, competence and caring is co-constructed by
teachers and students. A student attempts to find "what she knows and how she

knows it" (p. 65). Conversely, a teacher is exhibiting his "act of care and respect" by "also discovering what the student knows and how she knows it" (Oakes & Lipton, 2006, p. 267). The five tenets of CRP are seemingly intended to steer teachers, students, and teacher educators toward "caring" but more of a transformative caring that disrupts narratives of automatic approval or automatic condemnation "for whatever knowledge or interpretation the student" espouses (Oakes & Lipton, pp. 266–267).

# Autoethnography Research and Pedagogy

Autoethnography is a relatively new research tool in education born in the discipline of anthropology only 50 years ago (Patton, 2002). The term *autoethnography* was introduced by Raymond Firth in 1956 when talking about a 1928 argument between Jomo Kenyatta (first president of the independent Kenya) and Louis Leakey (acclaimed 20th-century archeologist/anthropologist) during a public lecture in London (Elder, Bremser, & Sheridan, 2007). Both men were said to have claimed "insider" knowledge of Kikuyu customs regarding female circumcision. Born in Kenya and educated abroad, both Kikuyu tribal men also earned doctoral degrees in anthropology. Elder et al. (2007) aptly describe the center of their argument as "who has the right to represent a society," traditional hypothesis-driven anthropology, or autoethnography. Kenyatta's (1966) *Facing Mt. Kenya* is indeed recognized today as the first published autoethnography (Hayano, 1979), but to date his work is not without harsh academic criticism.

The work has been critiqued by Louis Leakey and other social scientists who essentially label either Kenyatta's style or any style of autoethnography as too subjective. Kenyatta's critics seem to be most bothered by his rendition of autoethnography for some reasons that I accept (i.e., limited triangulation of sources, limited disconfirming resources, and mismanagement of the delicate interweaving of a narrative literary style with social science inquiry), and for some reasons that I reject (i.e., use of first-person voice, biographical narratives, and native ethnography). Moreover, Kenyatta (1966) and his native Kikuyu people are noted as receiving more praise and admiration than critique in his autoethnographic account (Hayano, 1979).

Conversely, a quarter of a century ago, Hayano (1979) also spoke to the potentialities of autoethnography. He actually describes autoethnography's capacity to create an alternative venue for marginalized voices. The research genre appears to be gaining particular credibility and influence in education, communication studies, and qualitative research (e.g., Banks & Banks, 2000; Bochner & Ellis, 2002; Dalton, 2003; Denzin, 2003; Ellis & Bochner, 2000; Holt, 2003; Laubscher & Powell, 2003; Maguire, 2006; Roth, 2005; Sparks, 2000). Autoethnography includes among its representative publications the highly acclaimed article "White Privilege: Unpacking the Invisible Knapsack" by Peggy McIntosh (1989), which launched an international research movement that continues today.

Reed-Danahay (1997) describes autoethnography as enlisting "a rewriting of the self and the social" (p. 4). It is intended to ask questions such as, "How might my experiences of 'race' and 'class' offer insights about my ability to address these issues in any given educational event/situation?" Rather than seeking to escape subjectivity, authors considering autoethnographic techniques should do so precisely because of the qualitative genre's capacity to engage first-person voice and to embrace the conflict of writing against oneself as he or she finds him or herself entrenched in the complications of their positions. With such a focus on exploring and exposing the subjective self, how might one judge the merit of an autoethnography? Richardson (2000) suggests five guidelines to implement "when reviewing personal narrative papers that include analyses of both evaluative and constructive validity techniques" (Holt, 2003, p. 12). Richardson's (2000) guidelines seem to provide a framework for directing investigators and reviewers of autoethnography toward considering:

> Substantive contribution. Does the piece contribute to our understanding of social life? Aesthetic merit. Does this piece succeed aesthetically? Is the text artistically shaped, satisfyingly complex, and not boring? Reflexivity. How did the author come to write this text? How has the author's subjectivity been both a producer and a product of this text? Impactfullness. Does this affect me emotionally and/or intellectually? Does it generate new questions or move me to action? Expresses a reality. Does this text embody a fleshed out sense of lived experience? (pp. 15–16)

Similar to Denzin (2003), Richardson (2000) contends autoethnographic manuscripts might also include "dramatic recall, unusual phrasing, and strong metaphors to invite the reader to 'relive' events with the author" (p. 12). In his book titled *Performance Ethnography: Critical Pedagogy and the Politics of Culture*, qualitative researcher Denzin (2003) is credited for actually establishing the initial connection of performance to ethnography, autoethnography, critical pedagogy and critical theory. In the new millennium, scholars in the discipline of Communication Studies began to consider the possibilities of autoethnography as pedagogy (e.g., Banks & Banks, 2000) and as a tool for writing essays about critical pedagogy (Dalton, 2003). As mentioned earlier, CRP was recently rearticulated as emphasizing "the importance of . . . reflexivity . . . [and how the] exploration of one's 'place' within a stratified society has power to illuminate oppressive structures in society" (Jennings & Lynn, 2005, p. 27). A synthesis of the research streams from communication studies, qualitative methods, and educational studies points to at least three bridges connecting autoethnography to CRP (e.g., Banks & Banks, 2000):

1. Autoethnography teaches us about self,
2. Autoethnography teaches us to write, and
3. Autoethnography teaches us to inculcate and model. (pp. 235–236)

First, autoethnographic research is connected to CRP through its inherent reflexivity and positionality components that can teach us more about our racialized, classed, and gendered selves. It is a research method that challenges our assumptions of normalcy (e.g., what should be considered "right" regarding caring in schools). Researchers may find that instruction via autoethnography can also incite us to revisit our professional and personal participation in the socialization of classrooms and schools. Second, autoethnography can move researchers to practice writing as a cathartic endeavor to improve our craft for its own sake. For this qualitative research genre, sharing emotions with audiences is not only acceptable but expected. Third, autoethnographic research can provide scholars enough oxygen to live and breathe self-critical attitudes and self-disclosure in teaching and learning. The idea here is to force researchers to criticize themselves first and foremost and to be at least as critical of themselves as they are of others.

## Maggie and Me: Evidence of Autoethnography Projects Intertwined

### Maggie

Maggie was a White, middle-class, female teacher of predominantly Black, low-SES, urban high school students. Maggie was enrolled in my Intergroup/Intercultural Education course during the fall of 2004. I chose

Maggie from approximately 25 other students in her class because she represents an archetypal case of change in my graduate courses full of students whose voices speak to White, middle-class, female teachers finding themselves in the challenging position of both teaching and learning daily as an "other." Maggie had blond hair and she stood about 5'3. Her petite frame and raspy, assertive voice almost seemed counterintuitive. Maggie seemed to have what Weber (1914/1968) labels "legitimate authority" on "charismatic grounds." Evidence in support of this claim of legitimacy came during the part of the course where I assign autoethnographic research and the importance of finding a central question.

First, Maggie told the class that she might go with a question that she had considered prior to taking the course, "with only one negative experience with Black people in my entire life, how do I have the stereotypes in my head that I'm trying to get rid of." Her classmates listened and acquiesced. Maggie then shared a tale of that "negative Black experience."

As she recalls, her car was stolen in downtown Toledo. She began searching for her car because she "was so pissed off." Within an hour she found her car, ear-marked by its license plate and, of course, make, model, and color. She found a few middle- to high school-age Black males in her vehicle. When they were at a stopping point, she ran at them screaming, "Get the fuck out of my car." Startled, the boys said, "This ain't your car," and Maggie replied, "I know my license plate number and this is my car, get the fuck out of my car." Unbelievably, the boys complied, and to add insult to injury and immaturity, they asked Maggie to "drop 'em off somewhere." She neither dropped them off somewhere nor did she call the police. Her classmates listened and acquiesced. A class filled with talented, assertive students of color didn't even challenge Maggie's story. There was no such challenge partially, I think, because she told it so convincingly, partially because she didn't attempt to have the boys arrested, and partially because she seemed sincere about wanting to unlearn racial biases about Blacks and "others."

## Me

"You don't look like a professor," I am sometimes told. My body does not match the traditional older white-haired male authority figurine with verbal and nonverbal communicative behaviors that most of my White graduate students have come to expect and respect. I am a dark brown, 5'10, 248-pound former high school three-sport varsity athlete, and former college Rugby player. I have broad shoulders and a medium able-bodied build that one might expect of a former athlete who still maintains a brisk walking, occasional jogging, and weightlifting routine. I have most visible traditional Northwest African facial features, hair color and texture, and skin color. It is not unusual for me to wear a two-piece suit, button-down shirt, and tie the first day. Sometimes my head is bald, sometimes an inch thick, or at times I have a fade (similar to the crew cut but with a smoother "faded-looking" hair transition from the thicker hair on the top of the head to the thinner hair of the side of the head and side burns).

I am a product of post-*Brown* Southern schooling. I attended three predominantly White institutions in pursuit of the professoriate. Along the way, I taught as a teacher's aid in urban and rural grade schools. I am not a licensed teacher; however, most White practitioners give me some credence due to the fact that I have successfully taught grade-school students within the last 5 years and I have a PhD in education from the University of North Carolina at Chapel Hill. I am a Black man rooted in a poor working-class background in northeast Albemarle who became more academically, socially, and economically mobile through formal and informal education, when many of my peers did not. I am a first-generation college student who grew up approximately 6 miles from the Bartlett Plantation where my family was enslaved only four generations ago.

## Intergroup/Intercultural Course and Autoethnographic Research Projects

The fall 2004 semester of my Intergroup/Intercultural Education course stands as the first time I assigned an autoethnographic research project to any of my students. The course catalog describes it as focusing on the evolving role of intergroup and intercultural education in the United States, including the historical and contemporary relationship of schooling and "race" to educational outcomes. In this course, we examine racialized groups of people and the strength of intergroup/intercultural loyalties and divisiveness among and within these groups in the United States—thus, to some degree, we are interrogating ourselves. While learning about "others" and how to teach "others," we also engage in self-critique and learn how to be critical of who we socially construct as "others." This course tends to enroll approximately 20 to 25 graduate students per semester. Most of those graduate students are matriculating at the master's level.

Maggie and her classmates were expected to expend the bulk of their time and energy in the course on the autoethnography project. In light of this expectation, a comparable portion of my assessment of their progress or growth in the class was based on their autoethnographic research. Consequently, I began my own autoethnographic research to address how this method might be used in teacher education to inculcate a critical mass of resistance to race, class, and gender oppression in the classroom. I offered a few key preliminary activities and assignments to prepare students for the uniqueness of authoethnographic research. I later realized that such preliminary teaching tools were crucial to students' abilities to grasp autoethnography because it was a new method for all of them to learn.

## Preparation for Autoethnographic Research Projects

One preparatory activity that helps me get a sense of their predispositions and expectations is by learning about what they already believe about themselves. During this activity, everyone in the class is instructed to "name the three most problematic social identities in your life." The activity was intended to reveal the parts of social identity that individuals rendered most negative in their lives as educators. In the end, this activity works as a promising ice-breaker with predominantly White female graduate teacher education students. I quickly recognized a host of privileges and problems inherited by all of us. I recall a few social identity privileges and problems relating to religion, sexuality, and ability were shared, yet the race, class, and gender nexus was particularly poignant in our urban narratives.

A second preparatory tool was the creation of diverse groups. Throughout the 16-week course, I try to support diverse group work by creating in-class and out-of-class opportunities to engage the type of race, social class, and gender-reflexive writing posited by Berry (2005). Moreover, group approaches to "critically engaged dialogue" (Milner 2003, p. 201), "intragroup or same-group dialogue" (Taliaferro-Baszile, 2005), and "intergroup dialogue" (Gurin & Nagda, 2006, p. 22) are also promoted in the course. These approaches work in tandem to involve (a) creating diverse groups based on self-identified experiences of the matrix of race, class, and gender; (b) helping groups identify and define individualized decision-making roles; and (c) finding in-class time and space to balance intra- and intergroup socialization (Tatum, 2003).

The final preparatory tools are given to students in the outline form illustrated next. An in-depth class lecture accompanies this introductory guide to
"empathic validation, commitment, and confidentiality" (Hughes, 2007).
Follow-up lectures are applied as needed on this topic to guide class discussions
and activities.

## 1. Empathic Validation
   A. To listen to, acknowledge, and understand first and foremost
   B. To think and feel and thus to act (verbally and nonverbally) toward
      reasonableness
   C. To enlist reasonableness requires at least:
      1. Openness to counterevidence/disconfirming evidence/coun
         ternarratives/competing ideologies
      2. Openness to new syntheses of ideas and "new-self" experiences

## 2. Commitment
   A. To taking a "no fault" approach to conflict resolution with an anti-
      oppressive response
   B. To making a space "safe" for "productive conflict management" or
      "uncomfortable-comfortableness"
   C. To learning with and toward transformative resistance
   D. To unlearning malignant/anti-transformative resistance
   E. To collaborating for compatibility, at worst, and for consensus, at best

## 3. Confidentiality
   A. To maintaining the anonymity of names of places and people in nar-
      ratives
   B. To breaching confidentiality only when:
      1. Permission is granted preferably in writing by Informant(s) or
         Pertinent Legitimate Authorities
      2. Required by school law
      3. Confident (unequivocally) that shared information will lead to
         less oppression in the end for *All Parties Involved*—Triangulate
         and consider disconfirming evidence before proceeding

# Autoethnographic Reseach Project Assignment

There were five essential components of the autoethnographic research project. First, students were assigned to draft personal biographies that spoke to the intersection of race (without excluding accompanying experiences of class and gender) and education sometime during their K-12 or collegiate years. Their personal biographies had to offer positive or negative narrative "pictures" that waxed and waned in their memories from the initial moment of the experience. Second, students were assigned to locate a central question and guided to personalize the question (i.e., focus on first-person narration). As the central question was located, students were assigned during the same day to begin a review of research, where race intersected autoethnography, class/SES, gender, and education. There were several "givens" for this review that students received from me, including: Laubscher and Powell (2003), McIntosh (1989), Hill-Collins, (1990), and Jennings and Lynn (2005). These articles essentially constructed a foundation on which student pieces of autoethnographic research could grow.

Third, one class period was spent in their groups as a sort of autoethnographic writing workshop. Students were expected to share the parts they were willing to share as I walked around to each group. I tried to be consistent in my responses to each concern of the five groups. It was my sincere hope that such a workshop could yield questions and guide groups closer toward meeting and exceeding personal narrative writing style expectations (Richardson, 2000). Fourth, students were pushed to triangulate narratives or locate narratives of their raced-, classed-, or gendered-counterparts in order to address and interweave disconfirming evidence in their accounts. The idea here was not to hide subjectivity, but to name it, check it, and critique it with other voices on the subject in one's life. Finally, students were assigned to share portions of their autoethnographic research that they were willing to reveal in a public forum. Downtown Latte' provided such a forum. Owned and operated by two dedicated women who model social justice activism, "the Latte'" as it is sometimes called affectionately, was a near perfect stage for this assignment.

# Maggie, Me, and Autoethnographic Research Evidence

The following narratives represent topics discussed in manuscripts, in class, and during final presentations week, where students speak in front of both peers and

strangers. Ultimately, all of the narratives became part of the autoethnographic research of Maggie and Me. These narratives are intended to demonstrate
the potential of autoethnography as CRP for reflexive thinking in a manner
that doesn't position race versus class versus gender. Although race is central
in the descriptions and narratives of Maggie and me, class and gender issues
emerged unequivocally and therefore necessitated the centering of race without decentering class and gender (Hill-Collins, 1990, p. 230).

## Me:

Maggie says she had Black friends and even dated a Black guy in high school,
but those statements don't make her an expert on Black people and, besides,
she admittedly spends no time with non-White friends now. Because I notice
her charismatic authority in the class, I try to immediately disrupt her "more
diverse than thou" narrative by responding to her in the classroom forum, "I
feel like Whites and people of color are—to borrow from the Indigo Girls—
'intimate strangers.' " I relayed a poignant story from my new arrival to Toledo
from the South, "a White woman who had been a physical therapist of elder-
ly Blacks for years, looked at my finger when I took off my class ring and
replied sincerely, 'I didn't know Black people tanned!' " I then relayed another story of White families who adopt Black males but don't want them to
attend HBCUs, claiming "they don't prepare kids for a diverse world," as if the
predominantly White universities attended by their biological White children were known for their diversity programming. Maggie was relatively quiet
during this part of my lecture, but she gave me a look that suggests to me that
she was experiencing some cognitive dissonance.

## Me:

Maggie is obviously challenged by me and challenging to me as we engage
autoethnographic research and writing in her class. If I can just work with her
and her classmates through the personal biography, I think it will be okay. How
might I be part of the problem? I have to remember to introduce them to Freire
(1970) so they understand that this process involves struggle and caring and
that the relationship is reciprocal and not static. I need to tell the class to focus
on their K-12 or college experiences at the intersection of race and education.
I anticipate that there will be immediate questions about how one can do that
without discussing simultaneous gender and social class experiences. I'll have

to direct the class back to Hill-Collins (1990), Cleveland (2005), and my notes on CRP (Jennings & Lynn, 2005). I should say something like, "The idea is to center race for this course without decentering class and gender just like we talked about when we discussed Dr. Hill-Collins (1990) and others."

## Maggie: Elementary Years: "Niggers," "Spicks," or "Gooks"

My parents had just divorced, and Mom and I lived in the epitome of middle class. I was an only child, so I played with kids in the neighborhood. . . . My mom was a Godly woman who did not talk negatively about other races. My dad was a different story. I was only with him during the summer for a couple of weeks or at Christmas for a week. He was full of racism, with negative things to say about anyone other than White, rich people. . . . We moved . . . Mom got remarried . . . I was eight. Again, we lived in a middle-class neighborhood. . . . I was friends with everyone and did not think of what he had told me about "niggers," "spicks," or "gooks."

## Maggie: High School Years: "Nigger Lover"

The friends in my clique were all from middle-class neighborhoods. . . . Senior year I took typing class and became attracted to a Black sophomore also in the class. We started talking and eventually were a couple. . . . Our group of White girls continued to hang out with the Black girls and guys we had befriended years earlier, but now we were even more "in" [with Blacks than were other middle-class Whites]. We went to parties in an all-Black neighborhood outside our town. . . . One of the only times I felt the heat of dating out of my ethnicity was when one of my best friends (a raging alcoholic who is no longer my friend) called me a "nigger lover" just to hurt me. I have never forgotten the point of those words.

## Maggie: College Years: "Poor Little Rich Girl" White Preservice Teacher

[The Midwestern university I attended] has an awful reputation for being a school for rich, White kids; it was no different when I attended in 1993 through 1997. . . . One of my first horrible experiences with someone from another ethnicity took place during methods. I was assigned to an inner-city school. The teacher asked me one day if I was a P.L.R.G. She went on to inform me that the abbreviation meant Poor Little Rich Girl. I was hurt and embarrassed because I was enjoying my experience prior to that. . . . She was a nasty lady I have never forgotten. That experience stuck with me because she was preju-dice to me, but I was not to her. . . .

## Me: "It's Not That Hard"

Today in class, Maggie's like, "I get the personal biography part, but I can't fig-ure out my [central] question." "How's this going to be research," she said. Other students began to chime in, and it seemed to me that Maggie's question began a big snowball of questions that were worse than they would've been had she not been the one to ask it first, I thought. "It's not that hard," you're making it harder than it actually is," I said to myself. But, my frustration with Maggie aside, there appears to be a difficult challenge in locating a central thesis throughout the class, but this challenge is not so unusual for graduate students. After meeting with her group for in-class discussion and after talking with me after class, Maggie ultimately decided to focus on the central question, "Where does prejudice originate in my life?" Once the question is found, students need to move to further reviews of autoethnographic literature. Maggie seems to have limited experience searching for peer-reviewed sources, however, her reading comprehension skills and writing skills evident in the personal biography por-tion of the autoethnography project were what one would expect of an advanced master's student.

## Maggie: Finding the Central Question and Pre-Literature Review

I've sat in class week after week pondering about the beginnings of racism. How did it seep into my psyche if I have been friends with (and surrounded by) non-Whites all my life? It became apparent that I need to learn more when I did self-reflection to write my autobiography [personal biography component of the autoethnography assignment]. . . . I knew the racism comments my father made were wrong and ridiculous, so when and, more important, how did my prejudices solidly form and become readily accessible in my everyday life? I was anxious and curious to read scholarly journals and get an answer to my plagu-ing question. . . . I'm not sure if the prejudices I hold about Whites are as harm-ful as the ones [some] children had about their own race. Growing up in [the South], I was exposed to the prejudices of people called "White trash." This prejudice about what is presumably a poor White person stuck with me because I still hold those opinions. Jeff Foxworthy has made a living doing standup about this very group of people. . . .

## Me: 10/9/05, the Day Maggie and I took the Oxygen Out of the Classroom

I entered class feeling somewhat physically ill. I gathered my notes and myself and began the lecture portion of the course that day by saying, "All right, let's try to get through this." Maggie replied abruptly, relatively loudly, and with a half-smile, "What's the matter, you aren't prepared?" I immediately responded, "That's an interesting question, which leads me to ask, 'Why do so many White people suggest that I'm not prepared for my job?' " "I'm certainly prepared for today," I maintained. "We're discussing chapters from the book that I wrote!" Students self-identifying as "White" and "of color" in her assigned diverse discussion group raised their hands as did others throughout the class. Their answer unequivocally: "Because you're a Black man." Maggie's face turned red, and she refused to talk to me for the rest of class that evening. I learned from a trusted member of her class group, "She said, he better not come and try to talk to me today about anything else, I am so mad at him."Maggie, who from my purview had been rude to me that day and a few days of class before then in September, was now livid and no longer eager to discuss the tough issues, but now she was "dreading class" partially due to my previous response, partially due to the Toledo Race Riot. It is paradoxical that only 1–2 weeks before today's class, we experienced the Toledo Race Riot, which was international news, and we delved deeply into a course discussion of response bias through Swim & Stangor's (1998) description of Hits (e.g., I respond as if I was discriminated against and I was), Misses (e.g., I respond as if I wasn't discriminated against, but I was), False Alarms (e.g., I respond as if I was discriminated against, but I wasn't), and Correct Rejections (I respond as if I wasn't discriminated against, and I wasn't). A week later, Maggie reflected on the incident on her after class comment (ACC) sheet with the following remarks.

## Maggie: Regarding the Bad Oxygen Day in Class on 10/09/05

I was dreading class today . . . after the riots, I was dreading class. . . . You really embarrassed me today when you basically accused me of a prejudice statement. The reason I asked if you weren't prepared was b/c of what you said *prior* to that (something to the effect of): "just trying to get through this." I think what you felt I was accusing you of was a *total miss!* [actually, it would have been a false alarm] I guess the reason I was so embarrassed is b/c I'm taking this class very seriously. I talk about it constantly to my friends a+ students-black + white. I am trying so hard to unlearn those stupid prejudices. . . . I appreciate why you thought I was saying that b/c you've had lots of Whites say that, but you were absolutely wrong. It was what you said before that: + I only asked you what was bothering you b/c you looked upset. That was a Shitty Miss Dr. Hughes.

## Me: Thoughts Immediately Following Maggie's "Shitty Miss" Commentary

Except for the writing of White undergraduates on the qualitative component of anonymous end-of-course evaluations, I had never experienced any student being so blunt as to curse at or about me this way. The good news was that Maggie does seem to want to get better at teaching her urban Black students by exploring prejudices within herself, and in class she actually decided to focus her autoethnography on the more specific and personalized thesis, "Where does racial prejudice originate in my life and how might it influence my treatment of my urban, Black high school English students?" I should reply not only to her but to the entire class via email as I attempt to model how to confront rather than ignore race/class/gender conflict productively.

## Me: Attempting to Practice What I Preach on the Night of 10/9/05

My brain worked in a way tonight that triggered [what I thought would be] a teachable moment. It was more of an implicit association/critical pedagogical trigger. It wasn't a false alarm, hit, or miss because Maggie's comment triggered another general overall question in my head, not about her motives, but about student motives and particularly White student motives outside of her who have asked me the same question. It didn't trigger me to even consider whether Maggie's response was a hit, miss, or false alarm. Oftentimes, my students' comments trigger other thoughts and general questions in my head that I feel may be worthwhile teachable moments to pursue for all of us. Please know that I am not feeling your comments are signs of racial prejudice in those times where your words enlist responses from me that link to another experience of mine. I think your thoughts and my triggers might actually enhance our educational setting at that moment . . . at least most of the time. Tonight, I think it let some of the oxygen out of the room. Let's continue to work together and teach while we learn and learn while we teach. I apologize to Maggie and all of you for not clarifying the issue earlier [in class].

## Maggie: Post-Riot, Post-10/9/05, "White Trash and the Song Bird of Privilege"

If teachers are supposed to change the lives of the students they encounter, they need to be prepared for racial issues of every kind. I certainly was not prepared for this at [the university I attended]. I am personally trying to discover my White privilege, not enable it, since learning of it in this class. My White privilege is a topic I have thought about every day since reading McIntosh's [1989] piece. It is a songbird atop my shoulders singing a nasty tune that reminds me I have no idea what it is like to be a person of color. . . . Gordon [2005] goes on to tell how she tries to teach racial diversity more each semester she instructs at George Mason University. How lucky are those students!

## Me: Pedagogy Is a Two-Way Street

This decision to email the entire class regarding my confrontation with Maggie proved to be one of the defining moments of the course as it seemed to set the stage for meeting the other challenges of autoethnographic research. Maggie was rude, and I expected her to respect me more than to curse at me. Her knee-jerk responses had been unprofessional and she knew it, yet my knee-jerk "trigger" in class was by my own standards, shortsighted and we both knew that as well. So, we nonverbally seemed to call a truce. Maggie seemed to appreciate my mass email, which was evident in her immediate return to class participation, after initially giving me and her group members "the silent treatment." Her participation now, however, seemed more productive and insightful, and I think my participation was too. It's as if we challenged the very tenets of the course and its methodology and found that, in the end, it works, but not in some formulaic way, but in the tugging, trials, and triumphs of everyday life in any classroom. What a painful reminder that pedagogy is a two-way street?

## Maggie: "Autoethnography Lends Itself to Wondrous Self-Reflection"

My methods for this autoethnography have been pure and simple. . . . Needless

to say, this type of research has been useful because I have got to read scholarly opinions about the beginnings of prejudice while brooding over my own
beliefs and from where they stem. . . . The autoethnography lends itself to won-
drous self-reflection, while doing research at the same time. I cannot say I have
not been prejudiced toward children. I have thought many times in my head
horrid generalizations about certain students based on their skin color or
socioeconomic status. . . . Since day one of this experience [autoethnography],
I have spoken to my students about what I am learning. I have shared with several students many of our discussions. . . . I could not help but talk about it with
"D." D is a Black emotionally disturbed junior in my homeroom and English
class. I spoke with him about the way Whites rudely (usually unknowingly)
word their questions to Blacks about silly things like hair, tanning, etc. . . . Most
important, I have admitted outright my White privilege and how I am hum-
bled. Our relationship has developed wonderfully, I speculate, partly because I
give him hope [she shows she cares] about ethnic differences. He was one of the
only people who asked how my speech [autoethnography presentation] went!
Awesome!

## Me: Maggie Changes With "D"

By the end of the semester, it was clear to Maggie and me that autoethnography had transformed her relationship not only with me, but with "D."
Apparently feeling more validation than before from Maggie, "D" willingly discussed an article describing historical atrocities faced by the first Black male collegiate athletes. I remember the day she handed the same article to me and
explained how well her conversation about it had gone with "D." I did my own
thesis on this topic, and yet I still learned a tremendous amount of more specific details present in the article. I was taken aback by how Maggie now
seemed to have a better understanding of how White privilege works alongside
penalty and the inequity of the unearned physical birthrights that exist alongside misguided feelings of entitlement.

## Maggie: "Keep My White Middle-Class Privilege in Check" at the Potluck

Prior to this class, I had no friends of color. Just Whites. This course has offered
many blessings, including [Joe]. I told him just last week [at the potluck], I am
not losing him as a friend when we are finished. He has to keep my White priv-

ilege in check! . . . I am closest to the people I work with . . . and they are as White as snow. There are a few Black teachers in our district, and they certainly mingle with Whites—they don't have a choice! Of course there are tons of different ethnicities in our district. . . . Where I teach, has racial issues that plague the school. . . . It is certainly visible to me that there is not much black and white racial mixing, which is a shame . . . one would think there would be more racial segregation and issues [where I grew up] because it is considered part of "The South." I live in [a place] comprised mostly of White, middle-class people.

## Me: Potluck at Maggie's Place

My wife and I attended the end-of-the-course final presentation/potluck dinner party created and hosted by Maggie. Maggie proposed the idea during the last week or two of class to have a potluck to celebrate the diversity of our raced, classed, and gendered course makeup. I was skeptical at first when she posited what could have been a stereotypic theme of "authentic ethnic foods." Of course White students claimed there were no White ethnic foods, White was simply, "American." Laughter, acquiescence, and discussions followed my response: "Aren't rice crispy treats a White ethnic food?" Somehow, by including White as an ethnic group and not as "just American" for this potluck transcended the colorblind talk of the White students and motivated the class to really seek an "authentic" ethnic family recipe to bring to the dinner. The potluck was a success in that it fused the autoethnographic presentations of struggle and caring with a concrete artifact—food, a family artifact that was replete with its own raced, classed, and gendered narratives.

## Maggie: Post-Potluck "Validation, Commitment, and Confidentiality"

I have made a vow after this chapter, the speech, countless hours of pondering my place in the world, and reading for the Literature Review that I will not ever be color-blind. I want to celebrate our differences in the classroom. I want my students to be comfortable with who they are. I do not hush their innocently rude comments about other ethnicities. I stop my teaching and discuss it with them, and usually we come to the conclusion that their thought was a silly prejudice. I am also excited to share that I have used the three-step process we learned in September to validate, commitment, and confidentiality. I simply listen to their story about how they feel they have been discriminated against, validate what they shared, and end with the commitment to never do that to them. I am devoted to my unlearning of prejudice and racism, for their sake and my own. . . . I am taking my brain places it has not been in 30 years. Now my thinking is unlearning too. And that is what change [and caring] is all about.

When our narratives are considered in tandem, Maggie and I provide substantial evidence of how autoethnography can work as CRP. It forced us to face internal and external conflicts linked to the oppression we perceived in our lives. It moved us to consider how the matrix of domination works to bind and blind our pedagogy. It shaped our determination and willingness to participate in the struggle for an ethic of care. Her work became a template for how autoethnography can actually work. I am proud of us for engaging and sustaining autoethnography in this way to begin the difficult and vulnerable journey of personal-historical self-criticism, naming current positionality, and engaging reflexivity.

Indeed, our narratives relay a story of attempts by Maggie and me to translate and transfer what we learned about ourselves via autoethnography en route to unveiling more opportunities for "an ethic of care" (Noddings, 1992). Our progress seemingly hinges on our ability to adhere to CRP. Our narratives also speak to the internal and external pursuit of specific pedagogical help for overcoming the educational impediments of race, class, and gender oppression. After Maggie's "paper, the speech, countless hours of pondering [her] place in the world, and reading for the Literature Review paper" (personal communication, December 2005), I was convinced that autoethnography as a CRP might be initiated and sustained. Two years later, I see or receive messages from 5 to 10 students per semester from the course, including Maggie, who still speak of their transformation as educators confronting race, class, and gender in the classroom and at home. Several of them, including Maggie, even mention the sustained interethnic friendships they gained through the method and the course. I can't take credit for all of these occurrences. Clearly, students such as Maggie taught me important lessons about transformative resistance and pedagogical change by helping me find the light at the intersection of autoethnography and CRP. One latent example of how she influenced my work came after she accepted my request to review the first draft of the manuscript that preceded this chapter.

In an effort to seek disconfirming evidence, I gave a previous draft of this chapter to Maggie, but I had no reply for her for a couple of months. She offered a powerful and invaluable critique of the original manuscript. She felt that my argument initially polarized me versus White female graduate student-practitioners, which was certainly not my intention. Maggie actually exclaimed, "I just think it's like Dr. Hughes versus the White girl." She also noted two spaces where I had mistakenly left her real name in the original manuscript. Her constructive criticism forced me into several drafts that revisited and edited my underlying assumptions and dichotomies. As I had hoped, at the dawn of the fall of 2004, Maggie and I were beginning to find additional promising evidence of the utility of autoethnography in the social battle of grade-school disproportionality. By re-searching our fallible, but educable "selves," both of us began to acquiesce to the ever-humbling, yet exciting and hopeful episodes of *students becoming the teachers*.

# Conclusion:

## Toward Addressing Critics and Potential Threats When Connecting of Autoethnography to Critical Race Pedagogy

Critics at the American Educational Studies Association (AESA) and American Educational Research Association (AERA) annual meetings have asked me quite frankly, "Why waste your time with thinking about how your White graduate student-practitioners think, feel, and act when so many more deserving graduate students of color need you at the same time?" For the first part of my response this criticism, I draw again on Jennings and Lynn's (2005) CRP "for scholars of color . . . enormous power and privilege is embedded within our position as researchers and faculty members" (p. 27). The second portion of my response says, "White teachers are teaching kids of color in the traditional public schools (still serving approximately 90% of the nation's youth) more than people of color are, shouldn't I be concerned about not only their knowledge and skills acquisition, but also their predispositions and expectations for kids of color?" The third part of my response echoes the scholarly sentiments of Tillman (2002), who welcomes White students committed to social justice education and are willing to engage multiple non-White experiences, affording them the social currency to accurately interpret and validate an "other."

Delgado (1995) offers a chilling description of the nature of change/reform processes that tend to hinder such commitments and efforts toward validation in our society:

We postpone confronting novelty and change until they acquire enough momentum that we are swept forward. We take seriously new social thought only after hearing it so often that its tenants and themes begin to seem familiar, inevitable, and true. We then adopt the new paradigm, and the process repeats itself. We escape from one mental and intellectual prison only into a larger, slightly more expansive one. Each jail break is seen as illegitimate. We reject new thought until, eventually, its hard edges soften, its suggestions seem tame and manageable, and its proponents are "elder states-persons," to be feared no longer. By then, of course, the new thought has lost its radically transformative character. We reject the medicine that could save us until, essentially, it is too late.

Change by connecting autoethnography to CRP is certainly as painstaking as Delgado alludes. It is a change requiring my students and me to face the intersection of privilege and penalty, race, class, and gender long enough to inspire critical pedagogical tools for us to take back into the "real" world—to our work with urban youth suffering from both poverty and racial discrimination. The type of research-driven pedagogical change that emerges from applying autoethnography in this way necessarily involves (a) continuous development in teacher (Milner, 2003) and teacher educator reflexivity, as well as (b) the development of sound responses to potential threats of connecting autoethnography to CRP.

## Potential Threats of Reflexivity When Connecting Autoethnography to Critical Race Pedagogy

Luttrell (2000) conceptualizes reflexive researchers as those seeking to understand and appreciate differences and accept errors often made because of their blind spots and intense involvement. He actually coins the phrase "good enough methods" (Luttrell, 2000) to speak to a reflexive positioning that is not intended to celebrate mediocrity, but to acknowledge imperfections that surface despite meticulous procedural implementation. Luttrell elaborates on and clarifies "reflexivity" in the following statements from the *Harvard Educational Review*:

> Being reflexive is something to be learned in terms of degrees rather than absolutes (a good enough ethnography is more or less reflexive, not either-or in my view). I think of being reflexive as an exercise in sustaining multiple and sometimes opposing emotions, keeping alive contradictory ways of theorizing the world, and seeking compatibility, not necessarily consensus. Being reflexive means expanding rather than narrowing the psychic, social, cultural, and political fields of analysis. (Luttrell, 2000, p. 13)

From Luttrell's (2000) arduous goals of reflexivity also arise potential threats when considering the connection of autoethnography to CRP. Potential threats include but are not limited to:

- Facing the challenge of qualitative and quantitative scholars who dismiss the potential of autoethnography as critical pedagogy due to the way it merges narrative and social science writing styles,
- Accepting and appropriating subjectivity in one's own pedagogy rather than feeling compelled to hide it or to quantify it,
- Dealing with the emotional difficulty of writing against the "self,"
- Finding and confronting one's own *authentic* voice, and
- Coping with the vulnerability of revealing your old self and "new-self narratives" (Anders et al., 2005; Hughes, 2005).

The potential threats of connecting autoethnography to CRP and the narrative evidence presented earlier reveal the possibilities of this connection to unveil [more] opportunities for hope (Freire, 1996). This connection supports the imminent need for high school teachers and graduate teacher education programs to seek the myriad connections of race, class, and gender to educational reform. Our attempt at autoethnography seemed to move us through the painful and threatening processes of seeking and finding liberation in our democracy as being tied to each other (i.e., White students tied to non-White classmates tied to me). Evidence also supports the notion that connecting autoethnography to CRP can (a) increase empathic validation and commitment to socially just change; (b) increase knowledge, reasonableness, and empathy; and (c) increase an overall sense of one's own ability within the scope of teacher leadership to address and begin to ameliorate some of the threats of race, class, and gender-related oppression in the classroom.

## Connecting Autoethnography and CRP Toward Transformative Caring

The connection of autoethnography to CRP discussed here wasn't planned by Maggie and me. It happened through the daily necessity and demands of the course, the project, the social context, life outside the course, and the willingness of participants to learn, unlearn, share, care, critique, and be critiqued in stark contrast to traditional subtractive ways and means schooling. Valenzuela (1999) details how traditional White-only forms of caring actually render "subtractive schooling" for Mexican-American youth. Color-blindness implemented with intentions of masking race tends to coincide with class- and gender-blind approaches that seem to perpetuate subtractive rather than transformative schooling not only for Mexican American but also for other youth of color (Hughes, 2005). Autoethnography forces me to inquire "How does caring manifest in my classrooms as a one-size-fits-all endeavor?" "Does anyone like me benefit or lose with this form of caring?"

CRP also charges me to consider a different form of caring that affords one the tools to confront questions such as: "How might oppressive experiences of race concomitantly reflect negative experiences of class and gender in the classroom?" A connection of autoethnography to CRP then is a promising connection that can move graduate-level teachers and teacher educators toward becoming more transformative caring agents. Through this connection, a more transformative caring agent might promote more promising reflexive inquiries such as, "How does caring manifest in my classrooms as a subtractive one-White-size-fits-all form of schooling?" "Does anyone Black like me experience more transformative or more subtractive schooling with the form of caring I espouse?"

In the end, autoethnographic research pitfalls and promise of Maggie and me seem to reflect how we literally came to terms with each other, ourselves, and our students throughout the course of one semester. Our autoethnographic outcomes suggest at least three additional possibilities for professors and teachers in graduate teacher education courses attempting to take this route to transformative caring:

- Graduate teacher education courses can engage transformative caring by connecting autoethnography to CRP in ways that promote additional questioning of the curriculum, unit plans, and lesson plans in order to reveal and battle influences of race, sex, class, hidden single perspectives, and other forms of response bias (Swim & Stangor, 1998) and favoritism.
- Graduate teacher education courses can engage transformative caring by connecting autoethnography to CRP in ways that advance instructional leadership by inciting constructive self-critique in our students, our colleagues, and ourselves.
- Graduate teacher education courses can engage transformative caring by connecting autoethnography to CRP in ways that move beyond critical/analytic interpretation to action (e.g., Shultz, 2004).

The experience with Maggie challenged my taken-for-granted knowledge about CRP. It worked to teach me about checking my own response biases, professorial privileges and penalties, struggles, and cares while remaining cognizant of my students' experiences of oppression—to be at least as critical and caring with regard to my raced, classed, and gendered self as I am of my students. Perhaps autoethnography as illustrated here can be transferable to other teachers and teacher educators on our journey to disrupting assumptions about and responses to oppression in the classroom.

# References

Anders, A., Bryan, R., & Noblit, G. (2005). Levering Whiteness: Toward a pedagogy for Whites in denial of their privilege. In S. A. Hughes (Ed.), *What we still don't know about teaching race: How to talk about it in the classroom* (pp. 97–154). Lewiston, NY: Edwin Mellen Press.

Banks, S. P., & Banks, A. (2000, July). Reading the critical life: Autoethnography as Pedagogy. *Communication Education, 49*(3), 233–238.

Berry, T. R. (2005). At the crossroads: A community walk with a critical race feminist in teacher education. In S. Hughes (Ed.), *What we still don't know about teaching race: How to talk about it in the classroom.* New York: Edwin Mellen.

Berry, T. R., & Mizelle, N. D. (Eds.). (2006). *From oppression to grace: Women of color and their dilemmas within the academy.* Sterling, VA: Stylus Publishing.

Bochner, A. P., & Ellis, C. (Eds.). (2002). *Ethnographically speaking: Autoethnography, literature and aesthetics.* Walnut Creek, CA: AltaMira Press.

Campos, C. (2006). *Status of the American public school teacher.* Retrieved October 10, 2006, from http://www.nea.org/newsreleases/2006/nr060502.html

Cleveland, D. (2005). Creating productive space: Approaching diversity and social justice from a privilege perspective in teacher education. In S. A. Hughes (Ed.), *What we still don't know about teaching race: How to talk about it in the classroom* (pp. 53–74). Lewiston, NY: Edwin Mellen Press.

Dalton, M. M. (2003, Summer/Fall). Media studies and emancipatory praxis: An autoethnographic essay on critical pedagogy. *Journal of Film and Video, 55*(2/3), 88–97.

Darder, A., & Torres, R. (2004). *After race: Racism after multiculturalism.* New York: New York University Press.

Delgado, R. (1995). *Critical race theory: A philosophical position.* Philadelphia: Temple University Press. Retrieved May 6, 2006, from http://www.edb.utexas.edu/faculty/scheurich/proj7/crt-delgado.htm

Delpit, L. (1988). The silenced dialogue: Power and pedagogy in educating other people's children. *Harvard Educational Review, 58*, 280–298.

Delpit, L. (1995). *Other people's children: Cultural conflict in the classroom.* New York: New Press.

Denzin, N. K. (2003). *Performance ethnography: Critical pedagogy and the politics of culture.* Thousand Oaks, CA: Sage.

Elder, J., Bremser, P., & Sheridan, M. (2007). *Assigning personal narratives across the disciplines.*

*Exploring pedagogies and tools.* Retrieved July 6, 2007, from https://segueuserfiles. middlebury.edu/ctlr-workshops07/Assigning%20Personal%20Narratives%20 across%20the%20Disciplines.doc

Ellis, C., & Bochner, A. (2000). Autoethnography: Personal narrative, reflexivity: Researcher as subject. In N. K. Denzin & Y. S. Lincoln (Eds.), *Handbook of qualitative research* (2nd ed., pp. 733–768). Thousand Oaks, CA: Sage.

Freire, P. (1970). *Pedagogy of the oppressed.* New York: Continuum.

Freire, P. (1996). *Pedagogy of hope.* New York: Continuum.

Gordon, J. (2005). Inadvertent complicity: Colorblindness in teacher education. *Educational Studies, 38*(2), 135–153.

Guinier, L., & Torres, G. (2002). *The miner's canary.* Cambridge, MA: Harvard University Press.

Gurin, P., & Nagda, B. A. (2006). Getting to the what, how and why of diversity on campus. *Educational Researcher, 35*(1), 20–24.

Hayano, D. M. (1979). Auto-ethnography. *Human Organization, 38,* 99–104.

Hill-Collins, P. (1990). Black feminist thought in the matrix of domination. In *Black feminist thought: Knowledge, consciousness, and the politics of empowerment* (pp. 221–238). London: HarperCollins.

Holt, N. L. (2003). Representation, legitimation, and autoethnography: An autoethnographic writing story. *International Journal of Qualitative Methods, 2*(1). Retrieved May 6, 2006, from http://www.ualberta.ca/iiqm/backissues/2_1final/html/holt.html

Hughes, S. A. (2005). *What we still don't know about teaching race: How to talk about it in the classroom.* Lewiston, NY: The Edwin Mellen Press.

Hughes, S. A. (2006a). *Black hands in the biscuits not in the classrooms: Unveiling hope in a struggle for Brown's promise.* New York: Peter Lang.

Hughes, S. A. (2006b). Teaching theory as "other" to White urban practitioners: Mining and priming Freirean critical pedagogy in a body of resistance. In R. Helfenbein & J. Diem (Eds.), *Unsettling beliefs: Teaching social theory to teachers.* Greenwich, CT: Information Age.

Hughes, S. A. (2007). Why is family diversity education important in teacher and administrator education? In *Factis Pax: Journal of Peace Education and Social Justice, 1*(1), 5–9. Available at http://www.infactispax.org/2007/05/08/the-role-of-family-diversity-in-teacher-education/

Jennings, M., & Lynn, M. (2005, Summer–Fall). The house that race built: Critical pedagogy, African-American education, and the re-conceptualization of a critical race pedagogy. *Educational Foundations, 19*(3/4), 15–32.

Kenyatta. J. (1966). *Facing Mt. Kenya.* New York: Vintage Books.

Laubscher, L. R., & Powell, S. (2003). Skinning the drum: Teaching about diversity as "other." *Harvard Educational Review, 73*(2), 203–244.

Luttrell, W. (2000). Good enough methods for ethnographic research. *Harvard Educational Review, 70*(4), 499–523.

Maguire, M. H. (2006, March). Autoethnography: Answerability/responsibility in authoring self and others in the social sciences/humanities. Review essay. *Forum Qualitative Sozialforschung / Forum: Qualitative Social Research, 7*(2). Retrieved May 6, 2006, from http://www.qualitative-research.net/fqs-texte/2–06/06-2-16-e.htm

McIntosh, P. (1989, July/August). White privilege: Unpacking the invisible knapsack. *Peace and Freedom*, pp. 8–10.

Milner, R. (2003). Teacher reflection and race in cultural contexts: History, meaning and methods in teaching. *Theory Into Practice*, 42(3), 173–180.

Moll, L., Amanti, C., Neff, D., & Gonzalez, N. (1992). Funds of knowledge for teaching: Using a qualitative approach to connect homes and classrooms. *Theory Into Practice*, 31, 132–141.

Noblit, G. (1995, May). In the meantime: The possibilities of caring. *Phi Delta Kappan*, 77, 682.

Noblit, G., & Dempsey, V. (1996). *The social construction of virtue*. Albany, NY: State University of New York Press.

Noddings, N. (1992). *The challenge to care in schools*. New York: Teachers College Press.

Oakes, J., & Lipton, M. (2006). *Teaching to change the world* (3rd ed.). New York: McGraw-Hill.

Patton, M. Q. (2002). *Qualitative research & evaluation methods* (3rd ed.). Thousand Oaks, CA: Sage.

Reed-Danahay, D. (1997). *Auto/ethnography*. New York: Berg.

Richardson, L. (2000). New writing practices in qualitative research. *Sociology of Sport Journal*, 17, 5–20.

Shultz, B. (2004). *Project citizen* [DVD]. Chicago, IL.

Solórzano, D., & Bernal, D. (2001). Examining transformational resistance through a critical race and LatCrit theory framework: Chicana and Chicano students in an urban context. *Urban Education*, 36, 308–342.

Swim, J. K., & Stangor, C. (Eds.). (1998). *Prejudice: The target's perspective*. San Diego, CA: Academic Press.

Taliaferro-Baszile, D. (2006). Pedagogy born of struggle: From the notebook of a Black professor. In S. Hughes (Ed.), *What we still don't know about teaching race: How to talk about it in the classroom*. New York: Edwin Mellen.

Tatum, B. D. (2003). *Why are all the Black kids sitting together in the cafeteria*. New York: Basic Books.

Tillman, L. C. (2002, December). Culturally sensitive research approaches: An African-American perspective. *Educational Researcher*, 31(9), 3–12.

Tozer, S., Senese, G., & Violas, P. (2006). *School and society: Historical and contemporary perspectives*. New York: McGraw-Hill.

Valenzuela, A. (1999). *Subtractive schooling: U.S.-Mexican youth and the politics of caring*. Albany: State University of New York Press.

Van Galen, J. (2004). Seeing classes: Toward a broadened research agenda for critical qualitative researchers. *International Journal of Qualitative Studies in Education*, 17, 663–685.

Van Galen, J. (2006). *Class identity, teacher education, and pedagogies of critique: Toward conversations about class in education courses*. San Francisco, CA: American Educational Research Association Symposium.

Villenas, S. (1996). The colonizer/colonized Chicana ethnographer: Identity, marginalization, and co-optation in the field. *Harvard Educational Review*, 66(4), 711–731.

Weber, M. (1914/1968). *Economy and society: An outline of interpretive sociology* (E. Fischoff, Trans.). New York: Bedminster Press.

Wilson, W. J. (1980). *The declining significance of race: Blacks and changing American institutions* (2nd ed.). Chicago: University of Chicago Press.

Wilson, W. J. (1987). *The truly disadvantaged: The inner city, the underclass, and public policy.* Chicago: University of Chicago Press.

* Reprinted with permission with minor modifications for clarity. Originally published as: Hughes, S. A. (2008, Summer/Fall). Maggie and me: A Black professor and a White urban school teacher connect autoethnography to Critical Race Pedagogy. *Educational Foundations, 20*(3/4), 45–72.

· 8 ·

# Du Boisian Double Consciousness in the Multicultural Classroom and the Questions It Raises

HILTON KELLY

> It is a peculiar sensation, this double-consciousness, this sense of always look-
> ing at one's self through the eyes of others, of measuring one's soul by the
> tape of a world that looks on in amused contempt and pity. One ever feels
> his twoness—an American, a Negro; two souls, two thoughts, two unrec-
> onciled strivings; two warring ideals in one dark body, whose dogged strength
> alone keeps it from being torn asunder.
>
> —Du Bois (1903/1994, p. 9)

In a college course that I taught on social diversity in education, I used segments
from the award-winning *Eyes on the Prize* documentary film series to show students—who were born in the mid- to late 1980s—visual images of the protest
and the violence against school desegregation in both southern and northern
states. Although some students were disturbed by the visible inequality that
existed between White and Black schools, nearly all were surprised by the anger
and violence expressed toward Blacks. The most memorable reaction to the
film came from a White male student who had the courage to voice a negative implicit assumption, which foregrounds the ideas in this chapter. Waiting
until almost every student had given a response to the film, he exclaimed, "I
was shocked that the Black people were so articulate, more than some of the

Whites!" Without missing a beat, other students—Black and White—said that they had noticed it too. My students had assumed that before school desegregation Blacks were intellectually inferior to Whites due to bad schools, thus the need for the 1954 *Brown v. Board of Education* case, a unanimous U.S. Supreme Court decision to desegregate public schools.

Whether negative or positive, implicit assumptions can influence individual and group actions (Dasgupta & Rivera, 2006). Drawing from word of mouth and textbooks that seem ingrained in their consciousness, students assume that the 1954 *Brown* decision replaced *inferior* all-Black schools with *superior* desegregated schools. Such assumptions can make critiques of and actions against an unequal educational system nearly impossible. The dominant discourse among most students who enter my classes on social diversity resembles this: "Although there are still problems in education, Black people are much better off 'now' than they were 'then.' " Counterdiscourses, however, have the *potential* to support a "double consciousness" among students such that students are introduced to new logic systems. In this way, the prevailing logic among students (which most of my students eventually subscribe to) can become: "While all Black students have the right to attend desegregated schools today, not all Black students have the resources and the opportunities to succeed in a post-civil rights society." Ultimately, the issue really is whether students possess an oppositional consciousness that can lead them to seek social and educational justice in schools and society (see also Brandon, 2006; King, 1991).

This chapter brings "consciousness" back into analyses of DuBosian double consciousness. If we think about "two thoughts" as only about racial identity, then double consciousness seems anachronistic and has little value for people with multiple identities. Historian Darlene Clark Hine, for example, has pointed out the problem with linking double consciousness to "racial identity." Hine (1993) wrote: "Still, I suspect, had [Du Bois] considered the issue of gender, instead of writing 'One ever feels his twoness,' he would have mused about how one ever feels her 'fiveness': Negro, American, woman, poor, black woman" (p. 338). In what I consider a fair critique of Du Bois' work, the term *double consciousness* has serious limitations when you consider contemporary theories on multiple identities, matrix of domination, and intersectionality (Crenshaw, 1991; Hill Collins, 2000). Indeed, double consciousness does not apply to everyone. When "consciousness" is brought back to the center, however, the idea of a double consciousness (two souls, two thoughts, two unreconciled strivings, and two warring ideals) becomes relevant to all people with marginal identities in a White, male, heterosexual, able-bodied, Christian world.

Before I make the case that double consciousness should be promoted in multicultural classrooms today, especially when you consider the assumptions that students make about different social groups and their value in our society, I show how texts can shape our consciousness regardless of whether we have read them. After a discussion of the methodology that I used, I look at the 1954 *Brown* decision as a discursive text that has produced and reproduced a particular consciousness and vicarious memories (multigenerational sharing of memories) among students today (Errante, 2000). Next, I draw on oral narratives of former teachers who taught in legally segregated schools for Blacks in North Carolina as an example of oral narratives as discursive texts that reveal how they promoted "double consciousness" among their students in the Age of Segregation. Although I can make no causal argument that their teaching alone led to a social movement for Black civil rights and jobs, I do think that the teaching of a counterdiscourse promoted an oppositional consciousness to White supremacy and racism, a necessary condition for systemic change during the American apartheid (Massey & Denton, 1993). Finally, I end the chapter with a discussion about the development of a double consciousness among students in multicultural classrooms and the questions that it raises for teachers and schools.

# Methodology

These data are taken from a larger research project consisting of oral history interviews, archival research, and secondary historical materials (Kelly, 2007; Kelly, 2010). I selected the coastal plains region of North Carolina because several influential single-case and community studies already exist about legally segregated schooling in North Carolina (Cecelski, 1994; Noblit & Dempsey, 1996; Philipsen, 1999; Siddle Walker, 1996). These studies permit constant comparison and theory construction. In addition, this is the state where I was born and raised: I am familiar with the historical, social, and geopolitical terrain. I also taught in a middle school in one of the counties in the late 1990s, which gave me networks that I could tap into to assist me in soliciting participants.

I conducted semi-structured interviews with 44 former classroom teachers who taught in all-Black schools in Edgecombe, Nash, and Wilson counties in the coastal plains region of North Carolina. I interviewed 14 males and 30 females with an age range from 59 to 85. All participants were asked open-ended questions, such as, "What do you remember about teaching in all-Black schools before integration?"; "In the school(s) where you taught, what do you remember about the quality of education children received?"; and "What are your best and worst memories of teaching in all-Black schools before integration?" In a conversational manner, participants answered questions about how they remembered their work before school integration. Most of the interviews were conducted in the participants' homes, but three occurred in family-owned businesses. The interviews lasted approximately 90 minutes. None of the information about participants has been changed or altered.

## Oral History Interview Data

All of the interviews were collected in two waves from late December 2004 to late January 2005 and May 2005. I also conducted several pilot interviews with Black teachers who taught outside the tricounty area. Initially, through community nomination (see Foster, 1997), I derived a working list of 147 names of Black teachers who are long-time residents of Edgecombe, Nash, and Wilson counties. In the first of two waves of interviews, I used local telephone directories to locate individuals from my list of possible participants. Although there were more women than men on the list, it was difficult to find married women because their telephone numbers were usually listed under their husbands' names. In the interviews, I sought participants' assistance in my efforts to locate "missing" female teachers who still lived in the area. Participants were able to offer such assistance because, within a county, they usually lived across the street, down the road, or around the corner from each other. I asked every participant to identify additional teachers I should interview, which added only six names to my original list and gave me 153 teachers who could potentially be interviewed. Due to time and funding constraints, I chose to interview every fifth person on the list, and in seven cases I also conducted joint interviews with the participants' spouses who were teachers in the same school system. The total number of participants includes both individual and joint interviews from community nomination.

In a well-cited article, educational historian Jack Dougherty (1999) cautioned against an overuse of snowball sampling in historical and qualitative research on Black schools and teachers. Consequently, I adopted a strategy of "maximum variation" sampling to avoid a simple convenience sample (Patton, 1990; Strauss & Corbin, 1998). "Maximum variation involves looking for outlier cases to see whether main patterns still hold," according to Miles and Huberman (1994). Purposively and nonrandomly, I selected interviewees so that they included people from different social and political circles, intentionally seeking to create maximum variation. I deliberately asked informants to identify former teachers who might have a different experience from their own. For instance, I asked a participant who taught at the high school level to recommend an elementary teacher. As Patton (1990) explained: "Any common patterns that emerge from variation are of particular interest and value in capturing core experiences and central shared aspects" (p. 172). The total number of participants also includes participants who were chosen for maximum diversity of experiences.

Ultimately, I used what I had been told to determine which people I worked hardest to track down, with a self-conscious strategy of seeking to cover the full range of experiences. I talked to as many people as time and money would allow, and I ceased interviewing once I discovered that little new data (stories, topics, or people) were being presented (Merriam, 1998; Strauss & Corbin, 1998). I sought to achieve as diverse a sample as possible, being certain to include teachers of different sexes; teachers who taught in primary (Grades 1–3), grammar (Grades 4–7 or 4–8), and high school (Grades 8–12); teachers who taught in county and "city" schools; teachers from different types of colleges, such as normal schools, teachers colleges, state universities, and small liberal arts colleges; teachers who were in different age cohorts—60s, 70s, 80s, and 90s—at the time of the interview; teachers who left the classroom (quit or changed careers) and those who retired in education; and, finally, teachers who were married and those who had never been married.

## Collective Memory and Secondary Historical Sources

To be sure, the accounts from these teachers have been influenced by the days, months, and years since the 1954 *Brown* decision (Coser, 1992; Hamlin, 2002; Shircliffe, 2006). Although individual and collective memory is "always subject to the nostalgic interpretation of experience," as Beauboeuf-Lafontant (1999) explained, "points of convergence in these separate investigations of black segregated schools are many and they suggest in a compelling manner that

African Americans are recalling aspects of their history that warrant the atten-tion of educational researchers" (p. 710). Maximum variation sampling required me to search for "disconfirming instances or variations" among my list of liv-ing participants (Merriam, 1998, p. 63). In addition, secondary historical sources complemented the oral history interviews.

## Du Bosian Double Consciousness: A Brief Note

In his *The Souls of Black Folk*, W. E. B. Du Bois (1994) introduced the term *dou-ble consciousness* as an intellectual breakthrough and radical possibility in the education of African Americans. At the turn of the 20th century, in the midst of solemn efforts to maintain Black institutions and create opportunities along the color line, Du Bois and others saw the promotion of a double consciousness as the necessary condition for racial uplift, respectability, and mutual progress in an oppressive society (Alridge, 1999; Anderson, 1988; Gaines, 1997; Shaw, 1996; Wolcott, 1997). But it was Du Bois alone who articulated the "veil" as a social force impeding Black freedom, achievement, and progress. The veil stands as a metaphor for racial prejudice and discrimination at every level of society (individual, cultural, and institutional). As Du Bois (1903/1994) explained, "the Negro is a sort of seventh son, born with a veil, and gifted with second sight in this American world—a world which yields him no true self consciousness, but only lets him see himself through the revelation of the other world" (p. 5). Through formal education, however, Du Bois believed that an intellectual vanguard among the race could develop their gift of "second sight," acquire "true self consciousness," and challenge racial prejudice and dis-crimination (Du Bois, 1903/1994; Provenzo, 2002).

One of the most far-reaching challenges to racial prejudice and discrimi-nation in the United States has been the fight for school desegregation. At the turn of 21st century, more than five decades after the 1954 *Brown* decision, we continue to ponder whether segregated or desegregated schools are more effec-tive for the education of Black students. In a classic article, "Does the Negro Need Separate Schools?," Du Bois (1935) redirected the query and provided what I consider to be a clue about how teachers and schools might promote a double consciousness among students. Du Bois (1935) wrote:

> . . . theoretically, the Negro needs neither segregated schools nor mixed schools. What he needs is Education. What he must remember is that there is no magic, either in mixed schools or in segregated schools. A mixed school with poor and unsympathetic teachers, with hostile public opinion, and no teaching of truth concern-ing black folk, is bad. A segregated school with ignorant placeholders, inadequate

equipment, poor salaries, and wretched housing, is equally bad. Other things being equal, the mixed school is the broader, more natural basis for the education of all youth. It gives wider contacts; it inspires greater self-confidence; and suppresses the inferiority complex. But other things seldom are equal, and in that case, *Sympathy, Knowledge, and the Truth*, outweigh all the mixed school can offer. (p. 335; italics added)

Moreover, the fundamental question—at least to Du Bois—was not the type of school but the kind of education that Black students acquired. Whether in segregated or desegregated schools, Black students needed sympathy, knowledge, and the truth to "identify the contradictions inherent in white society's alleged devotion to the principles of equality, freedom, and democracy [and] to formulate creative strategies for survival and resistance" (Searls, 1997, p. 163).

According to Huey Li (2002), "the formation of double consciousness is a dynamic and never ending process striving to remove varied 'veils' that inhibit true self-understanding in order to re-integrate one's consciousness" (p. 144). Historically, Black teachers in all-Black schools have been critical about the promotion of a double consciousness among their students (Kelly, 2007). Jacqueline Jordan Irvine and Michele Foster (1996) pointed out that many White teachers of Black students in Catholic schools have promoted double consciousness in their classrooms as well. The success of these two different groups of teachers, I contend, rested on the degree to which they were sympathetic to the circumstances in which their students lived, they introduced the kind of knowledge that affirmed students' culture at the same time that they taught the "culture of power," and they challenged the textbooks, policies, and practices that yielded their students no true self-consciousness. Although the promotion of double consciousness also demanded that teachers point out the contradictions of equality, freedom, and democracy within the United States, it also required that they formulate creative solutions for survival and resistance themselves.

## Deconstructing the Dominant Discourse: *Brown* as a Discursive Text

Thinking back to students' assumptions about "inherently inferior" all-Black schools, I have tried to locate texts that may have shaped my students' consciousness about the way legally segregated schools for Blacks used to be. The most obvious text has been the 1954 *Brown* decision. As I stated earlier, through textbooks, word of mouth, television, and print journalism, my students (and I) have been influenced by dominant discourses. In *Brown*, for example, the majority opinion read:

> Segregation of white and colored children in public schools has a detrimental effect
> upon the colored children. The impact is greater when it has the sanction of the law;
> for the policy of separating the races is usually interpreted as denoting the inferiority
> of the Negro group. A sense of inferiority affects the motivation of the child to learn.
> Segregation with the sanction of law, therefore, has a tendency to [retard] the educa-
> tional and mental development of Negro children and to deprive them of some of the
> benefits they would receive in a racial integrated system. (Mullane, 1993, p. 629)

The stories that my students recalled and retold in my classroom resemble the wording and sentiments of *Brown*, a historical and cultural text. Although there are certainly other texts that have contributed to the production of students' vicarious memories of legally segregated schools for Blacks, I emphasize the *Brown* decision for its far-reaching and deliberate attempt to frame the need for school desegregation.

Through the authority and prestige of the U.S. Supreme Court, students have learned—many years after the fact—that "a sense of inferiority affects the motivation of the [Black] child to learn." Looking back at the previous quota-tion, notice that the effects of segregation only affect Black youth—not Whites. Moreover, students have read (or have been told) that "segregation," not White racism and discrimination, have "a tendency to [retard] the education-al and mental development of Negro children" and "deprive them of some of the benefits" of a racially integrated school system. When students and others draw on such texts (or sacred documents) to imagine what segregated schools for Blacks used to be, the danger involved is that it distorts the way that these schools might have been to the people who attended them.

" 'No narrative version can be independent of a particular teller and occa-sion of telling' and as a result 'every narrative version has been constructed in accord with some set of purposes or interests'" as Wertsch (2001, p. 516) quot-ing Smith explained. Deconstructing *Brown* as a discursive text, White cultur-al practices have rarely been articulated as detrimental to the well-being of Black youth in schools with the notable exception of emerging Critical Race Theory (CRT) in education scholarship (see Dixon & Rousseau, 2006; Ladson-Billings & Tate, 1995; Solórzano & Yosso, 2000). The problem was segregation, not the decisions of White educational authorities and state-sponsored racial discrimination. In addition, the dominant discourse assumes that Black chil-dren in segregated schools were mentally and psychologically damaged due to "inherently inferior" schools. Therefore, Black youth would benefit—socially, intellectually, and culturally—from the mixing of White and Black children in schools. I argue that such (racial) thinking is implicit in the *Brown* decision and has had a major influence on the way my students (and society) remember legally segregated schools for Blacks before federally mandated desegregation.

## Unveiling a Counterdiscourse: Oral Narratives as Discursive Texts

Although participants did not use the term *double consciousness* to convey their double aims of racial pride and the 3 Rs (Reading, 'Riting, and 'Rithmetic), the concept emerged from the data in explanations of how they prepared students for both a Black and White world. In the Age of Segregation, as it should be remembered, Black teachers could not produce "uppity Negroes," nor could they train "second-class citizens." Participants' accounts revealed that Black teachers supported a "healthy" double consciousness in which students struggled against White cultural practices but also sought to defy White supremacist ideology. Historian David Levering Lewis (1993) explained that, "in *Souls* the divided self would not remain flawed, compromised, unstable, or tragic. It would become in time and struggle stronger for being doubled, not undermined—the sum of its parts, not the dividend" (p. 282). It is from this perspective that I employ Du Bois' concept of double consciousness to examine how Black teachers before desegregation promoted "two thoughts" in their classrooms and schools—cautiously and responsibly.

As Du Bois foresaw, participants drew on a counterdiscourse to White supremacy to instill racial pride and academic achievement. Participants gave numerous examples of how double consciousness got promoted:

We were always taught that we were just as good as anybody. And, my parents instilled in us that the way you carry yourself is what counts. We never looked down or held our heads down. We always held our heads up. (Ada Pulley, personal interview, January 7, 2005)

But then what you are trying to do, you are trying to build your people up. You see what is going on, trying to prepare them for tomorrow so they can go out there and do better than you. Now our job was trying to prepare them for tomorrow you see. (Henry Davis, personal interview, May 19, 2005)

The students would march into the auditorium on baccalaureate or graduation night and you would see this big old sign, "Not finished just beginning." But you know, a few words can make you think. I am not finished here tonight. I am just beginning. I am going on to college. I am going to some school, you know, and further my education. (Nellie Hunter, personal interview, May 23, 2005)

Despite the common belief that Blacks should stay in their place and be subservient, Ada Pulley described her early socialization as reminiscent of racial uplift ideology, which started in her home and was later reinforced in classrooms and schools. Despite the idea that Black students should seek "Negro jobs" (Anderson, 1988), Henry Davis sought to prepare students for jobs and opportunities for "tomorrow," not just the reality in which they lived. Despite the prevailing ideas that Blacks only needed rudimentary or industrial education, Nellie Hunter pushed college and university training. Whether it was a directive to "hold your head up," a common goal to prepare students for tomorrow rather than today, or the use of a school motto to inspire, participants sought to instill ambition, hope, and pride in their students.

As a consequence, participants employed double consciousness to challenge White supremacy and White racism directly in their schools—carefully and responsibly. For example, Anniebelle Ricks (personal interview, December 28, 2004) told a story about how Amanda Cameron—whom I later interviewed—scolded the White superintendent in a faculty meeting. Apparently, on one of his rare visits to the school, the White superintendent gave a speech in which he kept referring to the entire Black faculty as "niggras." Cameron was so disturbed by the superintendent's tone and his "intentional" mispronunciation of "Negro" that she raised her hand in the middle of his speech to the faculty. The White superintendent stopped to take her question. Cameron said, "Mr. Humphreys. Can you say HERO?" According to Ricks, everyone's eye's dropped to their knees. After a quick, "yes," from the White superintendent, Cameron continued, "Well, Mr. Humphreys, you should be able to say "NEGRO." Ricks remembered that the entire faculty was on pins and needles; they were amused by Cameron's reprimand of the White superintendent, but they also feared she would be fired.

In her interview, Ricks speculated that Cameron was not fired because her father was a "big time" farmer who owned a lot of land in the community. When I asked her about the risk involved, Cameron (personal interview, May 23, 2005) remarked:

Wonder that I had not been fired. You know, at the time, we didn't know anything about what the Board [of Education] [was] doing because it was a lily white Board. All we had to do when the superintendent was coming over [pause] you know you got almost like tense—the superintendent is coming! . . . You had to be careful. I guess sometimes I would, at least, I would forget that. And then, I think they were afraid to fire me because my daddy was a tax payer in this county. . . . If you didn't own anything, you were just about a nothing, you know. So, I guess I might have said a lot of things and got away with more than maybe someone else because my daddy was a landowner.

Cameron's use of language to make a point is important here. Instead of confronting power directly, she chose to politely correct the way the White superintendent pronounced the word *Negro*. After all, the situation was a power-laden one. Was it not the duty of competent teachers to encourage the use of good speech, grammar, and pronunciation? Of course, Cameron refused to accept the disrespectful way that the White superintendent treated her and her colleagues. Cameron understood the "ways of White folk" in her small southern town—who often refused to use professional titles when talking to college-educated Blacks, so it was a particular discourse that she recognized (e.g., Black people are second-class citizens and do not deserve to be treated respectfully) and felt the need to disrupt. Still, she also recognized the limits of her resistance to White power. Although it was not completely safe (she could have been fired), it was hardly reproachable when you consider that the superintendent was addressing a group of college-educated faculty.

In addition to being able to identify contradictions (e.g., differences in addressing Whites and Blacks) and formulating creative solutions (e.g., speech correction), participants recalled numerous examples of sympathy, knowledge, and the truth as fundamental aspects of their pedagogical repertoire in legally segregated schools for Blacks.

## Sympathy

Working against a societal myth of Black inferiority, participants cared for and sympathized with their mostly poor and working-class students. According to Siddle Walker and Tompkins (2004), "caring had a purpose. . . . To care intensely for the students for whom they had been given responsibility was to provide them with a storehouse of tools for challenging and thwarting a deeply imbedded system of inequality" (p. 91). Participants revealed that caring usually involved expressing sympathy and compassion:

> The sympathy that we had for our poor children who had to stay out of school and work the farm, who came to school with a hole in the bottom of the shoe with a piece of cardboard in it, who came to school with a lunch bucket with a sausage biscuit or a

molasses biscuit and maybe a tea cookie that momma had made. . . . I think those are some of the good things that stuck with me for the love that we had [pause] and knowing how little we had but in spite of all of that—we forged. (Josephine Edwards, personal interview, December 21, 2004)

[Black students] had someone who could look at [them] and know what they actually needed. When I say what they actually needed, they needed more than just education: We talked about our health, character, self-respect first, and then how to respect others. . . . When we were all-black our children had a lot of self-esteem, they had a lot of character, they knew that they could do anything—anything that anybody else could do—and do it well. When you think about it, we were role models for our children. (Effie Smith, personal interview, December 27, 2004)

I think the first thing that you would write about black teachers before integration is that they cared about their children. They taught them yes but they cared about the children and that is where all the good teaching came from. (Catherine Taylor, personal interview, January 11, 2005)

Wishing and hoping for better lives for all of their students, participants possessed a sympathetic attitude toward the conditions in which their students lived. As bell hooks (1994) remarked, "To teach in a manner that respects and cares for the souls of our students is essential if we are to provide the necessary conditions where learning can most deeply and intimately begin" (p. 13).

## Knowledge

Participants also believed that the education students acquired needed to be grounded in "racial knowledge" that would help them endure the world outside the Black community. They prepared students with skills and knowledge, combined with good moral development, a positive racial identity, and a solid basic education to enter a world of state-sponsored segregation, racial discrimination, and economic deprivation. For example, participants recalled:

We didn't teach textbooks. Nor did we teach to tests. But we taught students as I hate to say it, but, the whole child. It has become such a cliché. How do you teach half a child? But, we met students' needs—not only educational[ly] but also socially, morally, spiritually. Whatever we saw that they needed to become a productive citizen, this is what we gave them. (E. J. Cummings, personal interview, May 24, 2005)

It wasn't just the Tigris and Euphrates rivers, you know. It also had to do with [pause] "Why is your hair so pretty? because God didn't make anything ugly. God gave you the hair that you have in order to fit the climate that [your ancestors] grew up in—the cli-

mate of Africa. . . . And God gave you pretty hair and God made everything beautiful. So don't let me see you sitting in the classroom and whining in reference to somebody's hair because it is straight. Your hair wasn't meant to be straight." So, this was
my way of teaching history: who you are and the beauty of you. (Nellie Hunter, personal interview, May 23, 2005)

We brought in a lot of resources from the community to let the children know that
these are some of the things that you can do—the dentist, the doctors, whatever profession these people were in. Students who had graduated from high school and had
come back from college—and they were doing well—were given time to talk to the
student body. (Athalene Emory, January 11, 2005)

In accordance with Monica White (2004), "black teachers at that time felt a
moral obligation to prepare each student for success in facing the challenges of
discrimination in a racially segregated world" (p. 150). These accounts and others should make us wonder whether all the textbooks, materials, and supplies
in the world could have replaced the kind of knowledge that Black teachers promoted, especially when you consider that the hidden curriculum emphasized
racial pride, morality, responsibility, and citizenship.

## The Truth

When Samuel Gray told me about the year he discovered that his school (a Black
high school) had to pay the White high school to play team sports in the "public park," his facial grimace and trembling hands betrayed the calm voice record-
ed during the interview. As a prominent coach in his county, Samuel Gray
complained often, loudly, and publicly until the Black principal asked him to
cease further protest. Samuel Gray (personal interview, May 18, 2005) remembered: "He asked me not to go over there [to the white high school]. And these
were his words: 'I am afraid of white folks.' If he had not told me the truth, I would
have dealt with it totally. But when he was so honest [pause] black men his age,
and my father's age, didn't have the courage that we had. And he said to me, and
I had just gotten out of the military, I was 25, he said, 'it's going to take young
men like you to change things." Samuel explained that he respected his principal's wishes, but he continued to talk to students and parents about the injustice.
Samuel explained, "Our kids needed to be motivated and inspired, but they also
needed to know the truth about the system—one Black and one White—that
existed in this country. And, I found myself talking about it quite often."

Other participants explained how they tried to tell their students "the
truth" in their classrooms:

But we were trying to teach them the things they were going to have to come up with and what they were going to have to experience. For example, we had to teach the black child that he had to be just a little bit better to get the same type job that the white child got. If a black child and a white child were to go and apply for the same job, all things being equal—if they had the same qualifications, same experience, same everything—then the white child would get that job. The only way the black child was going to get the job, he had to be a little bit better at doing a little bit better quality work than the white child. (E. J. Cummings, personal interview, May 24, 2005)

We could work close to kids—there was just camaraderie you know—and if I wanted to talk to you and tell you something . . . [I could] because being black myself I could come up and sit with you and tell you: "the only thing that is going to prepare you is an education—so get your act together now. (Henry Davis, personal interview, May 19, 2005)

I think that we were so [pause] trying to make our children [pause] wake them up. You know, this is a new day, you have to take off and do something. We tried to get them to study more, do more, you know, excel [pause] as much as you can. You see we could talk to them because it was a situation in which there were no white people there and you could motivate those children to get going. [pause] I mean that's something that I remember doing a lot—trying to get them to the place that they could go beyond the four year school—beyond the high school, you know, because some of them were a little complacent. They just didn't want to do anything beyond high school other than go get a job. (Carol Cooper, personal interview, January 3, 2005)

In each of these accounts, participants promoted double consciousness in response to societal beliefs of Black inferiority, which they understood to be dominant in the hearts and minds of some Blacks and Whites in the Age of Segregation.

## Double Consciousness in the Multicultural Classroom

Within multicultural classrooms, the suppression of the "gift of second sight" or the development of double consciousness has serious implications for social action. When schools and curricula fail to promote a "true self-consciousness" and only allow Black youth to see themselves through the eyes of others, for instance, Du Bois warned that this situation could lead to a negative self-consciousness as individuals conformed to how the world saw them (Allen, 1992). But the psychosocial pressures to conform do not exist for Blacks only; it is a mutual struggle for women, sexual minorities, the poor, and the disabled. "If a person's soul is double, then it is because he [or she] must live in two worlds at once," as Charles Lemert (2002) stated. With this in mind, double consciousness can lead to a positive and true self-consciousness for marginalized students as educators work to connect their personal troubles to social inequalities. According to Huey Li (2002), "It is common for the marginalized people perceived as 'others,' to develop a 'double consciousness' in the process of cultural hybridization" (p. 138). To the contrary, I have found that my students—of various shades, genders, sexualities, and classes—do not easily recognize how discourses and social structures shape their lives, desires, and consciousness. Although "marginalized people" may be gifted with "second sight" due to their social position(s) in an oppressive society, they are not always aware of how dominant discourses provide scripts for their lives and, ultimately, become ingrained in their consciousness.

As I have shown throughout this chapter, historically, some classroom teachers have been key players in the promotion of a double consciousness among their students. Although former teachers in legally segregated schools for Blacks did not work under the same conditions that today's teachers face, growing research provides strong evidence for the "re-segregation of public schools" throughout the United States (Boger & Orfield, 2005; Kozol, 2005; Orfield, 2001). According to a team of researchers at the Harvard University Civil Rights Project, now at the University of California at Los Angeles (Frankenberg & Lee, 2002; Frankenberg, Lee, & Orfield, 2003; Holley, 2005; Orfield, 2001; Orfield & Eaton, 1996), there is a pervasive pattern of resegregation in U.S. public schools due mostly to the reversal of desegregation court orders and the increasing segregation of White, Black and Latino neighborhoods and communities. Writing about segregated schools today, not in the Age of Segregation, Frankenberg, Lee, and Orfield (2003) reported:

> Segregated schools have much higher concentrations of poverty and other problems and much lower average test scores, levels of students, teacher qualifications, and advanced courses. With few exceptions, separate schools are still unequal schools. (p. 11)

Although the politics of resegregation in U.S. public schools is beyond the scope of this chapter, any evidence of a return to "the way we were" calls for a discussion of consciousness as we seek to address some of the educational problems that our society faces today.

Regardless of school type (segregated or desegregated), students must become critically engaged and constantly question the world taken for granted. This should not be done accidentally. All teachers have a role to play in the promotion of a double consciousness among all of their students. Fully aware that double consciousness is usually identified with racial identity (e.g., twoness—an American, a Negro), I argue that the term must become strongly linked with "consciousness" (e.g., two thoughts), which raises new questions for teachers in multicultural classrooms:

1. How can possessing a double consciousness make a difference in the lives of the students I teach?
2. How does my pedagogy promote a double consciousness among the students I teach, especially historically underserved multicultural students?
3. How can I become more knowledgeable about the lives and the histories of students I teach (ethnic minorities, working poor, homosexual, disabled, and women) so that I can affirm them while promoting double consciousness?
4. How can the school encourage, promote, and develop a double consciousness among its students, especially in resegregated environments in an oppressive world?

These questions need to be addressed through personal reflection and research. Like the teachers who taught in legally segregated schools for Blacks, teachers must possess a double consciousness rooted in the social and political circumstances in which their students live. As Jonathan Kozol (2005) articulated well:

> Teachers in these schools must work, and know that they must work, within "the box" of segregated demographics and extreme inequities . . . but in their temperaments and in their moral disposition many also stand outside that box, because they are aware of its existence, and this sense of double-vision, being part of something and aware of what it is at the same time, regenerates the energy they bring with them each morning to the very little place (one room, one set of chairs) in which they use what gifts they have to make the school day good and whole and sometimes beautiful for children. (p. 287)

In the contemporary United States, as Kozol inferred, teachers must be able to identify the contradictions in which they work (looking and thinking inside and outside of the box), and then they must work with others to find creative solutions for survival and resistance. Although I do recognize that some teachers possess a double consciousness but are simply overwhelmed by the lack of resources in their schools and communities, the best advice that I can give to these teachers is to continue being sympathetic to the issues that their students face, to keep introducing knowledge that affirms every student, and to always tell the truth.

# References

Allen, E. (1992). Ever feeling one's twoness: "Double ideals" and "double consciousness" in the souls of Black folk. *Contributions in Black Studies, 9/10*, 55–69.

Alridge, D. P. (1999). Guiding philosophical principles for a Du Bosian-based African American educational model. *Journal of Negro Education, 68*(2), 182–199.

Anderson, J. (1988). *The education of blacks in the South, 1860–1935*. Chapel Hill: University of North Carolina Press.

Beauboeuf-Lafontant, T. (1999). A movement against and beyond boundaries: "Politically relevant teaching" among African American teachers. *Teachers College Record, 100*(4), 702–723.

Boger, J. C., & Orfield, G. (Eds.). (2005). *School resegregation: Must the South turn back*. Chapel Hill: University of North Carolina Press.

Brandon, L. T. (2006). On dysconsciousness: An interview with Joyce E. King. *Educational Studies, 40*(2), 196–208.

Cecelski, D. (1994). *Along freedom road: Hyde County, North Carolina and the fate of black schools in the South*. Chapel Hill: University of North Carolina Press.

Coser, L. A. (Ed.). (1992). *Maurice Halbwachs: On collective memory*. Chicago: University of Chicago Press.

Crenshaw, K. W. (1991). Mapping the margins: Intersectionality, identity politics, and violence against women of color. *Stanford Law Review, 43*(6), 1241–1299.

Dasgupta, N., & Rivera, L. M. (2006). From automatic anti-gay prejudice to behavior: The moderating role of conscious beliefs about gender and behavioral control. *Journal of Personality and Social Psychology, 91*, 268–280.

Dixon, A. D., & Rousseau, C. K. (2006). *Critical race theory in education: All God's children got a song*. New York: Routledge.

Dougherty, J. (1999). From anecdote to analysis: Oral interviews and new scholarship in educational history. *Journal of American History, 86*(2), 712–723.

Du Bois, W. E. B. (1935). Does the Negro need separate schools? *Journal of Negro Education, 4*, 328–335.

Du Bois, W. E. B. (1994). *The souls of Black folk*. New York: Gramercy Books. (Original work published 1903)

Errante, A. (2000). But sometimes you're not part of the story: Oral histories and ways of remembering and telling. *Educational Researcher, 29*(2), 16–27.

Foster, M. (1997). *Black teachers on teaching*. New York: New Press.

Frankenberg, E., & Lee, C. (2002). *Race in American public schools: Rapidly resegregating school districts*. Cambridge, MA: The Civil Rights Project, Harvard University.

Frankenberg, E., Lee, C., & Orfield, G. (2003). *A multiracial society with segregated schools: Are we losing the dream?* Cambridge, MA: The Civil Rights Project, Harvard University.

Gaines, K. (1997). *Uplifting the race: Black leadership, politics, and culture in the twentieth century*. Chapel Hill, NC: University of North Carolina Press.

Hamlin, F. (2002). "The book hasn't closed, the story is not finished:" Coahoma County, Mississippi, civil rights, and the recovery of a history. *Sound Historian, 8*, 37–60.

Hill Collins, P. (2000). *Black feminist thought: Knowledge, consciousness, and the politics of empow-*

*erment.* New York: Routledge.

Hine, D. C. (1993). "In the kingdom of culture": Black women and the intersection of race, gender, and class. In G. Early (Ed.), *Lure and loathing: Twenty Black intellectuals address W.E.B. Du Bois's dilemma of the double-consciousness of African-Americans* (pp. 337–351). New York: Penguin Books.

Holley, D. (2005). Is *Brown* dying? Exploring the resegregation trend in our public schools. *New York Law Review, 49,* 1085–1107.

hooks, b. (1994). *Teaching to transgress: Education as the practice of freedom.* New York: Routledge.

Irvine, J. J., & Foster, M. (1996). *Growing up African American in Catholic schools.* New York: Teachers College Press.

Kelly, H. (2007). *Jim Crow's teachers: Race, remembering, and the geopolitics of teaching in the North Carolina coastal plains.* Unpublished doctoral dissertation, University of Massachusetts, Amherst.

Kelly, H. (2010). *Race, remembering, and Jim Crow's teachers.* New York: Routledge.

King, J. (1991). Dysconscious racism: Ideology, identity, and the miseducation of teachers. *Journal of Negro Education, 60*(2), 133–146.

Kozol, J. (2005). *The shame of the nation: The restoration of apartheid schooling in America.* New York: Crown Publishers.

Ladson-Billings, G., & Tate, W. F. (1995). Toward a critical race theory of education. *Teachers College Record, 97,* 47–68.

Lemert, C. (2002). *Social things: An introduction to the sociological life* (2nd ed.). New York: Rowman & Littlefield.

Lewis, D. L. (1993). *W. E. B. Du Bois: Biography of a race, 1868–1919.* New York: Henry Holt.

Li, H. (2002). From alterity to hybridity: A query of double consciousness. *Philosophy of Education.* Retrieved April 16, 2007, from http://www.ed.uiuc.edu/EPS/PES-Yearbook/2002/138-huey-li%2002.pdf.

Massey, D. S., & Denton, N. A. (1993). *American apartheid: Segregation and the making of the underclass.* Cambridge, MA: Harvard University Press.

Merriam, S. B. (1998). *Qualitative research and case study applications in education.* San Francisco: Jossey Bass.

Miles, M. B., & Huberman, A. M. (1994). *Qualitative data analysis: An expanded sourcebook.* Thousand Oaks, CA: Sage.

Mullane, D. (Ed.). (1993). *Crossing the danger water: Three hundred years of African-American writing.* New York: Double Day Publishing.

Noblit, G., & Dempsey V. (1996). *The social construction of virtue: The moral life of schools.* Albany: State University of New York Press.

Orfield, G. (2001). *Schools more separate: Consequences of a decade of resegregation.* Cambridge, MA: The Civil Rights Project, Harvard University.

Orfield, G., & Eaton, S. (Eds.). (1996). *Dismantling desegregation: The quiet reversal of Brown v. Board of Education.* New York: New Press.

Patton, M. Q. (1990). *Qualitative evaluation and research methods* (2nd ed.). Newbury Park, CA: Sage.

Philipsen, M. (1999). *Values-spoken and values-lived: Race and the cultural consequences of a school closing.* Cresskill, NJ: Hampton Press.

Provenzo, E. (2002). *Du Bois on education.* Walnut Creek, CA: AltaMira Press.

Searls, S. (1997). Race, schooling, and double consciousness: The politics of pedagogy in Toni Morrison's fiction. In H. A. Giroux & P. Shannon (Eds.), *Education and cultural studies: Toward a performative practice* (pp. 153–176). New York: Routledge.

Shaw, S. (1996). *What a woman ought to be and to do: Black professional women workers during the Jim Crow era*. Chicago: The University of Chicago Press.

Shircliffe, B. (2006). *The best of that world: Historically black high schools and the crisis of desegregation in a southern metropolis*. Cresskill, NJ: Hampton Press.

Siddle Walker, V. (1996). *Their highest potential: An African American school community in the segregated South*. Chapel Hill: University of North Carolina Press.

Siddle Walker, V., & Tompkins, R. (2004). Caring in the past: The case of a Southern segregated African American school. In V. Siddle Walker & J. Snarey (Eds.), *Race-ing moral formation: African American perspectives on care and justice* (pp. 77–92). New York: Teachers College Press.

Solórzano, D., & Yosso, T. (2000). Toward a critical race theory of Chicana and Chicano education. In C. Tejeda, C. Martinez, Z. Leonardo, & P. McLaren (Eds.), *Charting new terrains of Chicana(o)/Latina(o) education* (pp. 35–65). Cresskill, NJ: Hampton Press.

Strauss, A., & Corbin, J. (1998). *Basics of qualitative research: Techniques and procedures for developing grounded theory* (2nd ed.). Thousand Oaks, CA: Sage.

Wertsch, J. (2001). Narratives as cultural tools in sociocultural analysis: Official history in Soviet and post-Soviet Russia. *Ethos, 28*(4), 511–533.

White, M. (2004). Paradise lost: Teachers' perspectives on the use of cultural capital in the segregated schools of New Orleans, Louisiana. In V. P. Franklin & C. J. Savage (Eds.), *Cultural capital and Black education: African American communities and the funding of Black schooling, 1865 to the present* (pp. 143–158). Greenwich, CT: Information Age.

Wolcott, V. (1997). "Bible, bath, and broom": Nannie Helen Borroughs, the national training school, and the uplift of the race. *Journal of Women's History, 9*, 88–110.

## · 9 ·

# An Academic in the Classroom

## Uncovering and Resisting the Barriers to Racial Equity in Public School

BENJAMIN BLAISDELL

After 5 years in graduate school and receiving a PhD in Education, I returned to teach English as a Second Language (ESL) in a public elementary school. When I decided to return to the classroom, I thought it would be a good opportunity to write about the experience of someone who claimed to an antiracist, social justice teacher educator/researcher working as a public school teacher. As a graduate student, I examined and wrote about my identity as a White educator who had been complicit in institutional racism and who was attempting to work against that complicity and pursue antiracism (Blaisdell, 2005a, 2005b). I taught several university classes on social foundations of education and multicultural education, further developing an agenda of antiracism as a teacher educator. So, I conducted an autoethnographic study of my year back in the classroom with the hope that organized reflection on my attempts at antiracism in a public school would give me insight into how to pursue that agenda more effectively in school settings and help me become more effective at communicating such an agenda as a teacher educator in the future. In addition, I hoped to use my graduate school experiences to promote culturally responsive and antiracist practices at the school. However, as the school year progressed, I became more and more aware of the barriers that prevent teachers from working toward racial equity. In this chapter, I discuss those barriers with that similar agenda of influencing the practice of teacher educators who promote racial equity.

Several factors limit the pursuit of antiracism in contemporary public schools. One is standards-based reform, especially in the high-stakes testing context of No Child Left Behind (NCLB). Standards-based reform has effects on school-wide practices that are inhospitable to culturally responsive teaching and the pursuit of racial equity. Second is the existence of an overly technocratic leadership ideology, which supports the ideology of and compounds the limiting effects of standards-based reform by perpetuating limited views of curriculum, pedagogy, and teachers. Third is the liberalism that dominates teacher ideology. Through an adherence to liberal ideology, teachers sustain institutional practices that support the limiting effects of standards-based reform and repress culturally responsive and antiracist pursuits.

As I lay out these barriers, I follow the diagnostic approaches of political race (Guinier & Torres, 2002) and Critical Race Theory (CRT). Political race analysis examines how the marginalizing effects of institutional practice on students of color point out inherent flaws in the structure of the institution. Toward that end, I describe how the effects of standards-based reform on children of color, and specifically Latino English language learners (ELLs), at one elementary school to highlight the marginalizing effects of standards-based reform on all students. I use CRT to inform this analysis by showing how institutional school practices limit the access of Latinos ELLs to rigorous curricula. The aim is to bring to light how this limited access can happen to any student when a school responds in technocratic ways to standardized curricula and assessment. The property analysis of CRT, in particular, can expose institutionalized inequitable access to curricula. Furthermore, I argue that such analysis can be done with teachers in a dialogic approach that creates room for teachers to resist practices that limit access. From such inquiry, educational scholars can then work with teachers to construct counterpractices, or practices that challenge the status quo of curricular distribution and racial disparity.

## Studying the School

During the school year, I carried a notebook with me at almost all times, following the approaches of participant observation and journaling (as described by Anderson, Herr, & Nihlen, 1994/2007). Every week, I would compile the notes from my notebooks. Later in the year, I coded the data from all of the fieldnotes and journal entries with the help of a colleague. After coding the data several times, we used domain analysis (Coffey & Atkinson, 1996) to analyze the ways in which teacher and administrators contributed to and justified the racial inequity at the school. After reviewing our coding, I came up with the three "accounts" (p. 99) for (and responses to) inequity: those according to the discourse of standards-based reform, those according to technocratic leadership, and those according to the ideology of liberalism.

In addition to my notes on the barriers to racial equity, I took notes on my own interactions and teaching experiences. To show the possibility of how current power structures can be challenged, I discuss my own transformation during the school year. In the beginning of the year, I started out supporting the same marginalizing instructional structures of the school. However, conducting the autoethnographic study helped me recapture the critical perspective I developed in graduate school and to resist the dominating ideologies at work. As Denzin (2003) and Alexander (1999) argue, autoethnography is a way to use personal experience to understand and even resist political forces in institutions. Likewise, Anderson et al. (1994/2007) state that practitioner action research can help teachers "challenge the mythologies and institutional and social arrangements that lead to school failure for a disproportionate number of poor and minority students" (pp. 7–8). The reflection process—informed by performance ethnography, political race theory, and CRT—helped me undertake such a challenge and shift my own teaching and work with teachers to promote racial equity. I do not want to overstate my ability to fight racial disparity at the school.[1] Rather, I share my own story to show the possibility that education can look different and teachers can resist racially marginalizing practices even in a standards-based reform context.

## Barriers to Racial Equity

Southern Elementary (a pseudonym) was a school with a little more than 500 students. In terms of racial background, 54% of the students were White, 23% African American, 16% Latino, and 4% Asian. In addition, 36% of the students were on free and reduced lunch. In the district, there were nine elementary schools; of those schools, Southern was one of the two schools with the highest proportion of non-White students and the highest proportion of students on free and reduced lunch. The faculty at Southern often claimed to love the school's diversity. Teachers talked about how they liked that

Southern was more racially and economically diverse than the other schools in the district, and they often declared how they preferred to work with these diverse populations.

At the same time, there was a large racial achievement gap according to both test scores and grades, especially in math. On the reading end of grade (EOG) test, 99% of the White students and 82% of the African-American students passed, and on the math EOG, 90% of the White students and only 33% of the African-American students passed. In addition, only 52% of the ELLs passed the math EOG. Grades showed a similar achievement gap. In reading, more than 95% of White students were at or above grade level, whereas 79% of African-American, 78% of Latino, and 80% of ELL students were at or above grade level. In math, 88% of White students were at or above grade level, but only 33% of African-American, 47% of Latino, and 52% of ELL students were at or above grade level.

## School-Wide Responses to Standards-Based Reform

The faculty and administration's response to standards-based reform affected many of the school's educational practices and perpetuated the racial achievement gap. First of all, the discussion of curriculum started from and was usually limited to meeting the standards listed in the North Carolina Standard Course of Study (NCSCOS). Although many of those standards are reasonable on their own, the curriculum at Southern centered on the list of standards and indicators on the NCSCOS rather than on the students' lives or from any broader beliefs or goals on education. One area that was affected by such a limited vision of curriculum was the school's approach to reading, which was individualistic and incremental, especially for lower level readers (who were disproportionately African American and Latino). Despite the existence of a literacy program that did follow a broad approach to literacy and that involved an attempt to instill a love of reading, much of the time the focus of most teachers' energy was on how students fared on multiple-choice tests linked to leveled readers. The students would have to answer test-like comprehension questions aligned to the standards on the NCSCOS to determine their reading proficiency.

Scores on these tests drove most teachers' approach to reading. When students did not do well, they often received more remedial forms of instruction that was more directly focused on the lower level thinking skills. The result was that the curriculum that many of my Latino ELL students, the majority of whom received low scores, had access to was much more limited to a basic skills approach.

> I am noticing that [two of my students] often work on either test-prep reading passages or they work with leveled readers (books). These books are not inherently bad, but they are pulled away from the rest of the class, some of who are in book groups where they get to talk about the books. These two are making slow incremental progress in reading and receiving instruction that doesn't include higher order thinking skills.

As mentioned in the previous quote, teachers would create book groups, which were organized homogenously according to how the students scored on the standardized reading tests. The lower level groups received simpler reading activities that often involved worksheets of multiple-choice test questions that mimicked the EOG test. So, even when my students were in book clubs, their group work rarely focused on getting them to read texts that fostered higher order thinking skills. The teachers rarely pushed those lower level readers to work in heterogeneous groups that involved more interesting and rigorous reading and higher order thinking skills.

Even the reading specialists, who worked specifically with students who scored low on the reading tests, were rarely able to get those readers to catch up to their higher level peers. Their methods were effective at getting the students to progress to the next reading levels, but they did so incrementally so that those students would never catch up to their White non-ELL peers. Furthermore, the specialists' approach involved pulling students from class, segmenting their learning. So, my Latino ELLs and the other lower level readers, predominantly African-American and Latino students, were in effect segregated from access to higher level curricula.

A similar segregation occurred with math. First of all, some grade levels created separate homogenously leveled math courses, and the makeup of the courses was based on students' current proficiency levels. Again, these proficiency levels were determined by periodic standardized assessments using the EOG test format. In the third grade, for example, the students were pulled from their regular classroom teacher and assigned to one of five math classes based on their current test scores. I worked with one of the two lowest level groups because it had a high number of ELLs. This class had no White students. The other low-level math class did have a few White students, but most of those students were also labeled as Exceptional Children (EC), the district's term for special education students. Incidentally, the highest math group had only two African-American students and no Latino students. Neither of the teachers of these two classes mentioned the racial difference in class makeup, and both were a little surprised when I pointed it out them.

## Technocratic Leadership

The administration at Southern adhered to a technocratic leadership approach. I base my definition of technocratic ideology in what Apple (2004) calls authoritarian populism. According to Apple, authoritarian populism is an ideology that creates a myth of a common culture, a culture that is already created and taken for granted. People, especially people without power, are positioned as consumers—as opposed to creators—of the predetermined common culture and valued knowledge. I argue that such an ideology—as it exists in educations settings—promotes the belief that what counts as valued school knowledge is already and unarguably set in place. The job of schools and teachers, then, is only to facilitate and then measure the acquisition of that knowledge. In turn, such an understanding of knowledge leads to a technical approach to education in which the goal of schooling is the teaching of measurable skills. At Southern, the administrators' overly technical view of education and knowledge caused the administration to hold a narrow definition of curriculum and instruction. They adhered to a definition of successful teaching that was limited to how teachers could align lessons to the state standard course of study and to how well the students would perform on standardized assessments. Efforts by teachers, which link to indicators on the standard course of study, were often discouraged. Furthermore, both of the administrators believed that their authority made their observations and interpretations of teaching incontestable.

For example, the principal observed me during a lesson I was working on with five of my Latino ELLs. I consciously designed the lesson—part of a unit that lasted several weeks—to give these students an opportunity to read extended text (rather than the worksheets they often received) that was complex and above grade level (rather than the below grade-level readers three of those five students were usually given) and was of high-interest to them (the students and I together chose the topic—animals—and the text—a national geographic website). Having the students work together on their project, I was trying to follow a teaching approach that stemmed from a color group consciousness for Latino students.[2] This approach involved having joint, group goals and a chance for the students to find and make meaning about the animals they read about together. The goal was not only to be more culturally aware[3] in my methodology but also to use the ideas from color group consciousness to make the curriculum and learning my students received more rigorous. Toward that aim, I followed the scaffolding techniques for ELLs as put forth by Walqui (2006) and tried to use the students' understandings, observations, and descriptions of the text to push them to restate and re-present the text in other ways (one key aspect of scaffolding), facilitating the process with various graphic organizers (another key aspect) until they could discuss the animals with more fluency and in a more extended fashion. My intent was to foster academic success by reading above grade-level text and writing sentences and paragraphs beyond the formulaic writing they usually were asked to produce.

It is certainly possible that my attempts were not as culturally responsive as I wanted them to be. It is possible that I could have adapted my teaching to be even more successful at getting the students involved in more rigorous and complex learning. The principal's limited view or teaching, however, prevented our discussion from ever analyzing the cultural responsiveness of my teaching or the degree of effectiveness of my use of color group consciousness or scaffolding. Instead, the language in her review was dominated by the discourse of standards. Overall, I received a decent evaluation. I received mainly positive checkmark responses on the evaluation form. However, she made no comment about any of my attempts at culturally responsive teaching, scaffolding, or increasing the rigor of curriculum and learning. The primary verbal feedback she gave me was in relation to the standard course of study. She encouraged me to consider how much the language objectives from the lesson fit into "what a year's worth of English language learning" should be. When I was unclear of what she meant, she referenced the standard course of study for ELLs and commented on how I should focus on getting the students to progress from their current English language proficiency level to the next level according to the list of skills and indicators. Leaving aside the fact that the standard course of study for ELLs is not designed for them to progress in such a linear fashion, her response indicated to me that she had an awareness of what I believed to be the larger issue—specifically, that these students were below grade level and that the current approaches by the school were not overcoming that gap. When I tried to explain my motivations for the lesson and how I was using their grade level content objectives (also according to the standard course of study) to get them to work on more age- and content-appropriate communicative activities, I felt like I wasn't heard. She again referenced the standard course of study for ELLs and how I needed to show how much language they learned in the course of the year.

This is just one example of how the administration often did not interpret practices that followed a culturally responsive approach as "best practice." If it was not clear to the administration how lessons met the indicators on the standard course of study and if it was not clear that those standards drove teaching, they tried to redirect teachers to use methods that more directly and overtly addressed those standards. My colleagues who did attempt to employ culturally responsive teaching often commented on how neither administrator looked favorably on their more interactive lessons[4] and how they both would focus more attention in observations on how the activities helped the students on standardized assessments. In the end, a school-wide response to standards-based reform that segmented and remediated the learning of my Latino ELLs was coupled with the administration's narrow view of curriculum and instruction and their attempts to control limit teachers' approaches to instruction.

## Liberal Ideology

Teachers often supported the administrator's technical view of education by adhering to the ideology of liberalism. Liberalism assumes that the institution of education—like all social institutions—is socially just. Specifically, liberal ideology understands schools as sites that work toward alleviating social inequality (Apple, 2004; Dale, 1976). This leads to a blindness to how the institution causes social inequity. Rather, the standardized practices of the institution are seen as the primary mechanisms to work toward social justice. In school settings, then, liberalism promotes following the standard approaches to instruction—those that fit into and support the current structure of the institution—to support the achievement of all students. When racial disparity in academic success occurs, the issue is not in these practices. Instead, teachers and other school personnel often believe the primary sources of racial disparity to be the students or their families. Even when these practices are critiqued, liberalism only promotes "tinkering" with them so as not to disrupt the overall institutional structure in which they exist (Tyack & Cuban, 1995). So as not to disrupt the "grammar of schooling," practices developed to alleviate racial disparity are incremental and individualistic or are relegated to the periphery on the school's way of functioning (Tyack & Cuban, 1995). In fact, those practices that end up segregating students of color (like the school-wide approaches to teaching reading and math I discussed earlier) are relied on to overcome the disparity.

Liberalism was the dominant ideology of the teachers at Southern, specifically with regard to race and inequity. By following liberal accounts of racial disparity, the teachers at Southern had difficulty seeing approaches to racial equity that did not fit easily into the current practices of the school. For example, many of my third-grade Latino ELL students were referred to a student support team because of their low scores on standardized reading assessments.[5] In those meetings (also used as the first step to referring students for special education services), a team of teachers and specialists (reading teachers, literacy teachers, the school social worker, and myself) would brainstorm practices that the teacher could use to help bring the student up to grade level. Many of these practices were not problematic when considered acontextually, but none of them offered ways to change the overall structure of the class to be more culturally responsive and to meet the needs of these students. Here is my reflection on one support team meeting:

> All of the methods they [the teachers and specialists] offer up are individually focused. They are designed to help [the student] in isolation. I tried to talk about doing more project-based learning in the class and including all of the ELLs in the projects the students labeled as gifted were doing. I felt like I wasn't heard. A few people nodded their heads.

In the support team process, all team members get to put out ideas, which are listed for the teacher to see. The teacher then chooses two of them to practice with the student. If they don't work, the team discusses the issue again until they decide what additional services the student might need, including special education. Of course, in the prior case, the teacher chose a couple of techniques that could be easily integrated into the current organization and routine of his class. Neither of the strategies was culturally responsive, involved scaffolding, or included the student in more contextually embedded[6] activities. This was the case in every support team meeting in which I participated. Therefore, like many teachers at Southern, these teachers contributed to the maintenance of a system dominated by a narrow response to standardized curricula, thus being complicit in institutionalized racial disparity.

Liberalism heavily influenced teachers' overall classroom instruction as well. Many teachers spent a large amount of their time preparing students for district- and state-mandated standardized assessments and focusing on individual indicators from the standard course of study. For example, even one of the more culturally responsive teachers in terms of cultural awareness[7] spent a large amount of the class time devoted to reading, having the students complete test-like short reading passages followed by questions with multiple-choice answers.

> I went in to the class on a couple of occasions today and [the teacher] was busy working with [the ELL] kids on worksheets. He has been asking me to help them with those worksheets as well.
>
> In the class I get the feeling that [two of the Mexican immigrant ELL boys] could really benefit from integrated, project-based activities. So much of their time scheduled for literacy is focused on reading out loud (guided reading), decoding words, answering pre-selected comprehension questions and making limited observations about the plot and characters of books. From my perspective there is little chance for them to think more globally or holistically about stories. What would really benefit these kids is gifted education. Because of being below grade level in reading, neither kid would test into gifted services.

The teacher often gave the lower level readers (primarily Black and Latino) these shorter acontextual readings, whereas his higher level readers (some Black but with more White students represented) read longer chapter books. This type of in-class segregation and a lack of awareness about it limited their ability to significantly improve their students' academic success.

This segmented the learning of the Latino ELLs with whom I worked and segregated them from the same curricular opportunities as the rest of the students. For example, here is my reflection on the instruction that one of my third-grade Mexican ELLs received:

> I fear that these boys are being ghetto-ized by the school—mostly unintentionally. What I mean by this is that they receive remedial (versus "gifted") instruction a lot of the time and the specialists and resource teachers that work with them work on basic skills. They are pulled from class to work on shorter reading passages that are not connected thematically or contextually to the rest of his instruction. In addition, they are in a more basic level math class . . . they do have a few teachers that care for them. However, I feel that the instructional approach they receive unintentionally positions them as remedial students.

# A Critical Race Analysis

The prior confluence of factors limited the access my Latino ELL students had to high-level, rigorous curricula and culturally responsive instruction. The teachers and administrators used the testing system to categorize my students as below grade level. Such use of categories can lead to the institutional marginalization of students of color (Delgado & Stefancic, 2001). Looking at the access to curriculum in terms of access to property can help describe how limited access to curriculum is a process that compounds itself and perpetuates institutional racism.

Harris (1995) discusses that one of the characteristics of property is that is bestows on people the right to use and enjoy certain privileges. Historically, the ownership of land afforded people certain rights of citizenship, such as the right to vote. These rights give people privileges and power that help them more easily acquire more property, a process that favors those with property over those without. When we look at curriculum as property, a similar process occurs. Students who score higher scores on standardized assessments have "acquired" a certain level/amount of curriculum, a certain amount of property. This ownership gives them the right to use and enjoy more rigorous curricula. They have better access to more property because they are given better texts and complex learning activities, put into higher level classes, and given gifted education services. Students like my ELL students, in contrast, have not done well on those assessments. In turn, they do not have the right to use and enjoy more rigorous curricula. In fact, the school has a "right to exclude" (Harris, 1995) those students from such activities. Instead, because they have not acquired certain levels/amount of curricula, the school, following institutional practices, only gives them to a more limited type of curricula, a less valuable form of property.

Such a process, one that regulates access to curricula based on assessment scores, limits the chance at educational success for students without certain levels of cultural, social, and economic capital, an effect that is compounded for many of my Latino ELL students. A process that inherently favors students from certain racial, ethnic, and economic backgrounds is inherently racist. The test scores and grades at Southern indicate that the current institutional practices are not effective in promoting racially equitable education. My accounts of the curricular, instructional, and administrative decisions of many of the faculty shed light on how such practices persist in schools.

# Hope?

Despite the dominance of such institutional practices, I was eventually able to begin to resist the remediating and segregating effects they had on some of the Latino ELLs at Southern. At first it was difficult for me—even as someone who had studied institutional racism—to break away from the demands of standards-based reform and testing. For example, this is from my journal a couple of months into the school year:

> I have been so caught up with testing and placing students and determining modifications for official purposes that I am falling into the same trap. I go through the day following the procedures that I don't follow the relationship building I should be doing with the students.

For those first couple of months, I didn't even think about how I could practice culturally responsive teaching. I pursued the daily demands of giving the state-mandated placement test and compiling lists of modifications that each student would be allowed to receive on their other required tests. Even as I integrated myself into the classrooms after the first few weeks of school, I allowed myself to be limited in my cultural responsiveness.

Luckily, I was able to break out of this pattern after a while. In fact, the research act (observing teachers, journaling on my own teaching, reflecting weekly with my colleague) helped me focus on how to become more culturally responsive, especially with regard to what Ladson-Billings (1995) calls critical consciousness.

> I have this academic lens and it is interesting, but does it actually enable me to do anything in the context of the school where I teach? Can it? Is it better suited to other avenues of influence, such as disseminating ideas through journal articles (if anyone reads them) or teaching pre-service teachers or doing performance (action) researcher? Am I then just using my job to support future counter-hegemonic work? How can I make the lens work at Southern? If I don't find a way am I then just adhering to (rather resisting) the dominant ideologies (like liberalism) that negatively affect the students I care about and want to advocate for? I guess what I'm asking myself is, "How can I resist the dominant and detrimental ideologies of the school now?

As the previous journal entry shows, the research act gave me a way to reflect on how to challenge the dominant institutional ideologies and practices. As the research and journaling progressed, I was able to use the reflection process to critically analyze specific school practices.

The winter break helped me think about some goals I have for the school year from here on out. I have commented on how I feel I have done some of my "Whitest" teaching at Southern. This has been because I have been learning how to teach at new grade levels. This has led me to follow a lot of what other teachers do and to support the literacy approach at the school. The literacy approach isn't entirely skills oriented, but I find that the way I have been used to support it is skills focused. So, I have decided to worry less about those goals—they end up working towards the tests anyway—and to practice more holistic teaching. I am setting up more project-based activities that focus on interests and life backgrounds of my students. I will not ignore skills, but they will be used to support broader goals. I will have to see how this affects the students' academic success, and I will also have to be sure to document their success in ways that the existing assessments do not.

Little by little, this type of reflection—that critically analyzed school practices—helped me refocus my teaching energies. I began to incorporate more project-based learning strategies with my students. For example, as I mentioned earlier, I used a culturally responsive teaching approach for Latino learners (based on a training from the Pacific Educational Group and the work of Rothstein-Fisch [2003], Trumbull [2001], and Ginsberg & Wlodkowski [2000]) and Walqui's (2006) articulation of scaffolding learning for ELLs to work with a small group of Latino immigrant ELLs. On a small scale, I was able to better the access some of my students had to more rigorous curricula. Although my successes with the students were moderate, I sensed a marked shift in motivation with two of the male students in particular. Here are my reflections on one of the students:

> He is coming up to me every time I come in the room now. Of course sometimes he just wants to work on the computer. But he also asks me if we are going to read together. At the beginning of the semester he just asked about games and now he asks me if I have any more books.
>
> I couldn't believe how much he was focused on reading [an on-line magazine]. When I asked him a question, he shooed me off because he wanted to finish the page first.

These may not seem like major accomplishments, but early in my work with him this student wouldn't stay focused on reading for even a minute at a time.

## Teacher Education and CRT

Coming out of a PhD program and a dissertation study highly focused on examining race from critical perspectives, I should have known better when I started working at Southern. That is to say, it should not have taken as long for me to see how the school's reform-based approach marginalized the racial minority students at Southern. I should not have allowed myself to support the remediating and segregating instructional practices to such an extent. That I did allow that to happen only points out how dominant the institutional practices that stem from the ideologies of technocracy and liberalism still are in schools.

My experience points out the marginalizing effect of these practices and ideologies on ELLs and students of color. Furthermore, these students' experiences can bring to light similar experiences of all students. To paraphrase Guinier and Torres (2002), the experiences of the students of color act as miners' canaries for the experiences of other students. This was true at Southern. Analyzing the institutional practices that the school developed in response to standards-based reform and high-stakes testing according to race (according to the experiences of many of the Latino ELL students) shows how basing access to high-level rigorous curricula on standardized measures unfairly limits the educational chances of any student who has not already acquired a certain amount of narrowly defined curricular knowledge.

The structure of schooling under standards-based reform and the dominant ideologies of public schools can make it extremely difficult for teachers to pursue culturally responsive and antiracist practices. My reflection on my own practice has shown me just how difficult that can be. At the same time, it taught me that the dominance of technocracy and liberalism can be resisted. CRT has been useful in examining the way that even well-intentioned individual teachers support institutional structural inequity. CRT, and its analysis of curriculum as property in particular, has also been useful, however, in helping me work against the institutional practices that sustain that inequity. As I transition into a teacher education position, this study has taught me that such analysis holds potential to help teachers resist inequity and promote more culturally responsive and antiracist practices. I hope to use these critical forms of analysis to affect the thoughts and practices of the teachers with whom I work, and I hope this account gives some insight into how teacher educators can use critical and political race theories toward antiracist goals.

## Notes

1. At the time of writing, I am conducting interviews with teachers who have managed to pursue racial equity in their practice. The focus of these interviews is on how they man-

age such a pursuit given the current climate of public schools.

2. I was involved in a training by the Pacific Educational Group that used the work of Rothstein-Fisch (2003), Trumbull (2001), and Ginsberg and Wlodkowski (2000) to develop an approach to teaching that accounted for and responded to the cultural learning styles of Latino students.

3. Ladson-Billings (1995) identifies three components of what she calls culturally responsive teaching: cultural awareness, academic success, and critical consciousness.

4. Two teachers received comments from the principal and assistant principal, as I did, that the students were not showing the teachers enough respect and that the teachers' "tone" was not "professional enough" in the classroom.

5. These assessments were not created to take a student's status as an ELL and did not take second-language acquisition issues into account.

6. Cummins (2001) discusses the idea that language needs to be "context embedded" in order for ELLs to best achieve both language and content goals.

7. Again, this is a reference to Ladson-Billings' (1995) three components of culturally responsive teaching.

# References

Alexander, B. K. (1999). Performing culture in the classroom: An instructional (auto)ethnography. *Text and Performance Quarterly, 19,* 307–331.

Anderson, G. L., Herr, K., & Nihlen, A. S. (1994/2007). *Studying your own school an educator's guide to qualitative practitioner research.* Thousand Oaks, CA: Corwin Press.

Apple, M. W. (2004). *Ideology and curriculum* (3rd ed.). New York: Routledge.

Blaisdell, B. (2005a). Sitting with ourselves: How to work against White guilt in anti-racist teacher education. In S. Hughes (Ed.), *What we still don't know about race: How to talk about it in the classroom.* Lewiston, NY: Mellen Press.

Blaisdell, B. (2005b). Seeing every student as a 10: Using critical race theory to engage White teachers' colorblindness. *International Journal of Educational Policy, Research, and Practice, 6*(1), 3–22.

Coffey, A., & Atkinson, P. (1996). *Making sense of qualitative data: Complimentary research strategies.* Thousand Oaks, CA: Sage.

Cummins, J. (2001). *Negotiating identities: Education for empowerment in a diverse society* (2nd ed.). Los Angeles: California Association for Bilingual Education.

Dale, R. (1976). *Schooling and capitalism a sociological reader.* London: Routledge & Kegan Paul, in association with Open University Press.

Delgado, R., & Stefancic, J. (2001). *Critical race theory: An introduction.* New York: New York University Press.

Denzin, N. K. (2003). *Performance ethnography.* Thousand Oaks, CA: Sage.

Ginsberg, M. B., & Wlodkowski, R. J. (2000). *Creating highly motivating classrooms for all students a schoolwide approach to powerful teaching with diverse learners* (The Jossey-Bass Education Series). San Francisco: Jossey-Bass.

Guinier, L., & Torres, G. (2002). *The miner's canary: Enlisting race, resisting power, transforming democracy.* Cambridge, MA: Harvard University Press.

Harris, C. I. (1995). Whiteness as property. In K. W. Crenshaw, N. Gotanda, G. Peller, & K. Thomas (Eds.), *Critical race theory: Key writings that defined the movement* (pp. 276–291). New York: New Press.

Ladson-Billings, G. J. (1995). Toward a theory of culturally relevant pedagogy. *American Education Research Journal, 35,* 465–491.

Rothstein-Fisch, C. (2003). *Bridging cultures teacher education module.* Mahwah, NJ: Lawrence Erlbaum Associates.

Trumbull, E. (2001). *Bridging cultures between home and school a guide for teachers: With a special focus on immigrant Latino families.* Mahwah, NJ: Lawrence Erlbaum Associates.

Tyack, D., & Cuban, L. (1995). *Tinkering toward utopia: A century of public school reform.* Cambridge, MA: Harvard University Press.

Walqui, A. (2006). Scaffolding Instruction for English language learners: A conceptual framework. *International Journal of Bilingual Education and Bilingualism, 9*(2), 159–180.

## · 1 0 ·

# Understanding Equity

## A *Brown* Lesson in a Teacher Education Program from a Critical Race Feminist Perspective

THEODOREA REGINA BERRY

"That's not fair!" It's the famous battle cry of children. Whenever children feel they are not getting something they want or need that they see another child (or other children) receiving, we hear these familiar words of protest. Many of us have been callers of the cry in our childhood. Oftentimes, recipients of the battle cry are teachers.

But how do prospective teachers come to understand fairness in the context of the classroom? And why is it important for future teachers to not only know that fairness is an important issue in teaching and learning but also that fairness should be a concept they begin to learn and understand as emerging educators?

This is a story in the teaching of fairness in a teacher education program. Using a lesson about *Brown v. Board of Education* of Topeka, Kansas, I, as a teacher-educator, conceptualized, developed, implemented, and engaged in an interactive class session with 22 preservice teachers in a social foundations course. This is a story about what we learned, together, about equality and equity.

# Why *Brown*?

In a typical social foundations course for undergraduate students in a teacher education program, there are various areas of study: Teaching as a Profession; Issues in Teaching and Learning; Students, Families, and Communities; Foundations of Education; History of Education; Philosophy of Education; Political and Economic Issues in Education; and Legal Issues in Education. The landmark 1954 *Brown v. Board of Education of Topeka* case, although situated primarily in the law, is the context of this study within the social foundations.

*Brown* historically addresses the long history of discrimination in the United States, particularly against African Americans, how it was "officially" established, socially accepted, and legally dismantled through a number of local, state, and federal laws and court cases. *Brown* also addresses philosophical and social issues embedded in de jure and de facto segregation as it questions naturally occurring segregation. I would argue that de jure segregation occurred because of the social order or unspoken laws of the times. Such unspoken laws often served as justification for numerous acts of intimidation inflicted on African Americans of that era. There were also political and economic influences on the *Brown I* decision that, in part, precipitated the *Brown II* decision of 1955. In the opinion delivered by Chief Justice Warren, *Brown II* stated, "All provisions of federal, state, or local law requiring or permitting such discrimination must yield to this principle . . . these cases arose under different local conditions and their disposition will involve a variety of local problems, we requested further argument on the question of relief" (Reutter, 1994, p. 892). Politically, this meant that state governments and local school officials would be required to change statutes, policies, and procedures that were in conflict with the *Brown I* decision. Economically, *Brown II* would require a restructuring of resources, human and monetary, to address the question of relief at the local level. Politically and economically, it was clear that the Court understood that a variety of measures would need to be implemented to enforce the *Brown I* decision.

Some would question the equality and equity promises embedded in the *Brown* decisions. Hess (2003) points out that the *Brown* decisions have been identified by law professors, high school teachers, and judges as significant information to be learned in schools. However, scholars such as Orfield and Eaton (1996), among others, recognize the limitations of the *Brown I* and *Brown II* decisions that have subsequently borne costs to the education of all children in this country on which we have only begun to make payment. Ladson-

Billings (2004) takes issue, in general, "with the *implementation* of *Brown* as endorsed by the [Supreme] Court" (p. 5). While supporting the purpose for the work toward the *Brown I* and *Brown II* decisions, she defines the *Brown II* decision (Tate, Grant, & Ladson-Billings, 1993) as a mathematical solution to a social problem rather than viewing *Brown II* as an equity solution.

But the intended focus of this lesson in social foundations was to address issues of equity in the context of the classroom for preservice teachers. The *Brown* decisions clearly had (and continue to have) a significant impact on U.S. society, its laws, and its culture or ways of being. Subsequently, the *Brown* decisions have impacted U.S. education because the case challenged the doctrine of separate but equal in the context of education. *Brown I* and *Brown II* serve as individual invoices submitted to this country for the debt of inequity incurred. Among the invoice holders, those responsible for relieving or realizing the promissory notes of *Brown* are teacher education programs in schools, colleges, and departments of education (SCDEs). To realize the promise, one must understand the meanings of the invoices submitted. While *Brown I* addresses the doctrine of "separate but equal' established by the *Plessy v. Ferguson* case, *Brown II* deals with issues of equity in the implementation of *Brown I*. *Brown I* clearly established equality based on "tangible factors" and their sameness (Reutter, 1994). In the *Brown II* decision, Chief Justice Warren states, "traditionally, equity has been characterized by a practical flexibility for adjusting and reconciling public and private needs" (Reutter, 1994, p. 893). In other words, where *Brown I* established equality on sameness, equity through *Brown II* became established based on needs, tangible and intangible factors. As a teacher-educator standing on the shoulders of such scholars as Ladson-Billings (1994, 2001), Irvine (2002, 2003), Cochran-Smith (2004), Foster (1997), Obidah (2000), and others who have significantly contributed toward payment of this debt, I have a responsibility through my teaching, praxis, and research to engage in work that promotes both equality and equity for preservice teachers. For my students, I wanted to demonstrate the purpose of both *Brown I* and *Brown II*. I wanted them to "see" that it wasn't enough that their students would have equality.

## Setting the Scene

I taught this lesson to a group of preservice teachers in a Social Foundations course at a historically Black university in North Carolina. There were 22 students in this class; 3 of the 22 students were White: 2 female and 1 male. The university is situated in a large college town with two other colleges/universities in the same town, one in the neighboring town to the south and five in the neighboring town to the east.

I used critical autoethnography through research journals and exit cards for my research methodology and data collection and critical reflection for data analysis and interpretation. Reed-Danahay (as cited in Wolcott, 1999) defines *autoethnography* as "a form of self-narrative that places the self within the social context" (p. 173). Further, she identifies this methodology as an "ethnography of one's own group" (p. 173). I added the critical marker to signify an "explicitly political project" (Burdell & Swadener, 1999); this was a means of examining power relationships in my role as a teacher-educator and as a member of the selected culture: African Americans. Adding "critical" to create "critical reflection" denotes making reference within the reflective process to power, power relations, conflict, and/or oppression within a social context. Subsequently, I define critical reflection as contemplation in relationship to power issues within a social context. These ways of acquiring and understanding myself and my students in the context of the curriculum were well suited to my theoretical framework: Critical Race Feminism (CRF).

CRF, a theoretical genre developed from Critical Race Theory (CRT), is the lens I use to understand myself as a teacher and an African-American woman, to understand my students as African-American men and women, and to understand and deliver the curriculum of *Brown*.

Critical race feminism (CRF) is a theoretical multidisciplinary genre that firmly places women of color at the center rather than the margins of the experience and acknowledges that their experiences are distinctive from those of men of color and White women. Multiplicity and intersectionality of identities is central to this theory. As an advocate of CRF, I believe that abstract theorizing must be supported with actual concerns of the community. This lesson on Brown was in direct response to an educational experience of a student in this course documented in an earlier assignment where students provided their educational memoirs. This particular story highlighted the disparities in treatment of students within a school providing the same resources to each student. As an African American female teacher educator wedded to the social foundations, I also realized that there was more to the *Brown* story than what the textbook revealed. There is more to any story than just the content of the story; there is context and emotion. And story does not function, live, exist, in isolation (Harris, 1997). It is connected and interwoven with other stories and counterstories (Delgado, 2000). As an advocate of CRF, I desired to engage in a discourse of resistance by providing a counterstory (Delgado, 2000) to the text, using a story from one segment of a student's life as the impetus for developing and implementing this lesson. In this way, I hoped to have these students gain multiple understandings of the *Brown* cases and how premise of equity, as proposed by *Brown II*, may exist in a classroom environment.

## Constructing the Lesson

Stephanie was a third-year undergraduate student who transferred from a state university in her home state of Georgia to this institution in North Carolina. At age 24, she was a little older than most of the students in my Social Foundations course as she took 2 years from school to care for her ailing mother as the youngest of her siblings. Now married to a medical student receiving his education at a nearby university and financing her own education, Stephanie was eager to be fully engaged in her education. When the class was assigned to complete individual educational memoirs, Stephanie included this story in her memoir.

> School was just something else I had to do. It wasn't very pleasant. The teachers weren't very nice. I felt more like an outcast. The teachers were very closed-minded. No sense of humanity. All of your differences were pointed out—judged before you were even spoken to or tested. I hated school. . . .
>
> On the first day of school, I was in the first grade, I was in a classroom full of White students. I was the only Black. The second day I was transferred to a classroom with all Black children and the classroom and the teachers were totally different.
>
> The teachers were rude and treated us as though we were tamed animals. Giving commands rather than asking. The room was not as colorful as the first classroom I'd been in and, instantly, my attitude changed. Disappointment set in. I couldn't wait for my mom to pick me up at the end of the day. This continued throughout my career at [school].

These lines prompted this initial reflection in my research journal.

> *The first line on Stephanie's story is so powerful that there are nearly no words to adequately express the emotions they evoke in me. And yet, I wonder how through all of the experiences she overcame, she acquired and maintained the desire to teach others. Her choice of closing commentary to this first paragraph, "I hated school," is like a voice in the wilderness, alone and struggling to survive. And she did.*
>
> *The incident she describes from her first year in school is clear and blatant racism of the institutional kind. I was angered by what appears to be such blatant disrespect. I find it surprisingly appalling that a student more than 10 years my junior would have experienced such*

*upfront, in-your-face discrimination at such a young age. I also find it interesting that she was aware of the difference in her overall environment at such a young age.*

As I continued to reflect on her story, I came to realize that her story, like many other stories of education and schooling, tells a tale of equality and equity. While Stephanie was in the same school with the same resources as her White counterparts, her schooling experiences clearly did not meet her needs. In the same building, there were teachers who treated their students with kindness and warmth and teachers who were rude and disrespectful. There were classrooms that were bright and colorful and classrooms without teaching and learning décor. There were classroom with all White students and classrooms with all African American students. To address how teachers promote such inequity in the classroom, I constructed a lesson that followed a reading and discussion of the *Brown* cases.

## The Lesson

I arrived at the classroom early to lock the classroom door to prevent students from entering the room before the exact start of the class. I went back to my office, gathered my teaching materials, and returned to the classroom at the precise start time of the class. Several students were standing outside of the classroom door awaiting my arrival. "Dr. Miss Berry, why is the door locked?" asked Derrick*, an African American male student. "Class, I would like for everyone to line up against the wall in size order, shortest to the tallest," I instructed. The students, looking rather puzzled, complied with my request without question. I was nervous. I wasn't certain how well this exercise would work out, but I tried to remain calm. I counted the number of students in the line and divided them exactly in half. I stood at the halfway point in the line. "All of the students facing me please walk to the classroom door," I instructed. As the students in the rear portion of the line moved toward the door, one White female student from the front section of the line started toward the door. "Did I tell you to move?" I snapped. She returned to her position in the line. "Why can't we go in?" Nancy*, an African-American female student, asked. As my heart sank, I responded in a firm tone. "I will provide you with instructions, and you will follow them." I unlocked and opened the door and then instructed the students standing at the doorway to take seats on the far side of the classroom near the windows. I turned to the students standing in the line. "You are to remain standing here until I provide you with further instructions." I walked inside of the classroom and closed the door.

Tracey*, an African American female student, was the first to speak up. "What's going on, Professor Berry?" I explained to the group of students in the classroom that they were about to engage in an exercise dealing with discrimination based on teacher perception. I would explain the theoretical premise behind this exercise when it was complete. I then instructed the students to avoid conversation with the other members of the class and follow the instructions I would provide as the class proceeded.

I walked out to the hallway, instructed the remaining students to enter the classroom, and told them to sit on the side of the room opposite their classmates. I informed the class that they were about to view a segment of a video titled *Light It Up*. "Watch the video clip and write down as many issues about schooling and education as you notice them in this clip," I instructed. Nancy*, who was seated with the second group, asked, "Why did we have to wait to come in the classroom?" "And why didn't you raise your hand to be recognized?," I responded. (At the beginning of the semester, I insisted that students learn not to feel required to raise their hands in order to speak in class.) Nancy* raised her hand, and I nodded to indicate that I recognized her. "Professor Berry, why did we have to wait to come in the classroom?" I responded, "Because I said so." The taller group began to whisper to one another as if they were beginning to understand what was happening. I walked to the television/VCR console and started the tape. Just then, Jamila*, another African American female student, walked into the classroom. I immediately decided that students arriving late to class would be placed in the short group regardless of height (although Jamila* would have been placed in the short group if she had arrived on time). "Sit on this side of the room," I instructed as I pointed to where the short group was sitting. Jamila* complied.

Shortly after the video started, an African American male asked that the television be turned toward his group. I turned the television and immediately Joan*, an African-American female student, spoke up. "Hey, we can't see the TV over here," she exclaimed. I explained to her and the rest of the group that if I moved the television toward them, the other group couldn't see it. "Not everyone will be able to see it clearly no matter where I positioned it," I added. "Well, then, can I move my seat," Joan* asked after raising her hand. "That would be very disruptive to the rest of the class," I responded. "Yeah, we're trying to watch the video over here," Charles*, an African American male added. Kendra*, an African American female student who was seated with the tall group, said, "This is fun." Immediately afterward, Nancy* raised her hand. Joan* loudly whispered to her, "You might as well put your hand down. She's not going to give you what you want."

I stopped the videotape and started a class discussion about schooling and educational issues that the tape addressed. Throughout the discussion, I gave preference to the tall group while covertly ignoring the small group. Approximately 10 minutes into the discussion, I paused and let out a long sigh. "I don't know about you, but I'm wiped out," I started. I asked how the class felt. As I expected, the students in the short group were angry and upset. "I didn't know you could be so mean," Joan* responded. Students in the short group continued to vent their frustrations, whereas students in the tall group extended their sympathy toward the short group. They did, however, admit to feeling good about being treated well. I asked, "Have teachers ever treated you in this (negative) manner?" I heard lots of voices saying yes. Students began telling their stories of unfair treatment by teachers. Stephanie stated that her teachers often treated her unfairly based on the previous poor behavior of her older brothers and her family's low socioeconomic status. Derrick* explained that the students who dressed well and, seemingly, came from better neighborhoods were treated better than him because he was an African American from a low socioeconomic background. Charles* spoke about how a female relative whose White peers assume she is an athlete because she attends a predominantly White university. Furthermore, she and Charles* are majoring in the same field, yet she assumes he is receiving a better education than Charles* because he attends a historically Black university. This dialogue led to a discussion about deficit theory, stereotyping, and equity in the classroom.

## What I Learned

This lesson occurred near the middle of the semester. By this time, I had established trust with these students, a trust that served me well to conduct this particular lesson.

However, I realize that asymmetrical power positionalities (Ellsworth, 1989) harvest a myriad of complications in this particular lesson. While I was attempting to teach my students about issues of equality and equity in the context of a Social Foundations course, we were living the imbalance of power in the very way the lesson was delivered. Exerting my power via dominance in this exercise worked in opposition to my position as a teacher-educator and scholar who espouses CRF. It was my way or the highway with seemingly little to no consideration of the multidimensionality of these students' lives in the context of schooling even though I had used a portion of a student's schooling experience as a key factor for conceptualizing, developing, and implementing the lesson. Some readers might even believe that I, as the person in power in that moment, abused the trust established with my students in order to proceed with this lesson/activity. But in the larger scheme of things, engaging in this lesson/activity served to address the complexity of teaching and living a praxis of equity while existing in a historically powerful position.

Counterstory (Delgado, 2000), as a tenet of CRF, became rather complicated in this context. As mentioned earlier, the impetus of this lesson was based on one woman's story of inequality and inequity in education in the South. Her story challenges one of the commonly held beliefs about segregation and inequality in schools regarding its suggested demise by the early 1970s with perceived complete integration. Her story also challenges the suggested dismissal of the Black inferiority theory (Ladson-Billings, 2004). It is clear in the story presented by Stephanie that the teachers and administrators in her elementary school perceived an automatic inferiority of African American students through the delivery of the education they received, even when occupying the same physical space as her White counterparts. Her story challenges the commonly held belief that all Black parents equally supported their children's education. Stephanie's parents failed to question the change that took place in this situation, thereby contributing to the inferior schooling experiences she describes.

But the selection of her story presents biases on my part. As an advocate of CRF, I wanted to center the voice of an African American woman. I desired to place front and center the voice representing the persons whose presence in the K-12 classroom as teachers is steadily decreasing. But in a classroom composed of mostly African-American women, is her story really a counterstory? Does it challenge what most of these students know about education based on their experiences as students and preservice teachers? Or does it challenge much of what they have been taught about education in the United States? Regardless of the possible responses to these and other related questions, it is clear that Stephanie and the other African American female preservice teachers in this class have had multiple and intersecting schooling experiences that create "stories/counterstories for educational uplifting of their students" (Berry, 2005a, p. 48).

CRF also encourages the acceptance of multidimensionality and intersectionality of being. As a northern-born and raised African American female teacher-educator, I recognized that I brought all of my self(s) into the teacher education classroom experience based on identities and experiences interacting simultaneously throughout my life as student, community activist, researcher, and scholar, among others (Berry, 2002). This exercise urged me to force out one version of myself with which I was not comfortable due to my perspectives on issues of power, oppression, conflict, and voice, especially in the context of race and gender. But as I reflected on this scenario that I created (understanding the power issues embedded in that), I learned that it was important to consider how this version of myself would impact on the (power) relationships I shared with my students. I learned that when the balance of power shifts, lessons on equity may create unwanted or undesired circumstances. But isn't that precisely the difference between equality and equity?

In the landmark classroom experiment Brown Eyes, Blue Eyes (Peters, 1987), Jane Elliott wanted to teach her students a lesson in equality after the assassination of Dr. Martin Luther King, Jr. As the person with the power in the classroom, Jane Elliott was able to help her students understand issues of equality in the context of the classroom. Twenty-five years later, her former students were able to articulate the effect of participating in such an exercise on their lives as adults. But how did such an experience influence the praxis of their lives?

These students were engaged in a similar exercise designed specifically to address both equality and equity in their future roles as teachers. These students fully understood the differences in equality and equity in the classroom, but I learned that some didn't fully realize the multiple ways in which they are demonstrated; others did not, until this lesson, have a name for what they were seeing or experiencing in the classroom.

CRF also advocates for the interaction of theory and praxis. I argue that CRF is only theory if it does not live in the way we teach. As such, it was important for me, as a teacher-educator who espouses such theory, to demonstrate, facilitate, and enact the life of such theory, the living praxis. My students and I were engaged in discussion and debate about Brown for several days leading up to this exercise. Some of them complained about the legalese of the written cases and the complexities embedded in the history of African-American education leading up to the Brown cases, whereas others were deeply engrossed and intrigued by its intricacies. However, participating, even involuntarily, in this exercise allowed me and my students to have some real sense of how equality and equity lives in a classroom setting.

In this way, CRF provides what Wing (1997) refers to as multiplicative praxis. This exercise, through the CRF lens, allows multiple ways of doing and being, including those ways often made less visible and those we determine to be uncomfortable, to bring to life the intersections of theory and praxis for the purpose of teacher education. Such praxis, considering all the ways we are, all of the things we know, and all of the things we don't know, promotes equality, equity, and social justice for preservice teachers that may find their way into the hearts and lives of their (future) students (Berry, 2005b).

# References

Berry, T. R. (2002). *Songs and stories: Lyrical movement in teaching and learning of an African American woman.* Unpublished doctoral dissertation.

Berry, T. R. (2005a). Black on Black education: Personally engaged pedagogy for/by African American pre-service teachers. *Urban Review, 37*(1), 31–48.

Berry, T. R. (2005b). Zooming social justice: A teacher educator's hopes and dreams for her students. *Democracy and Education, 15*(2), 3–5.

Burdell, P., & Swadener, B. B. (1999). *Critical personal narrative and autoethnography in education: Reflections on a genre.* Educational Researcher, *28*(6), 21–26.

Cochran-Smith, M. (2004). *Walking the road: Race, diversity, and social justice in teacher education.* New York: Teachers College Press.

Delgado, R. (2000). Storytelling for oppositionists and others: A plea for narrative. In R. Delgado & J. Stefancic (Eds.), *Critical race theory: The cutting edge* (2nd ed.). Philadelphia: Temple University Press.

Ellsworth, E. (1989). Why doesn't this feel empowering? Working through the repressive myths of critical pedagogy. *Harvard Educational Review, 59*(3), 297–324.

Foster, M. (1997). *Black teachers on teaching.* New York: The New Press.

Harris, A. P. (1997). Race and essentialism in feminist theory. In A. K. Wing (Ed.), *Critical race feminism: A reader* (pp. 11–18). New York: New York University Press.

Hess, D. (2003). *The classroom iconization of Brown.* Unpublished manuscript, University of Wisconsin, Madison.

Irvine, J. J. (Ed.). (2002). *In search if wholeness: African American teachers and their culturally specific classroom practices.* New York: Palgrave Macmillan.

Irvine, J. J. (2003). *Educating for diversity: Seeing with a cultural eye.* New York: Teachers College Press.

Ladson-Billings, G. (1994). *The dreamkeepers: Successful teachers of African American children.* San Francisco: Jossey-Bass.

Ladson-Billings, G. (2001). *Crossing over to Canaan: The journey of new teachers in diverse classrooms.* San Francisco: Jossey-Bass.

Ladson-Billings, G. (2004). Landing on the wrong note: The price we paid for *Brown. Educational Researcher, 33*(7), 3–13.

Obidah, J. (2000). Mediating boundaries of race, class, and professorial authority as a critical multiculturalist. *Teachers College Record, 102*(6), 1035–1060.

Orfield, G., & Eaton, S. (1996). *Dismantling desegregation.* New York: The Free Press.

Peters, W. (1987). *A class divided: Then and now, expanded edition.* New Haven, CT: Yale University Press.

Reutter, E. E. (1994). *The law of public education* (4th ed.). Westbury, NY: The Foundation Press.

Wing, A. K. (1997). Brief reflections toward a multiplicative theory and praxis of being. In A. K. Wing (Ed.), *Critical race feminism: A reader* (pp. 27–34). New York: New York University Press.

Wolcott, H.F. (1999). *Ethnography: A way of seeing*. Walnut Creek, CA: Alta Mira.

## · 1 1 ·

# Where Am I Going, Where Have I Been?

## A Critical Reflexion on Black-Jewish Relations, Jewish Political Shifts to the Right, and the Preparation of Young Jewish Women for Teaching "Other People's Children"

JOSH DIEM

This chapter is a product, an artifact. It is not a final product; naming it such would mean that it represents an end point, a point of completion where conclusions are reached and articulated. When it comes to the issues discussed in this piece, I don't think I will ever be able to reach a point of completion. The present conditions I describe beg for change. Therefore, this chapter serves as an artifact designed to reflect my thoughts on the issues addressed in this piece, up to the point at which I stopped the process of articulating my thoughts. It may be argued that there is never such a thing as a final anything, everything is partial, and what I have just stated is obvious, perhaps even trite. But this is not a piece on the limitations of our abilities to articulate total or final representations, perspectives, or truths. The process of writing this particular piece, and the feelings I have as I end working on this text mandate that I explicitly state what this piece is and what it isn't, as to clarify any possible confusion. I hope to demonstrate in the rest of this chapter that there are several important factors that make this claim essential to understanding the issues I raise here and the manner in which I raise them. The claims I make and the issues I raise all revolve around the central issue I seek to address—the current state of the relationship between Jews and Blacks in the United States and why the issue matters in the context of training future teachers. I use how I make meaning of what I see, hear, and feel from my Jewish undergraduate students when we address issues related to race and racism as both a metaphorical symbol of the larger issues and actual examples of the current state of said relationship.

The history of any heterogeneous group is complex, and Jews and Blacks in the United States are no exception. Neither group can rightly be conceptualized as monolithic. Jews in the United States can trace their familial lineage to countries throughout the world. The largest wave of Jewish immigrants occurred from 1900 to 1924 when 1.75 million Jews, the vast majority from Eastern Europe, migrated to the United States (Sarna, 1997). Since this period, Jews have come to America from across the globe. Eastern European Jews have continued to find the United States an appealing destination. This includes those fleeing persecution during the Holocaust and the resettlement of Russian Jews pre- and post-breakup of the Soviet Union. Additionally, Jews from Cuba, South America, and Africa (particularly Ethiopia) have all found their way to the United States (Heilman, 1995; Sachar, 1992; Sarna, 1997). The most recent estimate of the Jewish population in the United States is from 2006 when an estimated 5.275 million Jews resided in the United States (American Jewish Committee, 2006). This number represents roughly 1.7% of the total U.S. population (U.S. Census Bureau, 2006).

The population of Blacks in the United States includes those who can trace their ancestry to the African slave trade, as well as those who have voluntarily migrated from points across the globe. The number of African slaves in the United States swelled to its highest level in 1860, reaching an estimated 4 million (U.S. Census Bureau, 1860). In addition to Blacks whose roots in the United States can be traced to the slave trade, the Black population in the United States includes large numbers of individuals who have migrated from Caribbean nations, Central and South America, and the continent of Africa (Christian, 1998; Franklin & Moss, 2000). I should note that I use the term *Black* instead of *African American* as a means of paying respect to the fact that not all who are identified as Black in the United States believe this is a correct identification. This does not mean that they or I believe that their ancestral roots do not lie on the continent; rather, I use the term as a way to privilege the means by which many Blacks self-identify. For example, many Haitians, Jamaicans, and Bahamians do not self-identify as African Americans. They identify as Haitians, Jamaicans, or Bahamians. Additionally, many such individuals do not even self-identify as Black. That being said, I use the term Black as a larger, broader demographic category. It should also be noted that there are some specific differences in the historical evolution of the relationships between Jews and certain groups who fall under the classification of Black (African American, Haitian, etc.). The purpose of this chapter is not to paint with broad brush strokes or essentialize. However, as I focus more on the contemporary, I think it is important to use this broad term because I think it represents the mentality of American Jews who, unfortunately, too often see Blacks as a monolithic group. Currently, there are an estimated 39 million people identified as Black in the United States, representing approximately 12.8% of the total population (U.S. Census Bureau, 2009).

In addition to the individual history of these two broadly defined groups, the history of the relationship between these groups is equally complicated. Previously, this relationship could be aptly described as an alliance forged by two historically marginalized and oppressed groups brought together by the desire to fight for social justice and equity, each seeing in the other experiences and circumstances that resonated in themselves. But what was once a strong alliance has withered, virtually disintegrating to a point of nonexistence in any meaningful way. The reasons for this weakening in a previously strong allied relationship are important, but I do not focus my attention on describing the origins or historical evolution of the relationship between Blacks and Jews in the United States. Rather, I focus on the state of the relationship today. I use the particular experiences I have with the undergraduate students I teach as a symbolic metaphor for the current relationship. I make no claims of generalizability or the like, but what I experience with my students echoes what I experience outside the classroom in my daily interactions with people I know and love to complete strangers.

What I present here is a textual representation of a process that yielded six or seven different iterations of text that, in some way or another, all sought to address how I see the current state of Jewish–Black relations in the United States playing out in the attitudes, ideas, beliefs, and behaviors of the Jewish undergraduate students I teach.

The ideas expressed here are the result of an externally imposed culmination of this process. This imposition is otherwise known as the date the editors said they needed to have something or the chapter would not be included in the volume. It is also important that I note not only what this chapter is but also what I initially intended it to be. When I set out to write this chapter, I never imagined something like the text you are reading.

I initially envisioned a text organized and articulated in a much more linear fashion. The text I set out to write *was* to be a final product, an articulation of conclusions distilled from the presentation of literature and observations. I pictured a chapter that would briefly address the historical evolution of the relationship between Jews and Blacks in the United States, shift then to a focus on the current state of the relationship, and end with a discussion of how and why this subject is important enough to merit a chapter in this book. I believed my voice would give the subject a particular power that comes from my perspective—a Jew who teaches preservice teachers and is troubled by what I see and hear from American Jews about issues related to race and racism, both in my classes and my life outside the classroom. I intended to focus on the things I hear and see and in my classes, but only as a microcosm of what exists beyond the walls of the university and in the heads and hearts of my students. Further, it made sense to me to further contextualize and couch the issues within the larger context of the rightward shift in the social and ideological orientation of American Jewry. Not to exclusively serve as a textual means of self-expression and indulgence, I then planned on explaining why this matters to a larger audience interested in race, racism, and schooling. I believed then as I do now that these issues are important unto themselves, but they also serve as a symbolic metaphor of larger issues related to race, racism, and schooling. I had a plan and simply had to execute. It all seemed so simple.

But what I found is that for this socially, historically, and personally complex and complicated subject, there is no such thing as simple. I realized plans, outlines, and intentions were essentially useless, and I discarded them. This illumination was liberating, but only for a fleeting moment as I was then left asking myself, "Great, now what?" What seemed to be right in front of my face at the moment I conceived of the idea for this piece proved to be the most difficult to capture and articulate. As I read more and more about issues related to those I sought to address (literature) and began to write about my experiences with my students (observations), I became overwhelmed. What had started off as an idea that seemed easy to execute had now become something I saw no way to complete. How could I present all the necessary information in the space of a book chapter? How could I do this from the personal perspective I knew would give this piece its power while covering the necessary issues beyond their scope of the personal in a space that seemed to be shrinking before my eyes? These issues of space and learning more about a subject about which I already possessed a fairly comprehensive knowledge perplexed me more and more, but apparently that wasn't enough. As they always are, social and political issues were in flux, but there were particular issues that contributed to making this piece more complicated and relevant.

## Embracing the Partial: It Is All Any of Us Have

In order to deal with the simultaneously pressing issues of what to cover and what to exclude, and the rapidly changing issues of the day, I returned to a reading that provided me comfort when I was a graduate student grappling with the issue of creating a text that adequately represents the issue one wishes to explore and describe. I had assigned my graduate qualitative seminar participants Richardson and St. Pierre's (2005) seminal piece on the need to reconceptualize writing as a method of inquiry with little thought to how it articulated precisely the task in which I was struggling.

I remembered the feeling I had the first time I read the piece. It was as if I saw brilliance leaping off the page as I read of the idea that in the postmodern condition we do not need to feel that we know everything, that we have come to an end point, in order to write. We must understand that no matter what type of research we engage in and regardless of the privileged claims of others to the contrary, we always only write what we know, no matter when we decide when that end point is. That point is always arbitrary, always lending itself to a production of the partial. This particular quote states it perfectly:

> The postmodern context of doubt, then distrusts all methods equally. No method has a privileged status. But a postmodernist position does allow us to know "something" without claiming to know everything. Having a partial, local, and historical knowledge is still knowing. In some ways, "knowing" is easier, however, because postmodernism recognizes the situational limitations of the knower. (Richardson & St. Pierre, 2005, p. 961)

Rereading this piece was in a word: liberating. I didn't feel validated or vindicated because someone else had sanctioned my actions; rather, I had that feeling that comes over you when you're struggling to articulate an idea and then you hear someone say it poetically in a way so obvious yet so brilliant. All my efforts to devise a plan that would represent the whole were for naught because I would always, regardless of how much I included, be representing the partial. This notion was obvious and brilliant. It was with this reaffirmed sense of purpose that I pressed forward. I would sit down and write what I've seen, heard, and felt from my students about the issues without worrying about the completeness of the picture this would paint. Each of my interactions with my students is a picture just as important and complete as any other. But, getting to this point was not easy.

## Layers, Edits, Iterations, and Persepctive

When I stated previously that I produced several versions or iterations of a chapter that addressed the central issues of Black–Jewish relations in America and how they play out in my undergraduate students, I don't mean that I had large edits and spent hours cutting and pasting text. Everyone engages in that type of editing. But what I now have is several completely different texts that address the central issues, focusing on different subissues in each version. I have many partial views, many individual stories. But when the editor-imposed point of culmination came, I had to decide what to articulate. Which partial would I privilege? The sense of not being overwhelmed was temporary. All the individual "somethings" I knew seemed to merit discussion. In the end, I took the brilliant and simple advice of a colleague and friend who told me to simply think of the one or two most important things I wanted readers to remember. I hope I chose wisely, and I hope you remember.

When deciding on the most important things that I wanted the reader to remember, I thought of myself as a reader. When I read, what I remember more than anything else are ideas that are unique because of the author(s) writing the piece. As a reader, I need to feel that I am reading something that I need to read because the writer needed to write. That "partial, local, and historical" (Richardson & St. Pierre, 2005, p. 961) is what makes me want to read. Michael Lerner and Cornel West (1996) write intelligently and beautifully about the state of the contemporary relationship between American Jews and Blacks. They advance a discussion of the historical roots contributing to the relationship. This move marks the intelligent part. The beautiful part, although it too is intelligent, is the dialogue between the two as they discuss matters as they see them. They are well-read scholars informed by the history and the literature, but more important than that point is the fact that they are human beings who struggle to come to terms and make sense of the issues they identify as important come across as genuine and sincere. They do this scholarly work as individuals whose perspectives, beliefs, and actions are informed by what they experience.

Although much of what I write about focuses on the personal, I write from this perspective because it was the only means I found that accurately represents the issues as I see them. Obviously I only see things as I can see them, and this point is not a manifesto or groundbreaking piece on positionality, lenses, or the like. What I mean in this context is that how I see the issues, as a Jew who is concerned about what I and many others see as a departure from my people's commitments to social justice and equity, is imperative in understanding all else that I write. Although others who are not Jewish can very well see many, if not all, of the same things, their reactions and processing of the issues will not be the same. Try as I might to avoid making myself a central component to the piece, I could not do so without compromising the ability to articulate why these issues matters. That premise being said, I feel that while the piece is about my experiences, it is not at all *about* me. Perhaps, the best means of illustrating this point is by returning to the statement I made previously about the changing social and political conditions in the United States when I began writing this piece.

## A Black President? What Are You, Messugganah?

As the presidential primaries and general election of 2008 heated up, my email inbox became increasingly filled with forwarded emails that were almost exclusively focused on one candidate. And surprise, surprise—the candidate who was the focus of virtually all of these emails was the Black candidate. While the entire nation was subjected to rampant and increasingly inane conjectures regarding the secret Muslim life of Barrack Obama and discussions of Blackness that resembled a Goldilocks and the Three Bears metaphor of whether he is too Black, not Black enough, or just right, American Jews engaged in additional conversations focusing almost exclusively on matters of national security and, more specifically, Israel. The overarching question that framed virtually all these discussions was how friendly an Obama administration would be to the Jewish state. But there was a particular tone and biting edge to the questioning of this candidate, the Black candidate.

As you can imagine, mixing Israel, race, politics, and the warp speed by which information travels on the Internet and via email results in more emotionally fueled, yet intellectually lazy, disingenuous, or outright false claims than truths. There were no partial truths; there were lies. Add in a tone of good old-fashioned outright racism that many of these emails possessed and the facts that I am (a) a Jew, (b) not a Zionist, (c) a vocal critic of the actions of the government of Israel, and (d) sympathetic to the suffering and oppression Palestinians face, and you have a noxious mixture of name-calling and virtual shouting that became my world. It was clear to me that just as the visual images of the wrath caused by Hurricane Katrina had forced Americans to deal with the realities of poverty, race, and the legacies of slavery and Jim Crow in contemporary American life, this election would force American Jews to deal more openly with issues related to race and racism that for too long had remained silenced or confined to dinner table discussions and the like. But I was pessimistic and cautious, believing that these issues would only be examined in a superficial and fleeting manner, just as was the case with the issues that Hurricane Katrina unmasked. I knew the key to making this moment meaningful was how deep and honest the discussions and examinations regarding these issues would be. It is too soon to tell, but I fear that the interest in engaging in such conversations is absent. As long as the president, regardless of his race, displays his support for Israel, there will be less of a willingness to acknowledge and discuss matters related to race and racism, including those that played out in the campaign. In the unlikely scenario that this administration breaks with history and their own stated positions on the subject, there may be an opportunity to engage. Unfortunately, those opportunities may be tinged with racism and feelings of equating this lack of support with President Obama's Black identity and all Blacks' hatred toward Jews. But if this narrative is the honest representation of Jewish Americans' feelings, it would be unfortunate but vital for a real examination of the issues. We'll have to wait and see.

I saw the importance of the election and its relationship to the issues I had chosen to address in this piece increase, and I became increasingly apoplectic. What the hell was I supposed to do now? Fortunately, right around this time I was told that this volume was going to shift somewhat in its stated focus and attempt to explicitly link the subject of teaching about race and racism to the coming change in the executive branch of the U.S. government. This timing was both fortunate and unfortunate: It would free me to address the issues I now felt responsible to address, but it also required a great deal of work. This history is largely responsible for me producing several chapters' worth of text, most of which will never see the light of day.

# How and Why This Should Matter to Teacher-Educators

I need to stop here and state something about how I came to see the issues I present here as important and then explain why this matters not just on a broader, social level but specifically in relation to the preparation of teachers. Racism, in and of itself, and in this particular case racism and its role in the relations between two historically oppressed and marginalized groups of people, is always an important topic; but this text is specifically concerned with why this matters to me in the context of a teacher education program and why it should matter to others. It is also important to note that just as it is the case in virtually all discussions about race and racism, the issues that present themselves involve much more than just matters related to race and racism; you know because that wouldn't be enough. The issues as I see them play out, and the concerns I have that bring me to writing this chapter represent more than just the stated issues covered in this piece. They involve concerns I have held for a long time regarding what I have felt is the ease with which Jews influencing and influenced by my life ("my people") talk and act in racist ways. It is as if our history gives us permission to do and say things that can't be taken simply as racist. "Can't you take a joke?" or "Why do you have to make everything such a big, serious thing?" and similar refrains are common replies to my objections over racist statements and/or actions. I wish race was the only such issue I have found to be problematic among my people. What passes without challenge is an equally appalling discourse when it comes to sexism, misogyny, homophobia, heterosexism, and classism. So the issue of race and racism once again cannot be legitimately viewed alone. In this specific case, it must be viewed in the context of the intersections of the social constructions of race, class, ethnicity, gender, and sexual identity, and the history of a people, my people.

Therefore, in the remainder of this chapter, I put forth a representation, an articulated snapshot of the manifestations and constructions of said intersections of race, class, gender, and sexual identity, and the history of a people as they occur between and among my American Jews as they collide with the race, racism, social class, access to opportunity, social responsibility, and the historical sociopolitical evolution of Jews and Blacks (independently and in matters where relationships exist) in the United States. Much of this evidence emerges from how I discuss (or from the discussion of) the things I see, hear, and feel during the course of instruction, as well as during conversations I have with students outside of class. I also inject thoughts from periods of self-reflection on these issues. I hope to explain to the reader why the broader issue of social justice, and in particular racism, are so important to me not simply as an individual but as an individual whose ideas, beliefs, and actions related to social justice, equity, equality, politics, the functions of government schools, and racism are heavily shaped by the fact that I am a Jew. I come from a personal and historical background that demands I write this piece.

## Recognizing the Issue

I'm lucky enough to be friends with one of the editors of this volume, Sherick Hughes. I'm not just lucky because our friendship put me in a good position to contribute to this volume or because I was granted an extension on my chapter's deadline—thanks again for that accommodation! The reason I'm lucky to be friends with Sherick, at least as it pertains to this chapter and context, is that some of the most interesting, educational, and engaging conversations I have about race, racism, and privilege occur when Sherick and I meet up and talk about such issues until the wee hours of the morning. The fact that I identify as White and Jewish and Sherick identifies himself as a Black Presbyterian with Black Baptist roots is a foundational dynamic, as we clearly represent and can share two completely different perspectives related to our lived experiences dealing with racism and religion. But I don't have interesting conversations about race and racism with every non-White, non-Jewish person of color I know, and I'm sure it's a safe bet that Sherick isn't always engaged in the conversations he has with White Jewish people about the issues. There are plenty of White Jewish and non-Jewish folks with whom I have interesting and engaging conversations about race and racism. Our racial identities do not guarantee us anything in terms of interesting, meaningful dialogue. It is the combination of the fact that (a) we are friends with different racial and religious identities who can talk candidly and offer counternarratives about lived experiences, perspectives, and the like; coupled with (b) the fact that we are colleagues who are interested and familiar with much of the same literature on the issues that brings to our conversations certain dynamics that are almost impossible to replicate with other people.

I know the fashionable thing to do for White folks like me who claim to be down with/in the struggle for justice and equity is proudly announce and display the rainbow of humanity that is represented in the rolodex of my friends. But the reality of my lived experience is that while I have friends who are racial/ethnic minorities, and I have colleagues who are as well, I don't have a lot of friends who are colleagues or colleagues who are friends regardless of racial and/or ethnic group membership. When you filter that small list of those who are friends and colleagues down to those who are friends, colleagues, and racial/ethnic minorities, the list becomes quite short. I have a lot of relationships with colleagues whom I like, but I consider them more acquaintances, and more friendly relationships that I enjoy than friendships. I don't use the word *friend* as loosely as I feel others do, and because of that conviction, Sherick is one of only a few people whom I consider to be a colleague and a genuine friend.

This combination of colleague and friend allows for comfort and freedom in our conversations that just isn't there in most other situations—for both of us. Sherick and I have talked about this situation on numerous occasions, which is an interesting thing unto itself. We analyze critically the conditions that allow for the conversations that we have while having the conversations. Who else besides academics would do such a thing? These dynamics allow for many interesting topics of conversations regarding social structure and theoretical perspectives on race, religion, and society, and the exchange of vignettes about how the issues play out so differently in our lives. Yet there is also a specific focus in many of our conversations facilitated not only by the fact that we are colleagues and friends, but also by our particular lived experiences and identities. Specifically, my experiences as a Jewish American from Texas and Sherick's experiences as a Black American from North Carolina, both during the 1970s and 1980s, funneled us toward discussing the too often silenced topic of the disintegration of Jewish–Black relations. We find the promise of a once concerted effort toward profound and powerful political and social alliances of Jews and Blacks waning within our spheres of influence. Although it is not the case with all Jewish Americans, I grew up with an understanding of the relationship between Jews and Blacks in America, and in particular the role that Jews played early in the civil rights movement. I came to learn that Sherick was taught about much the same throughout his childhood. Our experiences as individuals, who belong to the groups Jews and Blacks, as well as our unique individual experiences and circumstances, bring us to a place where we understand the need for the conversation to occur not just between us but also on a larger scale. As is the case in many such instances, the silence we hear around us is indeed disheartening at best.

Our foray into this area of conversation began several years ago when Sherick told me of the profound influence one of his professors from his master's degree program had on his life. Prior to his retirement in 2005, this professor, Dr. Charlie Richman, was the first male Jew with whom Sherick ever had a relationship. Much the same as Whites have their one Black friend, this Wake Forest University professor of the Psychology of Discrimination was Sherick's Jewish friend. Dr. Richman actually contributed a chapter to Sherick's second book titled *What We Still Don't Know About Teaching Race: How to Talk About it in the Classroom*. Sherick told me that it was this relationship and Dr. Richman's chapter that reinvigorated his interest in the topic of Jewish–Black relations. Since then, we have discussed a number of issues related to the historical evolution and the present condition of the relationship between Jewish and Black Americans. But in 2007, we stumbled onto a conversational topic that Sherick felt would be a good fit for this volume.

That topic started somewhat broadly as we mused about how the current relationship between and among Jewish Americans and Black Americans, as well as the broader political and social climate of Jewish Americans, manifests in the manner in which younger Jewish Americans and younger Black Americans think and feel about each other. We took several zigs and zags as we discussed the issue and its various subissues, but we kept coming back to a dynamic I had just begun to notice and be troubled by in my undergraduate courses. I told Sherick that while I am never thrilled with the knowledge and perspectives on race and racism that a number of my self-identified White students possess, I was beginning to see some particularly disturbing things in many of my self-identified White Jewish students in terms of their thoughts about issues related to race, racism, and privilege.

I was disturbed because of the things they said and the attitudes they reflected, and although difficult to pinpoint, my response was triggered by more than words and attitudes. There was something more about hearing and seeing these attitudes and behaviors among my Jewish students that had a particular resonance. It wasn't that I knew that the students who would go on to become teachers would be in positions of power and authority, often in front of classrooms full of non-Jewish children of color. This issue, however, is something that did/does disturb me. It's analogous to the feeling of seeing someone you know and care about do or say something that goes against your core beliefs. As Jews, I see and feel a connection to all Jews, including my students, that facilitates and makes possible these feelings. I knew, as I do now, that there would be few other spaces outside the university classroom, where these future teachers would be required to think reflexively about these issues. I saw a future where my students became the same well-intentioned but misinformed and less promising teachers I have them read about in pieces such as, "How

White Teachers Construct Race" (Sleeter, 1993). I reminded myself about the ebb and flow of depression and hope that I experience every semester with virtually all my students when we talk about such issues. I then began to realize that this difference was, and is, significant, palpable, and visceral, and it deserves further examination.

After discussing the matter in depth, Sherick suggested the issue would make a good topic for this book. Sherick stated that he wanted this volume to capture some of the specificities that are represented in the manner that racial/ethnic, and in this case religious and cultural groups, act toward and think about each other. With the history that the Jews and Blacks in this country share, the documented shift toward "the [political] right" among Jewish Americans, and the changing demographics of our country, we both agreed that this chapter was an important one.

The reason I provide so much background information related to how and why I came to recognize the issues I write about here is that I think the nature of my relationship with Sherick is something that unfortunately is unique. Specifically, one of the fundamental issues to which both contributes and is a result of the current state of racist ideologies among my American Jews is a lack of personal contact and relationships with Black Americans and vice versa. Now that is not to say that I embrace what many have critiqued as the psychological view of race/racism that permeates our culture (Sleeter, 1993). I agree with this critique and do not believe that racism is simply the result of ignorance and/or fear of The Other. I am not making the simplistic claim that racism could be eliminated if every White person, Jews and Gentiles alike, simply got to know a person of color, thus seeing the error of their ignorant racist ideologies and resulting in an epiphany of the need for racial harmony. However, I do see this lack of personal contact as a barrier that, in combination with the deluge of messages from media sources about what it means to be Black, leaves American Jews and most White Americans in general with nowhere to go but to believe these images and messages as truth. This point does not say much about larger structural issues related to institutionalized racism, but it is a component of the overall problem. Oppressive mediated messages about what it means to be, act, talk, and live like a Black American as consumed by White Jewish Americans serves for too many folks as the complete (albeit, incomplete) basis of how my Jewish people make meaning of what Blackness is. Educational research might engage a similar process that brings messages to Black folks. But the degree to which such messages seem to further oppress White Jews in America is limited if at all present. When it comes to Jews and Blacks in the

in my Jewish students. The issue of the construction of gender in Judaism, as well as in other major religious traditions, has been written about extensively (see Elior, 2004; Hyman, 2005; Sharma & Young, 2007; Tirosh-Samuelson, 2004). The trouble and disturbance I feel related to the constructions of gender and gender roles and norms is shared by enough to spur the founding in 1998 of *Nashim: A Journal of Jewish Women's Studies and Gender Issues* and the publication of books devoted to feminism and Judaism (see Hartman, 2007; Plaskow, 1991; Ruttenberg, 2001). The variables and dynamics that I see manifest in the lives of my students is a source of constant questioning for me, as I often engage in trying to understand the current state of young Jewish women.

When I think about the state of the current female Jewish college student, I have let go of attempting to form rigidly defined categories into which I could neatly fit these young women—a futile activity I engaged in briefly. I gave up on this task primarily because this act of categorizing women, as performed by a man of privilege and in a position of power over the women he is critiquing, is an act possible only in a patriarchal social structure, and perhaps this act is a patriarchal, even sexist or misogynistic, act. I am, after all, a part of the society and social structures I critique. It is about we and us and not they and them. Although I would like to believe, and do, that my own personal and professional practices are not as sexist or misogynistic as most, I still recognize that as part of a society that bombards us all with such messages from the moment we enter the world, my desire to be an enlightened feminist is a struggle, and I often fail. Additionally, even if I could rationalize or justify this endeavor of categorizing women into this box or that one, the exercise is predicated on an act of essentialization. Although essentializing may not be possible or desirable, generalizations often are.

I use an example of explicit talk related to gender and women's reification and (re)production of sexist and misogynist constructions and roles of and for women because gender is openly spoken about in a manner race and racism is not. I do not mean to equate gender and race or sexism and racism. Rather, I use this example of an everyday lived experience to counter popular notions of Jews as progressive. This is our history, but it is not our present. If this is how women belonging to a so-called progressive group talk about matters related to gender and accompanying norms and roles, you can imagine how the discussions of race proceed. There are claims to contrary, and it is difficult to find a Jew who thinks of Jews as further to Left than most. But political affiliations, allegiances, and claims are not synonymous with how you conduct yourself on a daily basis. There is often dissonance or contradictions, but examples like this appear more like hypocrisy and/or lies than dissonance.

## Change Is Clearly Not Always Good

I see the issues related to American Jews and race/racism related to the overall phenomenon of American Jews becoming more socially and politically conservative since arriving en masse in the United States. In addition to issues related to race/racism, I see this play out most dramatically through my problematic everyday lived experiences, as well as those I bear witness to, related to gender. Although it cannot be said that Judaism, or any organized religion, is historically predicated on egalitarian relations or power structures among men and women, the time machine does seem to be in reverse when it comes to all matters social and political concerning American Jews. Again, I see these issues in the broader context of the changing ideological orientation of American Jewry. We have collectively morphed from a people with a deep historical commitment and connection to radical Left views in various forms to a people increasingly embracing neoliberalism and the radical Right.

I fear that we have lost our commitment to social justice and equity. As Karen Brodkin (1998) notes in her seminal work on the historical evolution of American Jews' sense of self and social justice, we have become White folks. This change did not happen overnight. In a pursuit of greater economic and social opportunities, too many of my people seem to have forgotten the place(s) from where they/we came. The ethos of the United States and the ideology of individualism appear to have trumped the values of equity and social justice. Our collective memory seems to have erased the advantages we inherently possessed, as well as those we were given. We ease our consciousness by giving to tzedakah while supporting policies and structures that facilitate and even cause the need to give. Perhaps concern for our own financial, educational, and social well-being has overtaken our concern for humanity at large, and the manner in which we construct and reproduce racist ideologies and practices is but one example. We demand and scream for the recovery of money, art, and other stolen resources from the period before and during World War II while raising our voices just as loud against the merits of reparations for the descendants of Black slaves in America.

# From Socialists and Freedom Riders to Playing the Blame Game: American Jews' Shift to the Right

The political and ideological climate of American Jewry today is a dramatic departure from our past. This historical evolution is a subject that has received a great deal of attention in numerous texts (Brodkin, 1998; Goldstein, 2007; Roediger, 2006). My people have a deep tradition of radical Left thinking that has been chronicled in such important works as *Revolutionary Jews From Marx to Trotsky* (Wistrich, 1976). Our past, in both America and our nations of origin (mostly Eastern Europe), is built on a foundation of ideological and intellectual Leftward leanings. But although Wistrich's and others works are important, it may be justifiably argued that equally important, if not more, was the passing down of these teachings and ideas through an oral and/or familial means of transmission. The messages and lessons in the writings and teachings of Marx and Trotsky, although not necessarily their texts, once were taught from grandparent and parent to children much like customs related to religious observance, cultural practices such as cooking, and the use of Yiddish have been replaced. They have not been replaced with updated versions of these lessons; rather, they have been replaced by a "take care of your own first" mentality. I have repeatedly heard the phrase "charity starts at home" from Jews I know. Although it may be argued that the phrase may refer to first helping those closest to you (i.e., helping domestically before abroad), this concept is not only ripe with contradiction, but it is also a huge departure from our past. We used to embrace the idea of charity, or giving to others, because we felt a sense of duty to do so. This giving has historically taken many forms, including the financial capital. The sense of responsibility to financial giving may remain, the current economic crisis notwithstanding, but a commitment to giving through social action has all but disappeared. This sort of giving, of doing for others, is about putting yourself and your own well-being on the line for a cause greater than and not directly related to you or those you identify with and/or love. Interestingly enough, the historical prominence of this type of giving through social action is what many Jews call on as a means of proving and justifying that present day is somehow excused.

When asked about use of the word *schwartza* (Yiddish for the n-word) and other racist comments and practices, many point to the work of Jews in the past on issues related to racism as evidence that they don't mean their comments in a racist manner. Young Jews, including my students, will call on the great deeds of Abraham Joshua Heschel and other well-known Jewish civil rights activists as proof of their own involvement in such matters. They romantically wax and wane about the role of American Jews in the Freedom Riders' activities, often overstating the importance Jews played in such events. This historical evidence of commitment to racial equity, equality, and justice is used as a means of proving oneself in the context of a people; this serves as a license to think, speak, and act in any manner without being questioned. When asked what they personally have done, committed, they have blank stares and no answer. A popular device for breaking this uncomfortable silence is the invocation of the tried and true rhetoric of ethnicity theory (Sleeter, 1993).

In addition to pointing to the accomplishments of their forbearers, my students love to engage in the practice of blaming racial and ethnic minority groups for what they see as pathologies instead of social conditions arising from the social structure and its imposition on the individual. The most popular tactic of all such practices is the "My family came here with nothing and made it, so I don't see any reason why everyone else can't do the same." This is all done of course without any recognition of the differences in skin color, nation of origin, historical contexts, conditions that precipitated migration, and so on. The coup de grâce is the invocation of the Holocaust, survival, and the realization of the American Dream of prosperity in the face of such obstacles. None of these stories of individual accomplishment should be diminished or marginalized, but neither should the fact that the triumphant crescendo of all of them being predicated on an acceptance of fighting such structural forces. My students recognize in the telling of their stories that their own families had to overcome much. But they don't ever stop and pause at the part of their stories that recognize the unequal and unjust social conditions their loved ones had to overcome. In addition, they lack any understanding of how and why Jews have been disproportionately able to overcome and achieve when other racial and ethnic minorities have not been able to do so. This shift in a focus to the individual and away from the structural is representative of a Rightward shift to an ideology concerned more with individualism than collectivism, and it is no surprise that it comes with greater economic success.

# Why This Matters to Me and in Schools of Education

These issues are clearly of particular importance and relevance to my life and my work. As a Jew, I am deeply concerned by the current inattention and reticence to meaningfully and critically engage in an examination of the intersections of race, class, gender, ethnicity, religion, and sexuality, as viewed through the lens of American Jewry. As a college instructor, I am equally troubled by the inadequate attention paid to these same issues in teacher education programs. Individuals who read this chapter are most likely engaged in this type of work and doing their part. This is most likely not all we have in common.

It is safe to assume that most readers can also relate to performance that takes place in schools and colleges of education when we turn our attention to the importance of requiring our students to take courses that directly address social justice, multiculturalism, equity, and diversity. Typically, these are the courses we teach. Our colleagues feel compelled to address the issues. They feel a collective tug in the direction of dealing with what matters. But the tug only gets us so far. There is talk of the importance of the issues, but actions say something different. The courses we teach and value are routinely marginalized, pushed into the corner as luxury items of sorts. Courses that address classroom management strategies, subject-specific pedagogical methods, and lesson planning are privileged. We scream that issues related to racism, sexism, homophobia, heterosexism, ageism, ableism, classism, language-based discrimination, and all other matters concerning social structure do not need to be set apart from such privileged courses, but instead need to be woven into their fabric. But our voices too often seem to fall on deaf ears.

The issues I attempt to raise by discussing the particularities of the dynamics of racism in the contemporary relationships between Jews and Blacks in the United States may be seen as both particular and broad. There are particular dynamics in this relationship shaped by a particular history. But the particulars of this relationship are representative of the larger problem of silence. Most Jews think of Jews in general as progressive or liberal. However they label it, they fancy their group as occupying space on the Left of the political spectrum. There is also a notion that this somehow is synonymous with progressive views on issues related to race. But as the election of 2008 shows us, we cannot make such simple assumptions.

Although President Obama overwhelmingly won the state of California, many suggest that his popularity and appeal also greatly contributed to the passage of Proposition 8 and the erosion of civil rights for nonheterosexuals in that state. The very people, particularly Latinos, Chicanos, and Blacks, who came out in such force to vote for the Democratic candidate also cast their vote for the reification and reestablishment of the legal differentiation of marriage rights for individuals based on sexual identity. This once again affirms that when it comes to matters of identity, oppression, and privilege, we can take nothing for granted. When it concerns matters related to racism, and the relationship between Blacks and Jews in the United States today, what I see, hear, and feel among my people is deeply troubling. When I hear nothing, I feel even more frightened. The silence I hear in the Jewish community, my community, is far too frequent, and it is deafening.

# References

American Jewish Committee. (2006). *American Jewish yearbook*. New York: Author.

Brodkin, K. (1998). *How Jews became white folks and what that says about race in America*. New Brunswick, NJ: Rutgers University Press.

Christian, C. (1998). *Black saga: The African American experience: A chronology*. New York: Basic Civitas Books.

Elior, R. (2004). *Men and women: Gender, judaism and democracy*. Jerusalem, New York: Van Leer Jerusalem Institute, Jerusalem, Urim Publications.

Franklin, J. H., & Moss, Jr., A. (2000). *From slavery to freedom: A history of African Americans* (8th ed.). New York: Knopf.

Goldstein, E. (2007). *The price of whiteness: Jews, race, and American identity*. Princeton, NJ: Princeton University Press.

Hartman, T. (2007). *Feminism encounters traditional Judaism: Resistance and accommodation*. Boston: Brandeis University Press.

Heilman, S. (1995). *Portrait of American Jews: The last half of the 20th century*. Seattle: University of Washington Press.

Hyman, P. (1995). *Gender and assimilation in modern Jewish history: The roles and representations of women*. Seattle: University of Washington Press.

Lerner, M., & West, C. (1996). *Jews & blacks: A dialogue on race, religion, and culture in America* (1st Plume printing ed.). New York: Penguin.

Plaskow, J (1991). *Standing again at Sinai: Judaism from a feminist perspective*. New York: Harper One.

Richardson, L., & St. Pierre, E. A. (2005). Writing: A method of inquiry. In N. Denzin & Y. Lincoln (Eds.), *The Sage handbook of qualitative research* (3rd ed., pp. 959–978). Thousand Oaks, CA: Sage.

Roediger, D. (2006). *Working toward whiteness: How America's immigrants became white: The strange journey from Ellis Island to the suburbs*. New York: Basic Books.

Ruttenberg, D. (Ed.). (2007). *Yentl's revenge: The next wave of Jewish feminism*. New York: Seal Press.

Sachar, H. (1992). *A history of the Jews in America.* New York: Knopf.

Sarna, J. (1997). *The American Jewish experience* (2nd ed.). New York: Holmes and Meier.

Sharma, A., & Young, K. K. (2007). *Fundamentalism and women in world religions.* New York: T & T Clark.

Sleeter, C. (1993). How White teachers construct race. In *Race, identity, and representation in education* (pp. 157–170). New York: Routledge.[AU: PLEASE PROVIDE NAMES OF EDITORS]

Tirosh-Samuelson, H. (2004). *Women and gender in Jewish philosophy.* Bloomington: Indiana University Press.

U.S. Census Bureau. (1860). Census of population and housing. *1860 Census.* Retrieved January 5, 2009, from http://www.census.gov/prod/www/abs/decennial/1860.htm

U.S. Census Bureau. (2006). U.S. and world population clocks—POPClocks. Retrieved January 5, 2009, from http://www.census.gov/main/www/popclock.html

U.S. Census Bureau. (2009). *U.S. Census quick facts: USA.* Retrieved, January 5, 2009, from http://quickfacts.census.gov/qfd/states/00000.html

Wistrich, R. S. (1976). *Revolutionary Jews from Marx to Trotsky.* New York: Barnes & Noble Books.

# PART III

# LIVING, LEARNING, AND TEACHING FOR A POLITICAL FUTURE

# · 1 2 ·

# La Política Vecindaria

## A Micro to Macro Lens on Immigrant Newcomer Students in U.S. Schools

LETICIA ALVAREZ & FRANCISCO RIOS

He told us to leave, and asked us what we were doing here? I got upset that day the teacher asked me what am I doing at school? I am not doing anything wrong! I said, I am not bothering anyone and he responded: you're bothering me! I told him I am not doing anything wrong, why are you throwing me out? He pulled me like so and said I told you to get out! I was leaving but he pulled me like so and I pulled my arm and told him I am going outside . . . then on my way out I stopped into the bathroom because it takes me half hour to walk home, and he saw me from a far and yelled get out now! I told him I had to use the bathroom. He said it doesn't matter, you will have to wait until you get to your house. I told him it would be about half hour before I would make it home and I couldn't hold it for that long. I told him I was sorry and he pulled me like this again and I pulled my arm away and told him I was sorry but I had to use the bathroom. He stood by the door while I went to the bathroom. When I finished and I told him I was leaving and he said 'well now you are not leaving' and he washed his hands so I sat down and I just waited until he felt like letting me out of the bathroom because he wouldn't let me out. Then he said 'we are going to the office' and when we got to the office he told me 'sit down clown' and we both starred at each other right on the eyes, the looks we gave one another were vicious, mean looks—mad looks. And I told him just because you are the teacher and because I am the student, because if not and he kept starring at me like he felt he had more power over me. Then he called my mom to set up an appointment. When we had the appointment he never mentioned that he pulled my arm and he never mentioned the altercation we had in the bathroom and in the office and that he was looking at me to intimidate me and starred at me like he was going to hit me. He never mentioned how I stood up and what we told one another. Since then, he doesn't direct a word toward me. I feel uncomfortable when he is around us students because he talks with everyone except me, and yes, I know he has to pass along information, he used to speak to me in Spanish but now he only speaks to me in English.

—TOMÁS (10TH GRADER)

In PE class, a friend who we call Shorty got slammed up against the gym lockers. A White guy, I don't know why, who knows what, but he started to demand and he was telling him [Shorty] to shut up and that nothing and he got him and slammed him up against the lockers. I didn't see anything but when I got into the locker room they told me that a White guy had hit Shorty and I asked who hit him? And he was crying because he got slammed agains the lockers. And that was the end of that . . . nobody did anything, and nobody said anything, and the truth is that nobody.

—ARTEMIO (10TH GRADER)

They changed my class because my teacher said that I wasn't going to pass the class, so they transfered me to into the Spanish class. The translator told my parents that it wasn't fair because there was still four months left before we would get out of school . . . my parents were upset. I say it is because I am Mexican and because I speak Spanish because the teacher said I don't under-stand him and he doesn't understand me. And we don't do anything because we don't even know what to do and the teacher gets bothered and yells at us, but it is because we don't understand him . . . he saids it is because I don't understand you and you don't understand me.

—BRIANA (9TH GRADE)

I don't know but there are many fussy people here who try to avoid us. That don't want to talk to us. I am not sure why that is, if it is because we are attending the same school as them or because we are Latinos. I don't know. I feel really bad because, well, there has been several ocassions that this one girl who is my same grade, and I am not sure why, perhaps because she doesn't like Latinos but everytime we would run into her she would say "too many Mexicans" and she would flip us off with her middle finger . . . and she would say it all in English. Oh yes and one time we were all at lunch and she was driving by in a car and she flipped us off again. I am not sure why she does that to us but we try to ignore her and not have any problems with her. And the truth is that we have never spoken to her . . . well when I saw her in the car during lunch and she flipped us off, i just thought wow she really doesn't like us!

—LUIS (12TH GRADE)

The previous immigrant newcomer students' narratives describe significant interactions that students had to encounter many times while attending a rural, wealthy resort high school in the West called Snow Town.[1] As the narratives suggest, the tension in relationships occurred with adults as well as with White peers in the school. Newcomer immigrant students seemed to be excluded from participating in the mainstream school culture, particularly due to their ethnicity and linguistic backgrounds. These interactions were detrimental to newcomer students' integration into the school's academic and social communities.

Due to the current educational policies and emphasis on high-stakes testing, often ignored in the educational system is the impact that everyday social interactions have on students' academic, social, and overall well-being, in particular for newcomer youth who are English Language Learners (ELLs). Unfortunately, the assumption is that ELLs must learn English and assimilate as quickly as possible to ensure academic and social success, but the reality is that, for ELLs to be successful in school, all other factors (e.g., social, cultural, linguistic, economic) have to be acknowledged and supported as part of the adjustment process (Collier, 1995; Suárez-Orozco & Suárez-Orozco, 2001; Walqui, 2002).

The relationships that ensued with White peers and adults in the school, we assert, are nested within the larger sociopolitical context of the school, the local community, and the nation. Particularly influential is the national rhetoric that emphasizes the negative impact that immigration, specifically undocumented immigration, has had for its citizens relative to the U.S. economy, lifestyle, and safety. Student narratives suggest that mainstream students and adults in the school did not believe that newcomer students had the same rights in the school as other students. Overall, these student narratives highlight how relationships between immigrant students and their White peers and adults in the school are nested within the larger sociopolitical context of the school, the local community, and the nation. Targeting newcomer immigrant students specifically because of their cultural and linguistic backgrounds in U.S. schools is a reflection of the larger hostile geopolitical and sociocultural attitudes toward people of different cultural backgrounds (e.g., culture, language, social hierarchies, and citizenship status) particularly immigrants from south of the border (e.g., Mexico). Immigrant student narratives also speak to the lack of preparation the school had to serve these students and how the lack of preparation was manifested in these relationships.

## Literature Review

Without question, the demographic profile of the nation continues upward toward greater cultural and linguistic diversity. In May 2008, the U.S. Census Bureau (2008) reported that the nation's minority population was more than 100 million, representing 34% of the total U.S. population. More important, in the 1-year period from July 2006 to July 2007, the Latino population grew 3.3%, Asians grew 2.9%, while the White population grew by only 0.3%.

Population estimates from the U.S. Census Bureau (2007) show that from 1980 to 2006, the Latino community grew from 15 million to 44 million, from 6.5% of the total U.S. population to 15%. The Asian community grew from 4 million to 13 million. All the while, the White population grew from 188 to 199 million but decreased in its percentage of the total population from 80% in 1980 to just 66% in 2006. Latinos currently make up 23%, Blacks make up 14%, Asians make up 4%, and Whites represent 59% of the K-12 school-age population.

A significant number of this increasingly diverse population are immigrants. By U.S. Census Bureau (2006) estimates (which can never fully identify the number of immigrants for a variety of reasons, not the least of which is that those who are here in the United States without proper documentation strive to live below the radar), about 37 million (12.6%) immigrants live in the United States. Of these, nearly half are from Latin America, whereas just a little less than 25% are from Asia; 84% of these immigrants speak a language other than English as home. ELLs represent the largest growing student population nationwide in U.S. public schools. This results in new challenges, most often for Latino students, exemplified in concerns about English language proficiency. For example, the number of students who are classified as limited English proficient grew from 3.2 million in 1995–1996 to 5 million in 2005–2006 (National Clearinghouse for English Language Acquisition, 2007), of which nearly 80% speak Spanish as their native language (Kindler, 2002). This represents a 57% increase in 10 years. Simultaneously, the overall school population went from 48 million to 49 million, a mere 3.6% increase during that same period.

Of note, the states with the largest increase of English learners (above 200% increase) are Colorado, Nebraska, and states in the southeast (Georgia, North and South Carolina, Kentucky, Tennessee, etc.). That is, the movement of immigrant students, for whom English is not their first language, to states that had been culturally insular has widened the number of locales that have experienced a new set of tensions and challenges for both schools and local communities. As one might imagine, for these newcomer students and their caregivers, this also represents a new set of challenges and tensions related to being physically distant from that which is culturally and linguistically familiar as well as community resources and social networks that serve as bridges between them and the long-standing gateway communities (i.e., New York, Los Angeles, San Francisco, etc.). This is the case for the setting, which is the focus of this chapter.

We wish to acknowledge that although immigrants are from many nationalities, most often people think of Latino immigrants due to their especially high representation as noted earlier. Consider that during the spring 2006 immigration rights rallies, most often the focus was not on those immigrants from Canada or Western Europe but rather from Latin America. That is, "immigrant" has become a proxy for race of the Latino community. Concomitantly, although ELLs may speak many languages other than English, most often people think of Spanish speakers because they represent the largest language group outside of English. Consider that in discussions of bilingual education, most people don't consider the use of Tagalog or Urdu; rather Spanish is the language that most often comes to mind. Thus, language is also often a proxy for race of the Latino community.

Despite the increase of ELLs in U.S. public schools, they continue to be underserved and excluded from meaningful integration into the mainstream school culture, just as in Snow Town High School. Although having limited English skills is a factor to their isolation from mainstream adults and peers, their isolation is intensified by the segregation and tracking they experience being enrolled in lower ability classrooms (Genesee et al., 2005; Ruiz de Velasco & Fix, 2000), having limited quality instruction (Harris, 2004; Quijada & Alvarez, 2006; Walqui, 2002), and being denied social status in the school by mainstream White peers and/or adults.

Along with these structural conditions, racism and antagonism toward immigrants make school settings a difficult place for newcomer immigrant students to adjust socially and achieve academically. The increase of immigrant students into U.S. schools is often viewed as a disruption because of the lack of qualified professional staff available to assist students with language development or provide them with best practices for their academic learning (Harris, 2004; Morse, 2005).

In addition to these structural conditions, racial tensions and stereotypes are barriers for ELLs and are counterproductive to their social adjustment, linguistic development, and academic achievement. The increase of community feelings against immigration has often set a platform for hostile school climates for immigrant students (Suárez-Orozco & Suárez-Orozco, 1998). The unwelcoming school climate plays out differently in different school contexts. In most school contexts, immigrant students are not allocated similar treatment or resources in the school and often times this unequal treatment allocates power and resources to mainstream students and further marginalizes immigrant students. This marginalization can be exhibited explicitly and, other times, is more subtle, as noted by student narratives at the beginning of the chapter. One thing is certain: The school climate has to be more welcoming to ELLs (Morse, 2005).

ELLs are at a disadvantage due to school infrastructures because they are segregated not only linguistically but also ethnically, which prevents them from being integrated into the larger school culture. Latina/os experience more segregation from Whites than other ethnic groups, which gives them fewer opportunities to form friendships with peers of other ethnicities as well as meaningful opportunities to learn and use English (Quillian & Campbell, 2003; Walqui, 2003). They are also segregated due to curricular tracking. In addition to the linguistic and ethnic isolation, demographic characteristics (e.g., gender, family, socioeconomic status [SES]) coupled with anti-immigrant political sentiments also play a factor in being integrated into the school culture. Current trends in policies (such as anti-immigration or anti-bilingual education legislation) at the national or state level aimed at immigrants may prevent newcomer students who are undocumented from ever adjusting within a particular community, let alone planning to pursue higher education.

In addition to these factors, there is a shortage of qualified teachers working with ELLs, and students have limited access to college prep classes that will give them the opportunity for social mobility (Quijada & Alvarez, 2006). The Hispanic Pew Center reported that newcomer Latino students who have experienced difficulties in school in their home country are 71% more likely to drop out of U.S. schools (Fry, 2005), whereas immigrant children who begin their schooling in the United States by the second grade are less likely to drop out than students who begin their schooling in later years (Fry, 2005). It is projected that one quarter of Mexican newcomer students are dropouts (or had never enrolled in U.S. schools) (Fry, 2005). Furthermore, half of the Latino students in the United States are attending larger schools that are typically underfunded and therefore have access to less educational resources (Fry, 2005; Quijada & Alvarez, 2006). The dropout is often attributed to the lack of academic and social support that ELLs receive in the school as well as their schooling experiences in their home country (Fry, 2005).

Despite these educational disparities, 88% of newcomer Mexican students described school in positive terms, and 60% had positive impressions of the adult administrators (e.g., principal) compared with 40% of the White students' negative views of the same administrators and teachers (Suárez-Orozco & Suárez-Orozco, 1996). It is important that all schooling dimensions pertaining to student learning be linked because these factors are all interrelated and do not operate in a vacuum. For example, students cannot be expected to rapidly learn English if they are confined in the same classroom with peers whose native language is also Spanish and are not given formal opportunities throughout their school day to interact with English-speaking peers.

## Theoretical Lens

We are guided in this work by the advice from ethnographers and cultural anthropologists whose work in education settings reminds us of the need to attend to both the microcultural context where one is working/studying as well as attending to the macrocultural context (see, e.g., Trueba, 1988). The macrocultural context often situates the microcultural context and thus creates conditions for what might (or might not) occur within the specific context. Given this role, then, we wish to turn our attention in this work to a theoretical framework that will help us attend to both the micro- and macrocultural contexts.

In their seminal work, Scheurich and Young (1997) asked, "Are our epistemologies racist?" They provide one such theoretical framework. Briefly, the framework provided suggests that racism may play out on four levels. At the smallest level, we see how relationships are playing out among individual people. This *interpersonal level* is probably the most often observed and most often considered. However, Scheurich and Young argue that the interactions that occur at this level are nested within the *institutional level*. At this level, the culture, policies, and practices of institutions (such as schools) play a role in creating the conditions in which these interpersonal relations play themselves out. As such, they influence in significant ways the kinds of interpersonal interactions that are likely to play out. At the next level, the *societal level*, the larger nation/state nests what happens within the institutions. That is, schools are a reflection of the values, beliefs, and assumptions of those powerful groups of the nation/state. Indeed, schools are often created to inculcate the young into the larger nation, to take on its cultural ways of being. Thus, if the nation/state harbors racism, then the institutions are structured to replicate that racism, which influences the kinds of interpersonal dynamics that occur. Finally, Scheurich and Young argue that that nation/state is nested within a particular philosophical (ideological) orientation, *civilizational level*, about being (ontology), valuing and believing (axiology), and knowing (epistemology) that guides and informs the kind of nation/state context that is developed. As described earlier, the philosophical orientation creates conditions for the nation/state, which creates conditions for the institution, which creates conditions for the interpersonal relationships that occur.

We find the framework helpful for the ways in which it compels us to think about both the interpersonal dynamics that we see occurring in hallways and classrooms as well as the larger sociopolitical context of the school, the local community, and the nation/state. This framework informs us in this chapter.

## Snow Town: A Specific Instance

Snow Town is a resort town located in the mountain West and started to attract a large Mexican population into the area for work in the service industry and construction about 10 years ago due to the decrease of available U.S. workers. Actually, many business owners filed H2B visas that would allow nonprofessional foreigners to work for a period of 10 months. In 2003, Snow Town businesses filed for 1,764 H2B workers. Currently, 14% of the county population is Latino, and 80% of the Latinos are from the same rural state in Mexico, 2.5 hours southeast of Mexico City. Due to the high cost of living in the area, many families share living quarters. The median income of Latino families in Snow Town is $15,000, whereas the median family income for White families is $59,500 (Snow Town County Statistics, 2004). Although the median income is so high, 57% of the jobs in Snow Town remain in the retail and service sectors, with the pay being between $18,200 and $21,840 yearly.

Due to the larger number of workers being recruited into Snow Town, the local high school has had a recent increase of immigrant newcomer ELLs. When this research was initiated, the entire school enrollment was 685 students, of which 8% (55) were Latina/o and the majority (50) were enrolled in the English as a Second Language (ESL) program. The school is said to have more than 80% of their graduating seniors pursuing a postsecondary education and is one (of only three) of the schools in the state to offer Advanced Placement (AP) courses; none of the students in the AP classes were Latina/os, yet the school had received the Blue Ribbon Award for Excellence in Education.

In 2004, when this research was initiated in Snow Town, the site for a larger research project in which we were engaged, there was a sixfold increase in kindergarten through second-grade students for whom English was a second language. Today, half of the kindergarten class is Latino and Spanish speaking. This large increase of Latino students into the Snow Town schools in is due to the workforce that Latinos bring into the town, particularly due to the available work in the service industry and construction as described earlier.

The immigrant student narratives presented at the beginning of this chapter reflect the tensions that exist between immigrant and White community members not only in the school but also in the larger Snow Town community setting. In particular, the narrative by Tomás was most directly linked to the events that were happening in the community at the time of the interview; additionally, other students were being treated as such due to the larger community and societal views on Mexican immigrants. In this setting, although the recent influx of Mexican newcomers to this resort town had caused upheaval in the community, it was exacerbated in 2006 due to an alleged rape reported by a teenage White girl. Unfortunately, the impact that this false report had on the immigrant males in the high school was direct and real. Tomás shared how he and other immigrant males in the school were not permitted to stay after school to lift weights or play any sports because they were being perceived and treated as "trouble makers" and "violators." The only description the girl gave the police was that she believed the men were both Latinos in their 20s and both were wearing hooded sweatshirts. A couple of weeks later, police confirmed that the girl's story was not true. Headlines in the local newspaper read "Police Reject Rape Report" (December 5, 2006), followed the next day with "Rape Report Exposes Labels: When Police Conclude a Teen Fabricated an Assault Story, a Community Is Left to Wonder About Racism" (December 6, 2006).

This incident raised the issue of how some residents stereotype members of the Latino immigrant community and also led many to purchase pepper spray and guns at local shops. Additionally, it elicited letters to the Snow Town newspaper calling for vigilante justice. The following is one of the letters submitted to the local newspaper:

> Was there a meeting I missed where the people of Snow Town voted to allow free reign for the gangs of illegal aliens that have formed in the valley? Did everyone just throw up their hands and say, "Oh well, they're here so there's nothing we can do about it?" What the hell is going on here, where is the public outrage? In the old West Americans formed gangs when elected officials and law enforcement were either indifferent to the citizens' safety or actually in league with the outlaw element. They called their gangs citizens' vigilance committees. They were kind of crude but they effectively got their point across. Perhaps their time has come again. (*Snow Town Newspaper*, December 2006)

The letter did not appear in the Letters to the Editor section because the editors thought the call for vigilante justice was too malicious, but rather the editors found a way to include these comments into an article discussing the alleged rape case (*Snow Town Newspaper*, December 2006). This particular community member had written to the paper before to attack illegal immigration. According to law enforcement officials, this local man's reaction was not typical. In addition to this type of response, there were some residents who wrote letters like the following:

> I would like to commend the Snow Town police department for the quick action regarding the alleged rape. Their actions appear to have prevented some type of hysteria. I was surprised to learn about the racial tension that appears to grip the community. Perhaps, this would be a good time for the "powers to be" in both the Anglo and Hispanic communities to ask, why do these feelings exist here, in paradise? Then open a community dialogue. (Jerry)

Prior to this false reported rape, there were continuous unwelcome outcries by White community members, mostly in the town newspaper, commenting negatively on this group's presence (e.g., taking jobs, lack education, criminals). Ironically, most of these same residents benefit from the labor the newcomers meet in the service industry (e.g., restaurants, hotels, and ski resorts), construction, and tending to the livestock on the local farms.

The elementary school principal reported that he often felt pressured by White parents in the community to group the school's Latino students into separate classrooms from the Anglos so that more focused grade-level learning would take place. One such parent, a businessman, shared the following with the principal: "We can't deal with the number of Hispanic children in those classrooms. It just has too much impact on the Anglo children" (*Snow Magazine*, p. 25). Ironically the man runs a business that employs Latino immigrants, and he further shared that he was going to pull his kids out of the public school and send them to a private school because he is now making a huge profit with his new employees. "I am now making so much of a profit margin because I've hired Hispanics that I can afford the private school" (*Snow Magazine*, p. 25), he told the principal. The principal expressed that "It's a sadness if Anglo parents recruit Latino adults to work but are unwilling to deal with the education of their children. If you think our Latino population drags us down too much, then we need to have a serious dialogue in our community" (*Snow Magazine*, p. 25). It is clear that the interpersonal relationships between immigrant students and their White peers and adults at the school are influenced by the local community occurrences. The school, just as the community, is structured so that immigrant students are segregated from the mainstream student population.

A letter to the editors of the local newspaper titled "Legal Immigration" stated the following:

> Just a note to say bravo to M.S. letter in response to "Abby's" article in your paper. Three of my grandparents immigrated from Europe to become legal citizens of the United States. When they made that decision, they left behind close relatives knowing they would never see them again. "Abby," did you even try to enter legally? (Marcy)

Although some of the community shares the previous sentiments, other community members don't share these views about the Latino immigrant population. In the *Snow Town Newspaper* (2007) when asked, "Given the valley's labor needs, what is your view of federal immigration laws?," the following were responses from local residents:

> An immigrant workforce would not be necessary if there was more affordable housing. (*Female, Bus Driver*)

> I think there needs to be a compromise. (*Female, Office Administrator*)

> They should hire more people to compensate for their needs. Especially in this county. (*Male, Loan Officer*)

> Immigrants should be given a chance to become citizens. (*Female, Waitress*)

> Other than Native Americans, I think we are all immigrants. (*Female, Pharmacist*)

## Discussion and Implications

We wish to make a number of points about what we have observed in this particular setting. First, the responses to this newcomer population fall along a range of possible responses. That is, although the students interacted with students and teachers who contested their right to a quality education, they also met others who willingly engaged them, befriended them, advocated for them. Likewise, although letters to the editor were often harsh and brutal, there were also those that were provocative and others that appealed to the community's humanity. Thus, we acknowledge that the responses within the school and local community were not monolithic. Notwithstanding, the question becomes which of these positions along the continuum was being privileged by these local institutions (i.e., the media and the school) such that it carried the most influence.

Second, these positions are often in tension with one another. But, as important, these positions often rest in tension with themselves. We find it ironic that a nation of immigrants would criticize immigration. We sense the tension in a community that is benefitting in profound ways from immigrant labor and sees the value of that labor while being critical of it (consider the example of the businessman who reported such high profits that he could send his children to a private school—away from the children of his workers, as described earlier). Consider the tension in the school community, an award-winning school that prided itself on the number of students who went on to postsecondary education, which now was compelled to provide services and programming for which they were not prepared (not with the resources nor the faculty nor with the faculty training). These tensions were added to existing unease about these students' mere presence on the school campus. Because of these tensions, there was an unclear message about what the people, school, and community really believed about the presence of these newcomers, what they really believed about schooling for all, what they really believed about cultural and linguistic democracy, and what they really believed about social justice.

Third, these tensions did not go unnoticed. The students and their families had ready access to the community newspaper (free). Local community leaders (and those who advocated on behalf of the Latino families) read these papers, shared them with others, and often formulated responses to those especially hostile submissions. In community forums, they often spoke for a more humane and just approach to the local immigrant community alongside those who were critical of these immigrant newcomers to the community. Thus, the

Latino students often got the message that they were a problem for the school and the local community. White students too got the message that these Latino newcomers were a problem. So we also ask the question that Murrillo (2002) asked from the perspective of Latino students: How does it feel to be a problem?

We wish to end with an important (general) implication for schools. As we have suggested, interpersonal relations, like those that begin this chapter, are nested within institutional cultures, which are nested within societal structures, which in turn are nested within ideological-philosophical orientations. Although these broader structures create the conditions for what happens at the more microcultural level, *they do not determine them*. Thus, individuals can respond in ways that are not sanctioned by the schools, schools can act in ways that are not sanctioned by the community, and communities can act in ways that work against the broader ideological orientation with respect to immigration. Concomitantly, we recognize that the microcultural can influence the macrocultural. Consider how social justice movements, often begun by small groups of individuals, can serve as the catalyst for a whole new way of living and thinking for a nation/state.

Hence, at what level might there be the greatest chance for powerful change toward a more humanizing, equitable, and just approach to education for newcomer immigrant students? For us, the answer is the school. Schools can, indeed must, be active agents in creating conditions, structural and organizational, to affirm student differences and adopt cultural assets approaches to teaching learning (see, e.g., Fránquiz & del Carmen Salazar, 2004; Yosso, 2006). But schools can, and indeed must, not only create the cultural conditions within it for productive and affirming relations of students with students and teachers with students, but they also must actively work to influence the local culture and do so actively, persistently, and sensitively. We recognize that this places a huge burden on schools already burdened by national mandates, which have been especially disempowering to schools and the professionals who work there. But we also believe that schools have a choice as described by Freire (1973):

> There is no such thing as a neutral educational process. Education either functions as an instrument which is used to facilitate the integration of the younger generation into the logic of the present system and bring about conformity to it or it becomes the "practice of freedom"—the means by which men and women deal critically and creatively with reality and discover how to participate in the transformation of their world. (p. 15)

# Note

1. Snow Town and the other names in this chapter are pseudonyms.

# References

Collier, V. P. (1995, Fall). Acquiring a second language for school. *Directions in Language and Education, 1*, 4.

Fránquiz, M. E., & del Carmen Salazar, M. (2004). The transformative potential of a humanizing pedagogy: Addressing the diverse needs of Chicano/Mexicano students. *High School Journal, 87*(4), 36–53.

Freire, P. (1973). *Pedagogy of the oppressed.* New York: Seabury Press.

Fry, R. (2005). The higher dropout rate of foreign-born teens: The role of schooling abroad. *Pew Hispanic Executive Summary.* Washington, DC: Pew Trust.

Genesee, F., Lindholm-Leary, K., Saunders, W., & Chrisitan, D. (2005). English Language Learners in U.S. schools: An overview of research findings. *Journal of Education for Students Placed at Risk, 10*(4), 363–386.

Harris, L. (2004). *Report on the status of public school education in California 2004.* Menlo Park, CA: The William and Flora Hewlett Foundation.

Morse, A. (2005). A look at immigrant youth: Prospects and promising practices. *National Conference of State Legislatures: Children's Policy Initiative—A Collaborative Project on Children and Family Issues.* Washington, DC: National Conference of State Legislatures.

Murrillo, Jr., E. G. (2002). How does it feel to be a *problem?* "Disciplining" the transnational subject in the American South. In S. Wortham, E. Murrillo, Jr. & E. Hamann (Eds.), *Education in the new Latino diaspora* (pp. 215–240). Westport, CT: Ablex.

National Clearinghouse for English Language Acquisition. (2007). *The growing numbers of limited English proficient English students: 1995/1996–2005/2006.* Washington DC: National Clearinghouse for English Language Acquisition. Available at http://www.ncela.gwu.edu/policy/states/reports/statedata/2005LEP/GrowingLEP_0506.pdf

Quijada, P. D., & Alvarez, L. (2006). *Cultivando semillas educacionales* (Cultivating educational seeds): Understanding the experiences of K-8 Latina/o students. In J. Castellanos, A. M. Gloria, & M. Kamimura (Eds.), *The Latina/o pathway to the Ph.D.: Abriendo Caminos* (pp. 3–17). Sterling, VA: Stylus Publishing.

Quillian, L., & Campbell, M. E. (2003). Beyond black and white: The present and future of multiracial friendship segregation. *American Sociological Review, 68*(4), 540–566.

Ruiz de Velasco, J., & Fix. M. (2000). *Overlooked & underserved: Immigrant students in U.S. secondary schools.* Washington, DC: The Urban Institute.

Scheurich, J., & Young, M. (1997). Coloring epistemologies. *Educational Researcher, 26*, 4–76.

Suárez-Orozco, C., & Suárez-Orozco, M.M. (1998). *Crossings: Mexican immigration in interdisciplinary perspectives.* Cambridge, MA: Harvard University Press.

Trueba, H. T. (1988). Culturally based explanations of minority students' academic achievement. *Anthropology and Education Quarterly, 19*, 270–281.

U.S. Census Bureau. (2006). *FactFinder: Selected characteristics of the native and foreign-born pop-*

*ulations (S0501)*. Washington, DC: U.S. Department of Commerce. Available at http://factfinder.census.gov/servlet/STTable?_bm=y&-qr_name=ACS_2006_EST_G00_ S0501&-geo_id=01000US&-ds_name=ACS_2006_EST_G00_&-=qr_name=ACS_2006_ EST_G00_S0501.

U.S. Census Bureau. (2007). *National population estimates for the 2000s*. Washington, DC: U.S. Department of Commerce. Available at http://www.census.gov/popest/national/asrh/ 2006_nat_res.html.

U.S. Census Bureau. (2008, May 1). *US Census bureau news*. Washington, DC: U.S. Department of Commerce. Available at http://www.census.gov/Press-Release/www/releases/archives/pop-ulation/011910.html.

Walqui, A. (2002). Structural obstacles that inhibit students' success. In *Module one: Sociocultural and linguistic context of educating English learners*. San Francisco, CA: Wested Publication.

Yosso, T. (2006). *Critical race counterstories along the Chicana/Chicano educational pipeline*. New York: Routledge.

# · 1 3 ·

# Race, Wealth, and the Commons

DEDRICK MUHAMMAD & CHUCK COLLINS

The Black–White racial wealth divide is a primary obstacle to racial reconciliation in the United States. The celebrated but brief heyday of the civil rights movement ended legal sanction of White supremacy, yet vast inequalities of wealth persist. There have been some advances in reducing the Black–White income gap. But if Black incomes rose at the same rate as they did between 1968 and 2001, it would take 581 years for Blacks to reach per-capita income parity with White America. It is in the area of wealth that we best see the sedimentary results of intergenerational inequality. In 2004, the median family net worth of Blacks was $20,400, only 14.5% of the median White net worth of $140,700. The median net worth for Latino families was $27,100.

Wealth and savings are a stabilizing force for families, and intergenerational transfers open up access to higher education, homeownership, savings, and investments. As a growing amount of sociological research reveals, the net worth of one generation contributes significantly to the wealth prospects of the next generation. Our nation needs to make a dramatic reinvestment in broadening wealth and opportunity. The massive past government investments in wealth-building, such as the Homestead Act and post-World War II "housing boom," were effectively "White-only" programs that bolstered the economic supremacy of Whites. Since the end of legal segregation and discrimination, there has not been a similar mass investment that Blacks and other people of color could benefit from as equal citizens.

## The Commons Sector: Source of Wealth

One barrier to such a mass investment is a mythology of how private wealth is created. No one builds wealth alone, although the myth of individual wealth pioneers is deeply part of our culture. In U.S. society, private wealth (savings, homeownership, investment wealth) is derived from a combination of individual activity and the "commons." The commons refers to the various forms of common wealth around us, what we have together. This includes the natural commons, such as fisheries, seeds, animals, air, land, water, soil, and airwaves. It includes the social or community commons, such as libraries, transportation infrastructure, property, and intellectual property. It also includes the cultural or knowledge commons, such as music, indigenous medicine, the Internet, and languages.

Some of these commons are gifts from nature. Others were built by people or community institutions, derived from shared funding and taxation. One way to view the commons, articulated by commons thinker Peter Barnes, is "the gifts of nature, plus the gifts of society that we share and inherit together—and that we have an obligation to pass onto our heirs, undiminished and more or less equally." The commons refers to forms of real wealth and property that can be counted and legally protected. Other forms of common wealth, however, don't have legal standing and may be difficult to quantify.

It is important to consider the struggle over the wealth divide as a contest over the distribution of common wealth. Corporations, benefiting their largely White and privileged shareholders, have looted the commons or shifted their costs onto it. Because most forms of common wealth are poorly defined, lack property rights, or are poorly managed, corporations see common assets as largely free for the taking. For example, most extractive industries—such as fishing, oil, coal, mining, and timber—take wealth from the ecological commons while paying little or nothing.

Corporations relate to the commons in several ways. They siphon off wealth created by public and community investments for private gain. They enlarge their profits by shifting costs off their balance sheets and onto the commons ledger. This is done by externalizing costs such as pollution, infrastructure, and employee health care. Finally, corporations enclose socially created and knowledge commons, placing them in private ownership and often charging us for their use. Enormous profits are made by corporations enclosing commons such as popular art, culture, Internet, and much more. All this is done largely within the framework of the existing legal and economic belief systems.

In 1995, during the shift from analog to digital television, a new set of broadcast frequencies were required. Congress obligingly gave them away—free of charge—to the same media companies to which it had previously given analog frequencies. This was an estimated $70 billion giveaway to some of the largest and wealthiest corporations in the country. Few Black businesses or corporations benefited from this historic subsidy, reinforcing White dominance in the broadcast industry.

Throughout U.S. history, Whites have had privileged access to different forms of the commons. At the same time, Black labor has added to the common wealth without adequate compensation or claim. Former Secretary of the Interior Walter Hickel quipped, "If you steal $10 from a man's wallet, you're likely to get into a fight, but if you steal billions from the commons, co-owned by him and his descendants, he may not even notice." A commons perspective is important in looking at current wealth inequalities and solutions.

## White-Privileged Wealth Creation

The story of "wealth creation" in the United States needs to be revisited through a race and commons perspective. There is a long and unseemly history of the U.S. government channeling common wealth to expand the individual wealth and opportunity of privileged Whites. Even before the existence of the United States as a nation, Europeans confiscated and enclosed land and natural resources from indigenous peoples, creating the base of wealth from which our modern economy derives. Similarly, the United States, often through military intervention, appropriated the resources of foreign nations, whether it be their natural resources or their markets, to the benefit of the United States.

For hundreds of years, African people were shipped out of their native lands to be tools of wealth production in the United States. Blacks were considered part of the wealth owned by Whites. Black labor built wealth for White America—while their communities have been later used as dumping grounds for the negative externalities produced by industrialization. Domestically, we can look back at the great "robber baron" fortunes of the Industrial Revolution that were based on White elites gaining free access to the nation's natural resources to exploit for personal enrichment. Great edifices and charitable institutions still carry the names of the individuals who cornered markets built on the natural commons, including oil, timber, and minerals—as well as socially created wealth such as railroads and capital markets.

But even the historical government programs most celebrated for building wealth for ordinary citizens were usually forms of "Jim Crow economic development"—providing Whites privileged access to the commons. The Homestead Act of the 1880s, the largest 19th-century initiative for individual wealth-building, essentially expropriated indigenous people's lands—and enclosed large tracts of common property—to grant private property titles to White homesteaders. In a similar way, the wealth-broadening programs of the New Deal and GI Bill are often lifted up as bold initiatives to broaden our middle class. But as Ira Katznelson chronicles in *When Affirmative Action Was White* (see his summary of the book in the March/April 2006 issue of *Poverty & Race*), Social Security, the educational benefits of the GI Bill, and homeownership programs of the 1950s all worsened the racial wealth divide.

These programs were designed by a Congress controlled by White supremacists and implemented in Jim Crow states so as not to upset local White rule. As a result, the first two decades of Social Security excluded agricultural and domestic workers, occupations disproportionately held by Blacks. During World War II, Blacks faced unequal treatment in the segregated military and in their ability to access the bountiful benefits of the GI Bill on their return. The postwar housing boom was fueled by subsidized assistance to more than 35 million Americans between 1948 and 1972. During these years, 11 million families bought homes and another 22 million improved their properties. The biggest beneficiary was "Whites-only" suburbia, where half of all housing could claim FHA or VA financing in the 1950s and 1960s. The home mortgage interest and property tax deduction also disproportionately benefited suburban homeowners, and interstate highway construction served as an indirect subsidy, as it opened up inexpensive land for suburban commuters.

Unfortunately, due to economic inequality and various White racist practices—including discriminatory mortgage lending, bigoted realtors, and outright White racist violence used to maintain segregated housing patterns—most Black families were prohibited from this government investment into the private wealth of America. Whites, in contrast, received privileged access to deeply subsidized government programs and common resources that catapulted them forward. At the end of World War II, 44% of U.S. citizens owned their own homes. In 2004, 76% of Whites owned their own homes, compared with 49.1% of Blacks and 48.1% of Latinos.

Today, the children and grandchildren of GI Bill recipients benefit from intergenerational wealth transfers that enable them to purchase homes, attend private schools, and start businesses. But they probably don't think of themselves as beneficiaries of "White affirmative action."

## The Myth of Self-Made Wealth

It will be difficult to overcome the racial wealth divide if we adopt a narrative of wealth creation that ignores the role of the commons. We must start with the seldom recognized premise that much of what we consider "wealth" derives from common wealth. Occasionally, the myth is exposed. In the debate over the federal inheritance tax, several thousand multimillionaires and billionaires signed a public petition opposing repeal of the estate tax. Many stated that the tax was justified because their personal wealth was the result of direct and indirect public investments in the commons. Bill Gates, Sr., father of the planet's wealthiest man, wrote:

> When someone has accumulated $10 million or $50 million or $50 billion (I can only think of one person in the last category), they have benefited disproportionately from society's investments in education, public infrastructure, scientific research and other forms of society's common wealth. Show me a first-generation fortune and I'll show you a successful partnership between a talented individual and society's invisible venture capitalist, the commons. . . . None of us can individually claim to own the commons but all of us benefit from it.

Still, the myth continues that one's wealth status is a reflection of one's individual effort and achievement. As long as Whites and privileged individuals believe their wealth derives largely from their own effort, it will be difficult to build political support for an inclusive wealth-broadening initiative, let alone any form of reparations.

In *The American Dream and the Power of Wealth*, sociologist Heather Beth Johnson interviewed more than 200 privileged White families about their attitudes toward family wealth and educational opportunity. Although these individuals saw the important role that modest "intergenerational wealth transfers" from their parents made in giving themselves and their children tremendous educational advantages, they still deeply believed one's station in life is determined by individual effort. These interview subjects saw no relationship between the power of their wealth in creating privileged advantages and the inability of others to achieve the "American Dream."

In this context, wealth- and asset-building programs assisting low-income people and people of color that teach "self-sufficiency" also risk perpetuating the myth that White and affluent people achieved their wealth status through some form of independent effort.

## The Real Wealth Story

A more accurate narrative of individual wealth creation starts with the fundamental truth that anyone with substantial wealth has gotten a lot of help from the commons. Anyone who boasts that they are "self-made" is ignoring the remarkable fertile soil of common wealth that we have all built together. Individual initiative matters, of course, but is often akin to adding the cherry and whipped cream to the top of the existing sundae of common wealth. Central to the moral claim to eliminate the historical racial wealth divide is recognition that each of us has a birthright to a part of our inherited commons for our sustenance and livelihood. People chafe at the notion of "giving people something for nothing." Yet we don't think twice about corporations and generations of White-privileged individuals receiving from the commons for nothing. These individual wealth "success stories" need to be unpacked. Even White middle-class achievement needs to be understood as privileged access to government programs and common wealth that was built through the efforts of many, some of whom have not benefited from their own efforts.

## Common Wealth for the Common Good

In *Capitalism 3.0: A Guide to Reclaiming the Commons*, Peter Barnes argues that we are at a historical moment where our common wealth must be reclaimed and secured or we risk permanent loss of which cannot be replaced. We need to find ways to protect the commons—and use its bounty for the common good, not for just the privileged few. While private wealth is distributed unequally, common wealth belongs to all, and its benefits should, wherever possible, be universally shared. Income from commons-based sources should be used to reduce inequality and expand opportunity.

At the same time, common wealth should be managed not just on behalf of those living now but also on behalf of future generations. Each generation has an obligation to preserve its shared inheritances and pass them on, undiminished, to the next.

Peter Barnes suggests that there are three large pools of common wealth that should be tapped at a national level to enhance the common good: the waste absorption capacity of nature, socially created wealth captured by individuals, and socially created wealth captured by corporations. Taken together, these pools represent trillions of dollars worth of shared resources and hundreds of billions of dollars in potential annual revenue. Our challenge is to identify possible uses of these pools of common wealth and organize to ensure their fair allocation. Barnes suggests that the criteria for selecting potential uses should be that they are: (a) universal, (b) permanent or perpetual, and (c) aimed at redressing historical inequities caused by unequal distribution of common wealth. We need to have a practical and political discussion about which common resources should be used for which common goods.

Collectively, we have a pretty good sense of what needs to be done to broaden wealth and opportunity. The "White-only" programs of the last 60 years were successful in lifting the opportunities for a segment of the population. Combined with some of the new innovations around asset creation, we can detail a wealth-broadening program that would close the racial wealth divide. The elements include:

- Debt-free higher education, like the GI Bill and Pell grants that enabled millions to graduate from college without deep debts.
- Matching savings programs, such as Individual Development Accounts (IDAs), that bolster private wealth.
- Kid Save accounts that contribute to greater asset-building and opportunity. One proposal is to allocate to every child born in the United States a tax-free inheritance of $5,000. When the child reaches 18, funds (greatly appreciated over nearly two decades) could be withdrawn for education, first-home purchase, or starting a business.
- Expanded homeownership, through various first-time homeowner mechanisms such as soft second mortgages and subsidized interest rates.
- Annual dividends to supplement wages. Alaska residents receive an annual dividend from the Alaska Permanent Fund, a portion of the state's oil wealth.
- Establishment of "Community Wealth-Building" funds, pools of capital to provide support for community development corporations, nonprofit housing organizations, employee-owned firms, social enterprises, community land trusts and other community-serving, and asset-building efforts.

Commons-based revenue can go to individuals or support commons institutions that expand opportunity. In Texas, a percentage of oil wealth contributes to several trust funds that pay for K-12 and higher education. How will we pay for this wealth-broadening program? An important source of revenue is to harness income from commons-based sources.

## Scarcity Rents for Natural Resources

Historically, polluters have dumped into the scarce natural commons without cost. If we charge for the use of our shared natural resources, we create both price incentives to reduce pollution and generate a revenue stream for the common-good uses described earlier. With the tremendous push to reduce carbon emissions and address our climate crisis, there will be new mechanisms to cap carbon and assess fees. The trouble with cap-and-trade systems to date is that they have been "giveaways" to historic polluters. A "sky trust" could capture this substantial revenue, probably in the range of billions of dollars per year, to broaden wealth and opportunity.

## Common Wealth Recycling Program

If we recognize that large accumulations of private individual wealth are the result of commons, we should more aggressively tax inheritances and recycle these opportunities. There is a clear moral rationale for taxing inheritances: Socially created wealth may be temporarily claimed by individuals but at some point should return to society. Inheritance taxes could be dedicated to a Wealth Opportunity Fund to serve as a source for several of the uses described previously.

In Washington State, the state's estate tax is levied on estates over $2 million ($4 million for a couple). This generates about $100 million a year that is channeled into the Education Legacy Trust Account. Funds are used to reduce class size in K-12 education statewide and provide higher education scholarships for 7,900 lower income students. Bill Gates, Sr., defended the tax, observing that: "If we abolish the state's inheritance tax we stop the opportunity-recycling program. We allow the common wealth to stop flowing and concentrate it in the hands of a few. And worse, we slow the investments in opportunity that aim to provide every young person a chance, whether they were born in South Seattle or Mercer Island."

# Socially Created Wealth
# Captured by Corporations

Corporations also hold socially created wealth—and we should look at the means to recapture some of this wealth for the common good. Peter Barnes describes the numerous ways that society transfers wealth to corporations. First, we grant them special privileges that are not available to real human beings, such as limited liability, perpetual life, and the ability to grow without limit. We supplement these gifts with other privileges, such as patents and copyrights that enable them to charge higher prices than a truly competitive market would allow. On top of that, society creates public infrastructure—roads, the Internet, regulated capital markets, and trade policies—that greatly enhances corporate wealth. On top of that, we often give corporations common resources (land to railroad companies, minerals to mining companies, spectrum to broadcasters, pollution rights to polluters) worth billions.

We rationalize these common wealth gifts to corporations by arguing that corporations create jobs and strengthen our economy. But in reality, most of these benefits flow to privileged elites who own most of the corporation's stock and are disproportionately White. Corporations pay back a portion of this through corporate income taxes, but this contribution is shrinking to nothing for some of the country's most profitable enterprises. Barnes proposes a levy on corporate wealth, placing a percentage of stock into an American Permanent Fund to be managed on behalf of the common good.

These are just a few examples of ways to creatively pair sources of common wealth with common-good uses. The Tomales Bay Institute is sponsoring a series of conferences and discussions aimed at fleshing out a series of policy initiatives (see below). Tapping the commons for initiatives to reduce the racial wealth divide is an appropriate and necessary remedy to centuries of exclusion from common wealth. Current contests over capping of carbon emissions and preserving the federal estate tax provide immediate opportunities to inject this commons perspective into public policy and the public consciousness.

# Note

\* Reprinted with permission. Originally published as: Muhammad, D., & Collins, C. (2007, May/June). Race, wealth, and the commons. *Poverty & Race*.

# · 1 4 ·

# Profiting From Racism

## A Family History of How Race and Class Privilege Created Wealth

Cooper Thompson

My chances for success in life were determined long before I was born. Generations of Thompsons, Middletons, and Watkins on my father's side and Austins, Guilds, and Shermans on my mother's side owned land and financial and material resources and then passed on whatever assets they had accumulated to their children and grandchildren. These assets, whether limited or substantial, gave my ancestors stability, opportunity, and, ultimately, a sense of security that they would survive and, in some cases, thrive. I am one of the beneficiaries of their foresight, thriftiness, and hard work. I am grateful for what they directly and indirectly have given to me.

I am also the beneficiary of systemic racism that has privileged me and my ancestors. It was racism that made it possible for my ancestors to first acquire land from Native People and then accumulate money from unpaid or underpaid labor of people of color. It was racism embedded in volumes of federal and state statutes and in long-standing cultural beliefs that allowed and even encouraged my ancestors to take advantage of their White skin privilege as they increased their wealth. Intentionally or unintentionally, my ancestors exploited people of color.

I am sure, like any family, my ancestors were a mixed lot: some kind and gentle, some mean and harsh. I am sure that some were troubled by the racism they saw, whereas others were blind to it. Some may have noticed injustice but failed to make the connection between their actions and the perpetuation of racism. Some rationalized what they were doing. They were all products of their culture and each a product of their unique family circumstances that socialized them into particular patterns of thinking, feeling, and behaving. I accept them for who they were.

I live in a different time. My ancestors in the 17th, 18th, and 19th centuries lived with cultural and political values that validated the oppression of people of African, Asian, and Native descent. "Old-fashioned racism"—overt, explicit, and intentional laws and actions designed to oppress people of color—was the law of the land. Today, most forms of old-fashioned racism have been "officially" abolished. Racism continues, however, as "modern racism"—covert, subtle, and sometimes unintentional discrimination directed at people of color.

Like old-fashioned racism, modern racism makes life difficult and sometimes impossible for people of color and, as I argue in the pages to come, makes my life easier and gives me opportunities to enjoy and improve my life. I am therefore the beneficiary of both the historical legacy and current patterns of racism. That means that my success as a White man and even my existence are directly due to racism. How much my success and existence are due to racism I cannot say. Sexism, classism, and other forms of oppression have also played a role. But I am sure that racism has been an important factor.

In the following pages, I'm going to present information about my family and my life to show how I have benefited materially from racism by answering these questions: How did my ancestors benefit from slavery and the theft of land from indigenous people? How have I benefited from this legacy and subsequent policies of racial segregation? How have I benefited from federal policies of racial discrimination at the time of my birth in 1950? How have I benefited from the exclusion of people of color from participation in most institutions of the society? How do I benefit now from the economic exploitation of people of color?

# How Did My Ancestors Benefit From Slavery and the Theft of Land From Indigenous People?

## The Thompson Family

My father was born and raised in West Point, Mississippi, with many genera-tions of southern families behind him. My mother was born and raised in Ridgewood, New Jersey, with many generations of New England families behind her. I begin with my father's ancestors.

My great-great-grandfather, William Thompson, was born in Tennessee in 1811 and moved to Mississippi sometime before 1868. Land records indicate that he bought property that year in a community known as Cairo, in Chickasaw County, about 16 miles west of West Point in northeast Mississippi. The name of the county is significant because the land was occupied by the Chickasaw and Choctaw people for centuries before the arrival of people of European descent.

In 1786, the Chickasaws signed the Treaty of Hopewell with the newly formed U.S. government, in which they declared themselves at peace with the United States. This treaty, however, was the first in a series that gradually diminished the rights of the Chickasaw people. White settlers entering Chickasaw County from the north and east wanted the land for themselves, as owners, in violation of Chickasaw beliefs of shared custodianship of the land. A series of treaties between the Chickasaws and the United States were aimed at moving the Indians out of the area to a new homeland in the west. Finally, in 1831, the Treaty of Pontotoc provided that the Chickasaw lands in Mississippi would be surveyed and sold as soon as possible.

While the Chickasaws were being relocated to the west in the forced march west known as the Trail of Tears, White settlers were buying this land. Public sales (of course limited largely to White men) began in 1836. At first, the land sold at $1.25 an acre, but prices decreased to a low of 12 and 1/2 cents an acre. This encouraged both settlement and speculation; land was often resold by speculators at $5 to $10 an acre.

In 1868, William Thompson purchased a quarter section of land (160 acres) from Robert Miller for $755.00. I don't know when or for how much the land was originally purchased; I assume that it was Chickasaw land purchased for far less than the $4.72 an acre he paid for it. I do know that the land was held in the family until 1926, at which point it was sold for $2,000.00, with the proceeds shared between my great-grandmother Mary Gilmore (Stephens) Thompson and her children, one of whom was my grandfather, John Gilmore Thompson. When I went to West Point, Mississippi, in 1997 to research my dad's family, my cousin referred to this land as the Thompson homestead.

I also know that, according to the 1880 census, my great-great-grandfather was illiterate and had two "servants" living in his household: Mariah Coggins, a Black female age 34, and Cate Coggins, a Black female age 10. Although I don't know for sure whether William Thompson or his father owned slaves before Emancipation, I do know that William Thompson's father-in-law, my great-great-great-grandfather, John Middleton, owned slaves. According to the census taken in 1820 and 1830, John Middleton owned from 3 to 14 slaves while living in Georgia and Alabama.

Now at this point, I have to do some speculation, as I continue to do as I move through the historical record, but I feel reasonably confident that what I'm next going to write is true. The only way that three generations of Thompsons could have lived on and profited from the land in Cairo was because the Chickasaws had been forcibly removed from the area. It is reasonable to assume that my great great grandfather, William Thompson, owned slaves; it is possible that Mariah Coggins had been a slave in his household before being considered a servant in the 1880 census. In 1860, the population of Chickasaw County was majority slave; there were 2,000 more Blacks than Whites. I believe that William Thompson owed his survival to unpaid Black labor.

My dad tells me that his father, John Gilmore Thompson, purchased a farm near West Point around 1918 and had a Black tenant farmer named Love*. Love's family, consisting of husband, wife, and two or three children, lived in a one-room cabin provided by my grandfather. In a letter to me, in which he describes his own childhood, my dad wrote,

> Love always had a cow, a pig or two, and a large vegetable garden. These were provided of course by my father. . . .Love was not paid in money, but he did have access to my father's charge account at a large general store in West Point.
>
> At Christmas each year, Mr. John, as my father was known to the Black people, would buy several boxes of bar candies and distribute a generous portion to Love and his family. I believe that he also gave Love an amount of cash, perhaps $5, at Christmas. This was a huge gift for people who saw no money at all the rest of the year.

(*My dad recalls only the name "Love" for this man and in correspondence with me refers to him simply as "Love." My dad believes that this was his first name

and that he had no surname; my suspicion is that my father was never told about
Love's surname. The cultural racism of the time allowed my father, a child, to
call an adult "Negro" by his first name. I wish I could refer to "Love" as Mr.
_____. )

This land, unlike the other Thompson property in Cairo, was held until my
grandmother's death in 1967; my father's share of the proceeds from the sale of
this property amounted to a few thousand dollars. In the context of my family, a few thousand dollars is not a significant amount of money. However, the
significance of owning land goes beyond any financial benefits that eventually accrued to my father.

Owning land brings a sense of security. It allows the building of a home you
know is yours; it provides food and wood for fuel and buildings. In an agricultural community such as West Point, I believe that land ownership was a pre-
requisite for emotional and material satisfaction. Some historians suggest that
the most significant reason that former slaves failed to prosper under
Reconstruction was because of the inability to own land due to racially discriminatory government land programs and lack of financial resources. Although
there were proposals and calls to provide land for freed slaves, the federal government provided some food and legal aid and established hospitals and schools
for people of African descent. For the most part, land that had been abandoned
or confiscated in the South ended up in White hands not Black. Throughout
Reconstruction, the Thompson family owned land. I can only conclude that
race was a primary factor, if not the primary factor, in determining the fortunes
of the Thompson family in comparison with the fortunes of Black families such
as the Coggins, whose options were extraordinarily limited.

## Other Branches of My Father's Family

In addition to the branch of my father's family that is descended from William
Thompson of Tennessee, there are at least three generations of Watkins, two
generations of Stevens, and one generation of Lowes that settled in Mississippi
after living in Alabama, Georgia, and Ohio, as well as several generations of
Bectons and Hilliards before that from North Carolina. The pattern of owning land previously occupied by Chickasaws and exploiting Black labor was
repeated in each of these families.

In a privately published book on various branches of the Watkins family, it is indicated that John Becton (born around 1700) was a "man of great
wealth" living in Craven City, North Carolina. His contemporary, the father

of Edith Hillard, was a "prominent planter" of Edgecomb County, North Carolina. Given the extent of slavery in North Carolina and the prominence of these two families, it is likely that they and their descendents owned slaves and profited directly from slave labor. The Becton and Hilliard families also owned land, all of which was originally occupied by Native people. It was this wealth that allowed their descendents—people such as Mary Watkins and Lewis Stevens, my great-great-grandparents—to move from North Carolina in the 1840s and purchase at least two slaves and land in Mississippi.

According to the 1860 census, my great-great-great grandfather, John Watkins (Mary Watkins' father), owned seven slaves, ranging in age from 12 to 51, and land in Oktibbeha County, Mississippi. Lewis Stevens owned land valued at $3,600, located next door to his father-in-law, and two female slaves ages 11 and 14. His personal assets were valued at $4,200. According to the 1880 census, my great-grandfather, John Wesley Lowe, had four Black servants living in a household that included his wife and two young daughters. The servants include a cook, Sallie Lowe (Black female age 49), a nurse, Ella Lowe (Black female age 12), the cook's daughter, Ginnie Lowe (Black female age 5), and the cook's son, Henry Gibson (Black male age 8).

I suspect that there are many more examples of the ways that my father's ancestors exploited Black labor; I have only begun to do research on slave holding and the use of servants on my father's side of the family. The same is true for lands originally occupied by Native people that were bought and sold by members of my family over the course of three centuries. But I believe that these limited data give strong support to my belief that the social architecture of racism helped created the conditions for my father's birth in 1918.

## How Have I Benefited From This Legacy and Subsequent Policies of Racial Segregation?

My maternal grandfather, Rupert Sherman Austin, is descended from at least nine generations of Shermans, five generations of Guilds, and three generations of Austins, all of whom lived in Massachusetts and Rhode Island. My maternal grandmother, Viola Estelle Lavendol, is descended from at least three generations of Lavendols and three generations of Potters. When I notice the other surnames that show up in genealogical records on my mother's side of the family—Rickerson, Palmer, Tabor, Whitford, Baker, Remington, White, Paine, and

Tripp—it becomes clear how deep my roots go into Anglo-Saxon culture.

I want to demonstrate the impact of historical racism on my life from two different perspectives, using each side of my mother's family to demonstrate an aspect of racism. Using Rupert Sherman Austin relatives, I explore the impact of slavery and theft of native lands; this is somewhat speculative given the lack of concrete data about my ancestors' participation in slave and land holding. However, the historical patterns are well established, and, given the length of time that his side of the family has been in New England—at least one Sherman lived in Roxbury, Massachusetts, by 1633—I feel confident that there was some direct participation in, and probably some support for, oppression of people of African descent and Native people. Using Viola Estelle Lavendol's relatives, I explore more directly the wealth that was created as a result of racial segregation.

## The Sherman and Guild Families

My maternal great-grandmother, Edna Elvira Sherman, was the daughter of William Chauncey Sherman, whose family goes back at least seven generations to a Samuel Sherman who lived in England in the 17th century. Her mother, Malzena Alice Guild, came from a family that goes back at least four generations to a Joseph Guild, who probably lived in Massachusetts in the 18th century. The majority of the Shermans lived in various communities in Rhode Island, the Guilds in Massachusetts.

It's easy to forget Northern participation in the institution of slavery and genocide of Native people. In the 17th and 18th centuries, slaveholding was legal and common in both Massachusetts and Rhode Island. In the 19th century, New Englanders of European descent were the beneficiaries of the Southern slave industry that supported the textile industry in the north; profits from the mills in New England were due in part to artificially low-priced cotton grown and picked by unpaid Black labor. Cotton was the essential raw material for factory jobs in New England. It provided employment for other workers in transportation, handicrafts, and wholesale and retail trade. Most of these workers were of European descent.

These patterns of slave holding and theft of Native land in New England are exactly the same as the treatment of African and Chickasaw people in Mississippi. I'm therefore led to the same conclusion about my mother's side of the family: Their existence, and in some cases success, in Massachusetts and Rhode Island was based on the privileges of racism. Population data alone prove this point: Although Native populations have been reduced to a fraction of what they were at the time of first contact with Europeans, there are thousands of Shermans descended from a Philip Sherman who arrived here from England almost 400 years ago. A privately published book on the Sherman family lists at least seven generations of Shermans who can be traced to Philip.

## The Lavendol Family

My maternal grandmother, Viola Estelle (Lavendol) Austin, died in 1990. She left an estate worth $600,000, of which I inherited $125,000 in 1993. At the time of her death, her financial assets included her home, cash deposits, and stock. My grandfather, Rupert Sherman Austin, was a salesman for an office supply company; my grandmother had a career as a ballet teacher, managing her own business from her home and a rented studio nearby. My grandfather died in 1957 at the age of 66; my grandmother continued to live in their home in Ridgewood for the next 33 years, until she died in 1990 at the age of 92. During those 33 years, she traveled to Europe several times, periodically took my sister and me on vacations, and spent part of every summer on the coast of Maine in a cottage she rented.

According to my parents, the value of my grandmother's estate is due to the fact that she and her husband saved and invested their money carefully over the years. I believe that this is part of the story. I also believe that grandmother's wealth, and thus my wealth through the inheritance, was derived in part from patterns of racial discrimination that are the legacy of slavery. As a way to trace the connections between racism and the acquisition of this wealth, I examine one of things I inherited from her, which she had inherited from her father: stock in the Bank of Commerce and Trust in Crowley, Louisiana.

My maternal great-grandfather, Everett Lavendol (Viola Austin's father), was born in 1862 and died in 1940. He was a resident buyer for "dry goods" stores. His office was located in New York City, although my mother recalls that his customers were in the southern United States, as were the workers who produced the cotton used in many of the products sold in the dry goods (textile) business. Slavery had been officially abolished for several decades when he started in this business, but the patterns of exploitation of Black farmers in the southern cotton industry continued into the 20th century via the institution of share cropping. In the early 1900s, therefore, when Everett Lavendol would have been in the prime of his career, it was still the case that the exploitation of people of African descent in the South was tied to the economic development of the North. He was only one or two generations removed from those who had profited in the same textile industry that had made its fortune on the backs of Black slaves.

In 1921, Everett Lavendol invested $500 in what is now known as the Bank of Commerce and Trust in Crowley, Louisiana. Crowley is located about 100 miles west of New Orleans. Today, as it was in 1921 when the bank was founded, Crowley is an area characterized by maldistribution of income and wealth based on race, as well as hostility toward people of African descent. In addition to Black poverty, there are certainly many poor White people, and I'm sure that there is hostility directed toward them as well. Race is not the only reason for the income and wealth gaps. But the Board of Directors of this bank are all White men, and the vast majority of stockholders are White and at least middle class.

Banks make money from various commercial, housing, and personal financial transactions. Given the legacy of racial discrimination since the bank's founding in 1921, and the likelihood that, today, a relatively small number of White people in Crowley own the majority of businesses and property that employ and house Black people, it is reasonable to suggest that some percentage of the profits of this bank are directly due to racial disparities and exploitation of Black people. As stockholders and recipients of annual dividends, my great grandfather, then my grandmother, and now I are the beneficiaries of racism through the dividend checks the bank has regularly distributed. Because of stock splits and increase in value over the years, the total value of the stock purchased in 1921 by Everett Lavendol is now worth about $500,000.

To put the original and current value of this investment in context, at about the same time as my great grandfather was investing $500 in the Crowley bank, my grandfather, John Gilmore Thompson, was giving Love his annual present of $5. Given his status as a tenant farmer, that $5 could have represented Love's total financial worth, money that was necessary for basic needs. And so it is highly unlikely that Love left an inheritance to his children, except, perhaps, for a few personal possessions. It even seems absurd to suggest that he could have left an inheritance. The contrast between Love's financial status and Everett Lavendols' financial status is profound.

Finally, I want emphasize the impact of inherited wealth as a means of maintaining privilege in some White families and denying privilege to most families of color. It turns out that the distribution of wealth across racial lines is more unequal than the distribution of income across race. While the income gap between Whites and people of color has been gradually closing (although there are significant income differences among various peoples of color), the wealth gap has been growing. In *Black Wealth, White Wealth: A New Perspective on Racial Inequality*, Melvin Oliver and Thomas Shapiro (1995) argue that wealth is a more significant determinant of success than income:

> Command over resources inevitably anchors a conception of life chances. While resources theoretically imply both income and wealth, the reality for most families is that income supplies the necessities of life, while wealth represents a kind of "surplus" resource available for improving life chances, providing further opportunities, securing prestige, passing status along to one's family, and influencing the political process. (p. 32)

I have to conclude that inherited money is a means to perpetuate the racial divide in the United States. I don't believe that my grandmother consciously intended this when she wrote her will; she did what most people do, which is to pass their wealth on to their living relatives in the spirit of generosity. Of course, she could have given all of her money away to people more deserving than I, but that would have been unusual, and I am sure that there would have been many people advising her against doing so. What I want to emphasize here is the racial impact of her decision and the decisions of many well-intended White people like her.

# How Have I Benefited From Federal Policies of Racial Discrimination at the Time of My Birth in 1950?

I was born on January 4, 1950, and spent my entire childhood, until I left for college, in Ridgewood, New Jersey. Ridgewood was known then as a "bedroom community." Located about 20 miles west of New York City, it was considered a desirable community for families in which the father commuted to work in Manhattan. During my childhood, Ridgewood was overwhelming White, middle to upper class, and Protestant.

After graduating from the U.S. Military Academy (West Point) and serving in the Pacific in World War II (WWII), my father held a variety of jobs in sales and management. (At West Point, his class was intentionally all White except for a single Black man; according to my father, his White classmates never spoke to their Black classmate for the entire 4 years they studied and lived together.) Although my father never made a great deal of money, he and my mom provided a comfortable home and always saved money. My mom helped her mother teach weekly classes in ballroom dancing, a small business that my mom took over some years later. For the most part, however, she was a home-maker and the person responsible for managing the family budget while my dad worked days and sometimes weekends and nights. We lived in a single-family house that my mom and dad purchased before I was born and lived in for the rest of their lives.

At first glance, this brief sketch of my background may look like the story of many middle-class Baby Boomers raised in the suburbs. But racism played some key roles here. Racially discriminatory federal policies impacted us dur-ing the 1950s and 1960s in ways that increased our economic opportunities and material standard of living. This process happened in at least three ways: My parents' ability to get a Veterans Administration (VA) mortgage when they bought their house, and my father's ability to get a job, especially after the war, were enhanced by their being White; the value of their house increased because of federal policies that explicitly supported the growth of White suburbs such as Ridgewood at the expense of Black urban areas; and my chances of getting into a "good" college were enhanced by living in White (and middle- to upper-class Protestant) Ridgewood.

## GI Benefits

As a WWII veteran, my father was entitled to a variety of benefits through the GI Bill. The only one he directly used, however, was the VA mortgage program. In 1947, he and my mother bought their house in Ridgewood for $10,500 with a VA mortgage of $7,500. Although the benefits of the GI Bill were, theoret-ically, available to all returning veterans, it was White veterans who principal-ly benefited from the GI Bill due to racial discrimination. In "How Did Jews Become White Folks?," Karen Brodkin Sacks (1998) writes,

> The GI Bill of Rights, as the 1944 Serviceman's Readjustment Act was known, was arguably the most massive affirmative action program in US history....GI benefits . . . included priority in jobs—that is, preferential hiring, although no one objected to it then—financial support during the job search; small loans for starting up businesses; and, most important, low-interest home loans and educational benefits....I call it affirmative action because it was aimed at and disproportionately helped male, Euro-origin GIs.
>      . . . the military, the Veterans' Administration, the U.S. Employment Service, and the Federal Housing Administration (FHA) effectively denied African-American GIs access to their benefits and to the new educational, occupational, and residential opportunities....African-American soldiers were disproportionately given dishonorable

discharges, which denied them veterans' rights under the GI Bill. Thus between August and November 1946, 21 percent of white soldiers and 39 percent of black soldiers were dishonorably discharged. those who did get an honorable discharge then faced (racial discrimination in) the Veterans' Administration and the U.S. Employment Service. (pp. 88–92)

My father never asked for or received any financial support through the GI Bill during his search for employment after the war, but I believe that he was, inadvertently, the beneficiary of racial-based (and gender-based) discrimination after the war. As a veteran and West Point graduate, he was able to land a variety of jobs in sales and management at a time when Black servicemen were having difficulty finding jobs in a wartime and postwar environment of explicit racial hostility in both the South and the North. In the South, the number of lynchings actually increased during the war; in 1946, there were White riots against Blacks across the region, and there were the ever-present laws mandating racial segregation. In the North in 1943, there were anti-Black race riots in several large northern cities and widespread racial discrimination in access to jobs. (At the same time, women of all races, but mostly White women, were being encouraged, and sometimes forced, out of the factory jobs they had held during the war and into unpaid domestic work as wives and mothers or low-paid service and clerical work.)

Regarding the issue of employment discrimination, Karen Brodkin Sachs (1998) writes,

> . . . black veterans did not receive much employment information and the offers they did receive were for low-paid and menial jobs. African-Americans were also less likely than whites, regardless of GI status, to gain new jobs commensurate with their wartime jobs, and they suffered more heavily....In one survey of 50 cities, the movement of blacks into peacetime employment was found to be lagging far behind that of white....In San Francisco in 1948, Black Americans had dropped back halfway to their pre-war employment status. (p. 92)

## Federal Subsidies

In addition to access to jobs and a mortgage, my mother, father, and I benefited from racial discrimination after the war in the form of federal policies that supported the growth of suburbs at the expense of urban areas. Suburbs were predominantly White, middle and upper class, and Protestant, whereas urban areas were more likely to be the home of African and Asian Americans, people of Eastern and Southern European descent, Jewish people, and poor people. Because Ridgewood was a New York City suburb, its residents were the beneficiaries of federal subsidies that made the town "attractive" and, over time, increased property values. Regarding these subsidies, Oliver and Shapiro (1995) write,

> The suburbanization of America was principally financed and encouraged by actions of the federal government, which supported suburban growth from the 1930's through the 1960's by way of taxation, transportation, and housing policy....[T]ransportation policy (for example) encouraged freeway construction and subsidized cheap fuel and mass-produced automobiles. These factors made living on the outer edges of cities both affordable and relatively convenient. (p. 16).

The house that my parents bought for $10,500 in 1948 was sold in 2005 for $650,000. Some of the increase in value is due to my parents' sweat equity in the house, and some of the increase is due to appreciation of property values. It seems to me that this is not an unusually high rate of appreciation for a 50-year investment; there are probably areas of the country where housing values have increased much more. I suggest, however, that a comparable investment by a Black family living in, say, Newark, New Jersey, would be worth far less today, assuming, of course, that this family could have even obtained a mortgage on a house in Newark in 1950. I believe that the increase in the value of their house from $10,500 to $250,000 has to be seen in the context of racism, as well as classism and anti-Semitism: Part of what made Ridgewood "attractive" was its identity as a White, middle- to upper-class Protestant community. Ridgewood's attractiveness was built, in part, on federal subsidies.

## Living in a "Good" Neighborhood

Finally, I believe that I have directly benefited from racism (and classism) through the perception, and perhaps reality, that communities such as Ridgewood, New Jersey, had a "good" school system that produced "good" students worthy of attending "good" colleges. Because of the financing of the school system through property taxes, the White, middle- and upper-class residents of the community could provide more than adequate financial support for public education. In addition, racial- and class-based prejudice on the part of college admissions officers undoubtedly supported the belief that students like myself, who had attended Ridgewood High School, were better students than, say, students who had attended a public high school in Newark.

In 1967, as a senior in high school, I applied to and was accepted at Brown University, a prestigious private university in the Ivy League. Although I had high grades and test scores and I worked hard on my application, I believe that my acceptance to Brown was enhanced simply by my growing up in Ridgewood. If it hadn't been for my grandmother's savings—she helped my parents pay for my tuition—I might not have attended Brown or any other private college. Having a degree from Brown has certainly opened doors for me that might otherwise be closed.

## How Have I Benefited From the Exclusion of People of Color From Participation in Most Institutions of Society?

I bought my first house in Denver in 1978 for $25,000. The house was located in what we politely called a "transitional neighborhood," which meant that it was undergoing gentrification: a predominantly African-American and Hispanic community where young, White, middle-class professionals were buying inexpensive property, moving in, and hoping to realize some future profit. I easily qualified for a mortgage of $23,750; I paid $750 down and $750 closing costs. Getting a second loan to buy the vacant lot next door and do extensive remodeling was also easy. When I sold the house 6 years later, in a period of economic growth, I made a profit of $30,000, which subsequently became the down payment for another home in Cambridge, Massachusetts. It's true that some of the profit I realized was due to sweat equity—the many hours I put into remodeling—and some of the profit was due to my luck at buying and selling at the right time. But my ability to borrow money and then realize profit from the sale of the house has to be seen in the context of White privilege.

First of all, I was able to get a Federal Housing Administration (FHA) mortgage. The FHA has a long history, beginning in 1934, of racial discrimination in deciding who gets loans and therefore which communities benefit from government support. For example, until 1949, the FHA explicitly recommended the use of restrictive covenants out of the belief that property values would decline if racial segregation was not maintained. Regarding these recommendations, Oliver and Shapiro (1995) write,

> The Underwriting Manual openly stated that "if a neighborhood is to retain stability, it is necessary that properties shall continue to be occupied by the same social and racial classes" and further recommended that "subdivision regulations and suitable

restrictive covenants are the best way to ensure such neighborhood stability." . . . While exact figures regarding the FHA's discrimination against blacks are not available, data by county show a clear pattern of "redlining" in central city counties and abundant loan activity in suburban counties. (p. 18)

But racial bias isn't limited to FHA loans and isn't just historical. There is every reason for me to believe that my skin color was a factor in my obtaining a second loan from a local bank; the existence of racial discrimination in bank lending is well established. Again, Oliver and Shapiro (1995) state:

> A 1991 Federal Reserve study of 6.4 million home mortgage applications by race and income confirmed suspicions of bias in lending by reporting a widespread and systemic pattern of institutional discrimination in the nation's banking system. This study disclosed that commercial banks rejected black applicants twice as often as whites nationwide. In some cities, like Boston, Philadelphia, Chicago, and Minneapolis, it reported a more pronounced pattern of minority loan rejections, with blacks being rejected three times more often than whites. (p. 19)

What might have been the outcome if there had been racial equality in access to home loans both before and during the period of time I owned this house in Denver? Presumably, rates of home ownership and property values in this African-American and Hispanic community would have been higher, making it more difficult for me to buy a home at such a low price. There would have been more competition for loans and presumably less money available to me for borrowing. A more stable community with higher levels of home ownership and less speculation might have meant a smaller profit at the time of sale. Theoretically, I might not have been able to buy this house at all if it weren't for policies of racial preference that benefited me.

## How Do I Benefit Now From the Economic Exploitation of People of Color?

In addition to the ways that I have benefited and continue to benefit from historical patterns of racism, I believe I benefit today from racism in at least two ways: as a consumer and as an investor.

As a consumer, there are many products I purchase that are produced by people of color working for low wages for companies operating both in and outside the United States. The result is that I pay lower prices than I would have if these workers were paid a fair wage based on the value they are adding to the product. And it's not as if these products are marginally profitable; management and owners are often making substantial profits on the products that I buy.

Several examples of products come to mind. The chicken industry, concentrated in the Southeast United States, employs high numbers of African-American, Caribbean-American, and Latin-American workers to process chickens; companies in the industry are known for paying low wages, union busting, and maintaining unsafe work environments. Service workers in hotels and restaurants are increasingly people of color; while there was growth during the 1990s in the number of jobs in the service sector, these jobs are typically low paid with few if any benefits. Produce from California—which is where most of the produce I consume originates—is often grown and picked by migrant workers and their children from Central America; the illegal status of many of these workers allows growers to pay low wages and provide substandard housing.

In the United States, companies have avoided paying fair wages by moving operations to regions of the country where there is high unemployment, an abundance of low-skilled workers, and little or no union organizing. Or companies have simply set up operations or contracted out work in countries where wages are low, unemployment is high, and there are few, if any, laws protecting workers. For example, the components for many electronic devices, such as personal computers, telephones, and stereo equipment, are assembled by workers in the Third World using toxic materials in unsafe conditions but marketed and sold by U.S. corporations using familiar trademarks. Much of the clothing in retail stores in the United States is produced in Southeast Asia by extremely low-paid workers, including children, sometimes in sweatshop environments.

When it comes to making investments, I have also profited from racism. Over the past 20 years, I invested my savings and the money I inherited from my grandmother in a variety of ways: certificate of deposits (CDs) in local banks, U.S. stock mutual funds, individual stocks, bonds, international funds, revolving loan funds, and money market accounts. Although I have chosen some investments that are considered socially responsible—from mutual funds that screen their stock picks to low dividend-paying revolving loan funds that help develop affordable housing—I certainly profited from the run-up in the domestic stock market during the 1990s. The mutual funds I hold include corporations producing and selling their products and services in both the United States and abroad.

In an effort to maximize stock value and thus increase shareholder satisfaction, many corporations have gone to great lengths to cut back on expenses, particularly manual labor costs. Although maximizing profits may be considered a fundamental rule of doing business in a capitalist system, many corporations have done so in a way that is particularly damaging to the communities in which they do business and the employees at the lowest levels in the hierarchy. Executives, and the shareholders in these corporations, made a lot of money in the past decade, whereas working-class people of color (and Whites) have seen no growth, or even decline, in their real income. In cases where corporations have sent jobs overseas (and hired people of color at extremely low wages) or contracted out work to nonunion shops, workers have lost jobs and seen their communities devastated. When corporations have pulled out of communities, they have done little to repair the damage.

I believe that the increase in the value of the domestic stock mutual funds that I hold is due, in part, to these corporate decisions. Using low-paid workers in Southeast Asia and Latin America to gain profit for mostly White people in the United States is the same kind of racism that motivated Europeans to trade arms for slaves in the 19th century; it is the same kind of racism that led to U.S. military involvement and support for right-wing dictators in Latin America as a way to protect U.S. investments in fruit production. It is racism when U.S.-based corporations exploit the resources of people of color, and I, and many other White people in the United States, reap the financial rewards of this exploitation.

# White People's Personal Reactions to My Comments Here

When I have talked with other people about the ideas in this chapter, in general, people of color have seen the truth in what I am saying. A few White people have also agreed with my analysis, even if they disagree with some of the details. But for most White people, the question I have asked myself—"How have my family and I benefited from racism?"—seems outlandish.

I acknowledge that some of my conclusions are speculative; I have no doubt that some of my analysis is faulty. And some White people reading this may decide that there is no similarity between my life and theirs, and that my conclusions have no relevance for them because I have more privilege than they do. I'm sure that's true in many cases. At the same time, there are many Baby Boomers who have or will soon have more wealth than I do. I think that my experience is instructive because I am not very wealthy by the standards of who is considered wealthy in the United States today. Instead, I think it's reasonable to consider my situation somewhat normal for many White, male, middle-class Baby Boomers.

Let me address one common response to what I have written here: The reason that White people like myself have been able to accumulate assets is simply due to our hard work. It is true that I have, at times in my life, worked hard. However, many poor and working-class people, both White and of color, have worked equally hard, if not harder, without being able to accumulate assets, through no fault of their own.

The truth is that luck has played an enormous role in my life, beginning with the luck of being born White, male, into a middle-class family with the chance to inherit some money from my grandparents. Of course, if I hadn't taken advantage of all the opportunities presented to me, things would probably have turned out quite differently for me. Said another way, I *have* worked hard for what I have, AND I believe that it's important to put hard work in the context of race, gender, and class.

Let me give a concrete of how I have "worked for what I have" and, at the same time, have not had to "work for what I have." The money I inherited from my grandmother in 1993—$125,000—was worth approximately $200,000 just 5 years later and probably worth double that amount by 2008. This increase is due to several factors, two of which I can claim some responsibility for, four of which I can't. I did decide to save all of the money, investing some of it in the stock market. I had been careful up to that point in my life to spend only what I had, so that my personal debt was limited to a modest mortgage payment on my home. That meant I didn't need to use the inheritance for paying off debts. I'll claim some responsibility for being frugal, even though my mother was an expert at frugality, and I must have learned some of it from her.

But it is also true that my ability to be debt-free is due, in part, to my status as a White, middle-class male with formal education. I can't claim responsibility for that; that status is largely an accident of birth. Connected to that status is the fact that my parents were able to provide for themselves, and so I did not bear the financial burden of supporting them, as is the case with many working-class families and people of color. Nor can I lay any claim to the rise in the stock market and my luck of being in the right place at the right time. Most important, I did nothing to get an inheritance from my grandmother; it was her generosity that helped create my wealth. So for someone like myself to attribute success simply to "hard work" is half-truth at best.

Rather than dismissing my conclusions or spending energy finding fault with my analysis, my wish is that White readers see themselves reflected in my story, find that my analysis does make some sense, and ask themselves the similar questions to the ones I have. For those White people who have thought of racism as a distant, abstract concept that applies to laws and institutions, my hope is that some of what I have written has brought racism home.

If we are serious about racial equality and justice in the United States, then there is much work to be done. A first and important step is that individual White people explore the continuing legacy of racism and how we continue to profit from racism. We can then take the material capital we've gained from White privilege and "spend" this capital in the service of racial justice and reconciliation. This could take many forms: supporting activist organizations, educating other White people, supporting community-based organizations of color, becoming activists ourselves, voting for political leaders who actively support racial justice, challenging media personalities who perpetuate racism, and making careful decisions about consumption and investing. One recent and powerful example of White people spending the material and social capital from their White privilege is "Traces of the Trade," a film by Katrina Browne and the DeWolf family of Rhode Island, documenting how the family profited from the slave trade. In a book I cowrote with Emmett Schaefer and Harry Brod, *White Men Challenging Racism*, we profiled the lives of 35 ordinary White men who work on a daily basis for racial justice.

## Acknowledgments

As I've thought and written about privilege and my own family's experience with privilege, I received support, comments, and helpful criticism from family and friends, including my parents, Joan and Pat Thompson; and friends, Harry Brod, Patti DeRosa, Emmett Schaefer, and Paul Marcus. My understanding of racism has been profoundly influenced by Wekesa Olatunji Madzimoyo, Valerie Batts, and Althea Smith. An early draft of this chapter was much improved by comments by Loretta Williams, Rita Hardiman, and Joe Barndt. Thanks to all of you. Finally, I want to acknowledge the generosity of my grandmother, Viola Lavendol Austin, whose financial support has given me the luxury of time to think and write about privilege.

# References

Oliver, M., & Shapiro, T. (1995). *Black wealth, White wealth: A new perspective on racial inequality*. New York: Routledge.

Sacks, K. B. (1998). How did Jews become White folks? In S. Race, S. Gregory, & R. Sanjeh (Eds.), *Race* (pp. 78–102). New Brunswick, NJ: Rutgers University Press.

Thompson, C., Schaefer, E., & Brod, H. (Eds.) (2003). *White men challenging racism: 35 personal stories/White men on race: Power, privilege, and the shaping of cultural consciousness*. Durham, NC: Duke University Press.

# · 1 5 ·

# The Myth and Math of Affirmative Action

GOODWIN LIU

With the arrival of spring, thousands of high school and college seniors have been anxiously checking the mail for word from the nation's most prestigious universities.

Although some envelopes are thick with good news, most are thin and disappointing. For many White applicants, the disappointment will become bitterness if they suspect the reason for their rejection was affirmative action. But such suspicions, in all likelihood, are misplaced.

Affirmative action is widely thought to be unfair because it benefits minority applicants at the expense of more deserving Whites. Yet this perception tends to inflate the cost beyond its real proportions. Although it is true that affirmative action gives minority applicants a significant boost in selective admissions, it is not true that most White applicants would fare better if elite schools eliminated the practice. Understanding why is crucial to separating fact from fiction in the national debate over affirmative action.

Any day now, a federal appeals court in Cincinnati will issue a decision in a major test lawsuit challenging the use of race as a factor in selective admissions. In that case, the University of Michigan denied admission in 1995 to a White undergraduate applicant named Jennifer Gratz. Charging reverse discrimination, Gratz said, "I knew of people accepted to Ann Arbor who were less qualified, and my first reaction when I was rejected was, 'Let's sue.'"

The Michigan case will likely end up at the Supreme Court. If it does, Gratz will try to follow in the footsteps of Allan Bakke, a rejected White applicant who won admission in 1978 to the University of California at Davis' medical school after convincing the high court that the school's policy of reserving 16 of 100 seats each year for minority students was unconstitutional. For many Americans, the success of Bakke's lawsuit has long highlighted what is unfair about affirmative action.

Giving minority applicants a significant advantage causes deserving White applicants to lose out. But to draw such an inference in Bakke's case—or in the case of the vast majority of rejected White applicants—is to indulge in what I call "the causation fallacy." There's no doubt, based on test scores and grades, that Bakke was a highly qualified applicant. Justice Lewis Powell, who authored the decisive opinion in the case, observed that Bakke's Medical College Admission Test (MCAT) scores placed him in the top tier of test-takers, whereas the average scores of the quota beneficiaries in 1974 placed them in the bottom third. Likewise, his science grade point average (GPA) was 3.44 on a 4.0 scale, compared with a 2.42 average for the special admittees, and his overall GPA was similarly superior. Given these numbers, the only reason for Bakke's rejection was the school's need to make room for less qualified minority applicants, right?

Wrong. Although Justice Powell pointed out that minority applicants were admitted with grades and test scores much lower than Bakke's, he did not discuss what I found to be the most striking data that appeared in his opinion: Bakke's grades and scores were significantly higher than the average for the regular admittees. In other words, his academic qualifications were better than those of the majority of applicants admitted outside the racial quota. So why didn't he earn 1 of the 84 regular places?

It is clear that the medical school admitted students not only on the basis of grades and test scores, but on other factors relevant to the study and practice of medicine, such as compassion, communication skills, and commitment to research. Justice Powell's opinion does not tell us exactly what qualities the regular admittees had that Bakke lacked. But it notes that the head of the admissions committee, who interviewed Bakke, found him "rather limited in his approach" to medical problems and thought he had "very definite opinions which were based more on his personal viewpoints than upon a study of the total problem."

Whatever Bakke's weaknesses were, there were several reasons, apart from affirmative action, that might have led the medical school to reject his application. Grades and test scores do not tell us the whole story. Of course, affirmative action did lower Bakke's chance of admission. But by how much? One way to answer this question is to compare Bakke's chance of admission had he competed for all 100 seats in the class with his chance of admission competing for the 84 seats outside of the racial quota. To simplify, let's assume that none of the special applicants would have been admitted ahead of any regular candidate.

In 1974, Bakke was 1 of 3,109 regular applicants to the medical school. With the racial quota, the average likelihood of admission for regular applicants was 2.7% (84 divided by 3,109). With no racial quota, the average likelihood of admission would have been 3.2% (100 divided by 3,109). So the quota increased the average likelihood of rejection from 96.8% to 97.3%.

To be sure, Bakke was not an average applicant. Only one sixth of regular applicants (roughly 520) received an interview. But even among these highly qualified applicants, eliminating the racial quota would have increased the average rate of admission from 16% (84 divided by 520) to only 19% (100 divided by 520). Certainly a few more regular applicants would have been admitted were it not for affirmative action. But Bakke, on receiving his rejection letter, had no reason to believe he would have been among the lucky few.

In fact, Bakke applied in both 1973 and 1974, and, according to evidence in the lawsuit, he did not even make the waiting list in either year. The statistical pattern in Bakke's case is not an anomaly. It occurs in any selection process in which the applicants who do not benefit from affirmative action greatly outnumber those who do.

Recent research confirms this point. Using 1989 data from a representative sample of selective schools, former university presidents William Bowen and Derek Bok showed in their 1998 book, *The Shape of the River*, that eliminating racial preferences would have increased the likelihood of admission for White undergraduate applicants from 25% to only 26.5%.

The Mellon Foundation, which sponsored the study, provided me with additional data to calculate admission rates by SAT score. If the schools in the Bowen/Bok sample had admitted applicants with similar SAT scores at the same rate regardless of race, the chance of admission for White applicants would have increased by one percentage point or less at scores of 1300 and above, by three to four percentage points at scores from 1150 to 1299, and by four to seven percentage points at scores below 1150.

It is true that Black applicants were admitted at much higher rates than White applicants with similar grades and test scores. But that fact does not prove that affirmative action imposes a substantial disadvantage on White applicants. The extent of the disadvantage depends on the number of Blacks and Whites in the applicant pool. Because the number of Black applicants to selective institutions is relatively small, admitting them at higher rates does not significantly lower the chance of admission for the average individual in the relatively large sea of White applicants.

In the Bowen/Bok study, for example, 60% of Black applicants scoring 1200–1249 on the SAT were admitted, compared with 19% of whites. In the 1250–1299 range, 74% of Blacks were admitted, compared with 23% of Whites. These data indicate—more so than proponents of affirmative action typically acknowledge—that racial preferences give minority applicants a substantial advantage. But eliminating affirmative action would have increased the admission rate for Whites from 19% to only 21% in the 1200–1249 range and from 23% to only 24% in the 1250–1299 range.

These figures show that rejected White applicants have every reason not to blame their misfortune on affirmative action. In selective admissions, the competition is so intense that even without affirmative action, the overwhelming majority of rejected White applicants still wouldn't be admitted. Still, isn't it true that minority applicants are admitted at rates up to three times higher than White applicants with similar SAT scores? Isn't that unfair?

To answer that question, it's important to observe that racial preferences are not the only preferences that cause different groups of applicants with similar test scores to be admitted at different rates. Geographic, athletic, and alumni preferences also weigh heavily, to the detriment of applicants such as Jennifer Gratz at Michigan. Gratz hailed from a Detroit suburb, not from a rural area or the inner city. She was not a star athlete. And her working-class parents were high school graduates, not University of Michigan alumni.

Yet preferences for athletes, although occasionally criticized, have never galvanized the kind of outrage often directed at affirmative action. Similarly, there is no organized legal campaign against geographic preferences, even though where one grows up is as much an accident of circumstance as one's skin color. Neither Gratz nor her lawyers at the Washington-based Center for Individual Rights have publicly denounced alumni preferences, much less launched a moral crusade against them.

Such preferences reflect institutional interests that are unrelated to an applicant's grades or test scores. But the same is true of affirmative action when it is used to enhance educational diversity. The question, then, is not whether unequal treatment is unfair as a general rule but whether unequal treatment based on race should be singled out for special condemnation.

As the Supreme Court said in 1954, unequal treatment based on race can inflict on members of a disfavored race "a feeling of inferiority as to their status in the community that may affect their hearts and minds in a way unlikely ever to be undone." But social stigma is not the complaint pressed by White applicants such as Bakke or Gratz. Despite 30 years of affirmative action, White students continue to dominate most of the nation's best colleges and all of the top law and medical schools. Against this backdrop, not even the most ardent foe of affirmative action would say that it stamps White applicants with a badge of racial inferiority. Indeed, just as athletic and geographic preferences do not denigrate applicants who are uncoordinated or suburban, affirmative action is not a policy of racial prejudice.

For White applicants, the unfairness of affirmative action lies not in its potential to displace or stigmatize but in its potential to stereotype. Minority applicants are not the only ones who contribute to educational diversity. Were a school to use race as its sole "plus" factor in admissions, then White applicants could legitimately complain that the school failed to take into account nonracial attributes essential to genuine educational diversity.

Putting the complaint in these terms is an important first step toward rethinking the conventional view that a race-conscious admissions policy pits Whites against minorities in a zero-sum game. Instead of attacking affirmative action, White applicants such as Jennifer Gratz might do better to urge top schools committed to educational diversity to place a higher premium on first-generation college attendance or growing up in a blue-collar home. Ironically, the stories of affirmative action's "victims" could spur America's colleges to further widen the elite circles of educational opportunity. That would be a result students of any color could applaud.

# Note

\* Reprinted with permission. Originally published as Liu, G. (2002, April 14). The myth and math of affirmative action. *Washington Post*, p. B01. Available at http://www.washingtonpost.com/wp-dyn/articles/A41620–2002Apr12.html

# Reference

Bowen, W. G., & Bok, D. (1998). *The shape of the river: Long-term consequences of considering race in college and university admissions.* Princeton, NJ: Princeton University Press.

# · 1 6 ·

# Toward an Informed and Transparent Philosophy of Racial Diversity for Colleges of Education

Sherick Hughes & Dale Snauwaert

When colleges of education prepare for National Council for Accreditation of Teacher Education (NCATE) accreditation, diversity commonly emerges with the assumption that all faculty, staff, and students understand its meaning and its connection to their own self-interests. This assumption is dangerous. Even after decades of study in the area, we were challenged positively by members of a Minority Recruitment and Retention Subcommittee at the University of Toledo to offer a robust response to the question: "Why is diversity important?" We[1] later took the question one step further to ask more specifically, "Why is it important to work toward an informed and transparent philosophy of racial diversity in colleges of education?" The following commentary offers what we believe to be a sound response to diversity education supporters and critics alike. There are at least four tenets of the democratic ideal supporting our pursuit of an informed and transparent philosophy of racial diversity: (a) checks and balances of the law, (b) optimal decision making, (c) social justice, and (d) peace.

# Checks and Balances of the Law in Colleges of Education

Checks and balances of individual rights and societal ideals can potentially benefit not only local individuals and families but also learning communities at large. Because majority and underrepresented families depend on the educators we educate, our universities/school communities can be only as strong as past, current, and future teacher education faculty, staff, and student members— members who are equipped ideally to deal with the challenges and build on the strengths of diversity in our society of learners. The ultimate task of checking and balancing the diversity components of teacher education is to enhance the college of education climate in a manner that requires all of us to revisit and critique notions such as political correctness. This part of our education may allow us to extend ourselves to address how the strings of liberation in our democracy tie each child to our own.

An informed and transparent philosophy of racial diversity might also address the law or legal tenet from a democratic rights and responsibilities purview. Individual families have the right to separate life, liberty, and the pursuit of happiness so long as that separate pursuit does not encroach on the democratic rights of others. Through this philosophy, we might help preservice, novice, and veteran educators and teacher/administrator educators revisit the rules and norms that govern political correctness and provide a platform from which we may argue for a democratic ideal to ensure that numerical and ethnic minority rights aren't being ignored, forgotten, or discredited. In the end, the checks and balances of the law bring us to one level of problem finding/solving without taking us to higher order thinking and feeling levels necessary for the democratic ideals of optimal decision making, social justice, and peace.

# Optimal Decision Making in Colleges of Education

Horticulturists use the term *variegation* to describe the blending of various patches of plants and flowers for expanding the possibilities that optimize diverse beauty and utility. Each flora's brilliance is enhanced by its counterpart. Recent research supports the notion that diverse human groups also render the spoils of variegation and socialized hybrid vigor in the realm of decision making and problem finding/solving. When working to seek and resolve problems, diverse human groups (ethnicity, gender, social class, social status, religion, etc.) excel beyond homogenous groups in terms of final product excellence irrespective of the degree of complexity of the problem or pending decision.

In 2003 and 2005, recent MacArthur Fellow, Dr. Jennifer Richeson, and her colleagues' social neuroscience research suggested that high ethnocentric bias strains cognitive ability. This study involved, (a) pretesting of participants for high/low Black ethnic bias, (b) subjecting participants to speaking briefly with a Black experimenter, (c) subjecting participants to a test of cognitive ability, and (d) comparing cognitive ability test results of participants pretested for high/low Black ethnic bias. Results indicate that participants pretested with high Black ethnic bias performed more poorly on Stroop cognitive ability tests when the stimulus (a Black experimenter) of their bias was present in the testing situation. Researchers conclude that participants with high Black ethnic bias spent so much cognitive energy toward coping with their biases that it was detrimental to their ability to maximize their cognitive potential.

Steele and Aronson (1995) explore life from the target's perspective to understand how stereotype threat informs us. To counter ethnocentric bias, for example, participants may need a frequency and intensity of positive educational experiences and expectations to overcome mental barriers linked to being part of a stigmatized group (Steele & Aronson, 1995). These research findings suggest that the lack of positive, frequent, and intense exposure to diverse appraisals can hinder our ability to complete cognitive tasks at our highest potential. Moreover, we might learn from the degree that our ethnocentric bias influences our cognitive ability to give or receive information from the object of our biases in the classroom.

University of Michigan research in the new millennium (Page, 2007) suggests that group think may get in the way when homogenous groups represent similar backgrounds and thereby limited variation on ideas about how to proceed when given a difficult task. Homogenous groups tend to fall more often into the trap of structure and agency as described in the pioneering work of Anthony Giddens in 1979. In short, Giddens alludes to the point that our decision making is only as "good" as the structures we create lets it be, and our human agency (ability to act) is limited by how we learn and teach each other and tell ourselves to act within the structure. Perhaps revisiting diversity in colleges of education might also move educators to take leadership responsibilities to form diverse co-equal community partnerships where they are more likely to invite local family members to the table as legitimate authorities and actually build some generative knowledge that may transcend the incessant challenges still facing diverse colleges (Tanaka, 2003). An informed and transparent philosophy of racial diversity in colleges of education can promote the type of diverse, co-equal partners that Page (2007) and others connect to working collaboratively toward optimal decision making.

## Social Justice in Colleges of Education

The following comment by John Dewey frames the central issue of social justice and democracy:

> schools *do* follow and reflect the social "order" that exists . . . accordingly, the problem is not whether the schools *should* participate in the production of future society (since they do so anyway) but whether they should do it blindly and irresponsibly or with the maximum possible courageous intelligence and responsibility. (cited in Tozer et al., 1993, p. 121)

Educational reflection and deliberation, however, require a normative frame of reference. Human beings interpret and understand experience, including values and moral and political principles, through frames of reference. We think, choose, and value within a context of frameworks of discourse and understanding (Lakoff, 2002).

It has long been recognized that education is contingent on the specific social and political organization of the society within which it is situated (Dewey, 1916; Freire, 1970; Gutmann, 1999; Jaeger, 1953; Plato, 1979). For example, Aristotle maintains that citizenship and civic education are logical expressions of the constitution (*politeia*) of the society (Aristotle & Everson, 1988). The *politeia* is not merely the formal juridical structure of the legal system. It comprises the basic structure of values that define society's view of the world (Aristotle & Everson, 1988; Jaeger, 1943; Karier, 1986; Marrou, 1982).

Democracy, understood as not only a political system but more fundamentally as a way of life grounded in specific values and principles, historically constitutes the *politeia* of the United States. The United States possesses a democratic self-identity and, in fact, claims to be a beacon of democracy for the world. Normatively, democracy should be adopted as a frame of reference because it is the ideal most consistent with human well-being and flourishing (MacPherson, 1973; Snauwaert, 1993). The alternative would entail the adoption of *intrinsic superiority*/inferiority, from which follow the principle of *unequal consideration* of the goods and interests of persons *as well as* the Platonic ideal of *unequal qualifications* to participate based on superior expertise/knowledge—

leading to unequal voting, hegemony, and exclusion—would apply (Dahl, 2000).

Democracy is an appealing and powerful normative frame of reference. As Dewey suggests, "unless education has some of frame of reference it is bound to be aimless, lacking a unified objective. The necessity for a frame of reference must be admitted. There exists in our country such a frame of reference. It is called democracy" (cited in Tozer, 1993, p. 125). At the heart of democracy are the values of moral equality and liberty, understood as an equal right to self-determination. Self-determination requires that there should be careful reflection on and rational deliberation concerning social values and, in turn, the imperatives of justice. As Amy Gutmann (1999) puts it, democracy as a frame of reference requires "conscious social reproduction." John Dewey suggests: "Democracy also means voluntary choice, based on an intelligence that is the outcome of free association and communication with others. It means a way of living together in which mutual and free consultation rule instead of force..." (cited in Tozer, 1993, p. 125).

Democracy, understood as not only a political system but more fundamentally as a way of life grounded in specific values and principles, provides a powerful point of reference. In the context of a democracy, social justice involves validation of the rights of others, a commitment to working and learning with others, a commitment to safety while others' rights our in our hands, and a confidentiality when others trust us enough to share sensitive and volatile information. In short, the question of social justice becomes "what do we need, and do we need more or less of it to meet or exceed the same ideal standards imposed upon 'others'?" Social justice regards the ability of a society to balance the individual rights with the democratic ideals, and it involves societal choices. With social justice in education, *e pluribus unum* (of the many, one) could exist as Multicultural Education pioneer James Banks (1994) suggested, with an unum that is negotiable and diverse within a goal structure that renders social justice non-negotiable. Such a social justice goal structure may provide a venue where "authentic" learning is conceptualized unequivocally as (a) learning for understanding, and (b) learning for meaningful applications involving at least the anticipation and demonstration of informed, fulfilling, and socially just choices given a polyphony of social options.

In 2001, Kevin Kumashiro argues that indeed one obstacle to social justice emerges from our own colleges of education about "others" because we tend to talk about teaching the other and teaching about the other without being critical of "othering" and without critiquing ourselves as "other." Despite our noblest efforts, social justice may continue to slip out of our grasp in colleges of education without a comprehensive informed and transparent philosophy of racial diversity. Too often, we may not even be cognizant of how we tend to (at the very least, on occasion) do what Lawrence Blum (2002) suggests in *I'm Not a Racist But...*: exaggerate differences between others, overemphasize similarities within others, perceive characteristics of others as immutable or unchangeable, and concede to beliefs in group hierarchy.

Paulo Freire describes social injustice as oppression that is replete with "othering" in the forms of victimization, racialization, sexism, disenfranchisement, and human hierarchy. Prior to being exiled for his pioneering work in 1964, Freire's literacy teams of the 1950s and 1960s taught so-called peasants and field hands of Brazil not only to read and write but to do so as a form of resistance to oppression. On being asked to return in 1979, a now internationally acclaimed Freire further pursued his work in critical pedagogy. Critical pedagogy involves teaching and learning for social justice by facilitating situations against "othering" and against seeing oneself as a "destined to be doomed" other. In his work, empowerment is encouraged through education, teacher–student relationships, dialogue, critical consciousness, and action.

To act in pursuit of the democratic ideals of social justice in light of Dewey, Kumashiro, and Freire, colleges of education can reconsider how to build on the presence of diverse families. Engaging an education of diverse families may advance social justice and anti-oppression by helping teacher leaders and administrators of schools learn to involve families in their curriculum and school management planning. In addition, this condition can work for enhancing university support systems by creating more spaces to exchange any transferable information from families about hidden rules and norms that can influence present and future college of education-to-local community relationships. It seems that one must build an informed and transparent philosophy of racial diversity into our college of education plans in order to benefit from the social justice environment that diversity might induce, support, enhance, and sustain.

## Peace in Colleges of Education

One can argue that there are at least three interdependent moral resources integral to bringing peace in colleges of education through our social justice and democratic efforts: (a) knowledge, (b) reasonableness, and (c) empathy.

Diversity is a key component of the moral resource of knowledge because of the history, experiences, and praxis that knowledge engulfs. Without the daily presence of diverse influences, our knowledge banks are incomplete, and the experiential stages to engage knowledge and praxis are based on limited vicarious teaching and learning situations.

Reasonableness relates to our ability to be open to unfamiliar ideas, experiences, and counterevidence. When we are reasonable, we are pushed to examine our own lived contradictions and to accept change when our taken-for-granted actions, beliefs, values, and knowledge is challenged in a sound and substantial fashion. At the heart of democracy is the value of liberty understood as self-determination. Self-determination requires that there should be careful reflection on and rational deliberation concerning social values and, in turn, the imperatives of justice that inform the purposes and practices of education.

An informed and transparent philosophy of racial diversity may provide more fertile ground for colleges of education to cultivate the knowledge from which reasonableness feeds. Reasonableness may take us from what I have come to describe as malignant ignorant resistance to what we conceptualize as critical conscientious resistance that is conducive to upholding the law, to optimal decision making, social justice, and peace. For example, an informed and transparent philosophy of racial diversity may help college of education members respond with more knowledge, reasonableness, and peacefulness to claims of bias and discrimination involving faculty, staff, and students. Tanaka (2003) suggests that when such a philosophy is sewn into the very fabric of the college, faculty, staff, and students demonstrate enhanced willingness and abilities to distinguish hits (perceive bias and bias is present) from misses (don't perceive bias but bias is present), false alarms (perceive bias and bias is not present), and correct rejections (don't perceive bias and bias is not present). In the book *Prejudice*, social psychologists Swim and Stangor (1998) explain that the degree to which we perceive and/or act on a hit, miss, false alarm, or correct rejection is related to the social, psychological, emotional, and financial costs that we perceive. The estimated costs of a false alarm may greatly outweigh that of a hit for an underrepresented college member. Any threat of misses could also contribute to the pressure that prevents our ability to retain members that add to our diversity.

Being reasonable is predicated on the discovery, confirmed by cognitive science, that human beings interpret and understand experience, including ideas, through frames of reference. We think within context of frameworks of discourse and understanding. We need a philosophy of diversity that allows for competing frames of reference in order to enhance and enrich rational delib-

## · 1 7 ·

# The Race for President and a Precedent for Race

## Lessons from NCLB and Bringing Race to the Top[1]

ZEUS LEONARDO

Having weathered through the Democratic race with Hillary Clinton and dispatching with Republican John McCain, Barack Obama became the 44th and first Black president of the United States. On the G.O.P. ticket, Senator John McCain was the earlier confirmed winner, having a longer period to prepare for the next round, much like an NBA team that secures the conference finals earlier than its imminent opponents in anticipation of the Finals. Compared with the older statesman, Obama is a charismatic younger candidate and the first to break the color barrier, whereas McCain would have been the oldest president if he were elected to the highest office. Obama has had to confront the race question head on, even if the most public spectacle involved another Black man in the figure of his pastor, Reverend Wright. McCain lords over Arizona, a state that fought against turning Martin Luther King, Jr.'s birthday into a holiday and where a recent initiative removes ethnic studies programs from schools and universities, bundled with retrogressive immigration policies targeting Latinos.

Race has loomed largely in the entire run up to the candidacies, and race has become an opportunity for the presidency in an unprecedented and public way. But it did not start with Obama; rather, he inherited and will likely continue it, notwithstanding the power the Oval Office holds. Many reasons were responsible for Obama's rise, such as the weakened economy. But centuries-old race relations played out once again, and each candidate responded to the racial opportunities that arose, pushing one ahead of the other and ruining the other's chances. As a master politician, Obama deployed race discourse deftly, whereas Clinton's racial innuendos were arguably in bad taste and McCain just couldn't get it together. The race for president has been settled and a precedent for race ushers education into a new era. Obama's educational platform goes by the name of "Race to the Top," which arguably gestures an ambivalent nod to the dilemma of race relations in the U.S. As No Child Left Behind faces reauthorization, it behooves educators to take stock of the racial lessons contained in the Act. What have we learned so far?

## No Child Left Behind as a Racial Text

One racial lesson that is available to President Obama and the citizenry can be found in the most sweeping federal law involving schools: No Child Left Behind (NCLB). Things are always easier in hindsight but much of this analysis was available when NCLB was in full effect. It is the task of this chapter to introduce NCLB as a racial text that has become the most significant challenge to the Obama presidency with respect to U.S. schools. Whether or not President Obama succeeds in bringing race to the top of his educational agenda is to be determined. We should be clear that a vulgar kind of color-blindness does not frame NCLB because it recognizes the four subgroups that implicate race. It is to the left of color-blind initiatives that one finds in Ward Connerly and former California Governor Pete Wilson's sponsored and half successful campaigns to erase race from official governmental transactions, such as the identity privacy act and anti-affirmative action proposition. Vulgar color-blindness is the inability to deal with the reality of race. Its contours include the following tenets:

- Race and racism are declining in significance.
- Racism is largely isolated, an exception to the rule.
- Individualizes racism as irrational and pathological.
- Individualizes success and failure.
- Blames people of color for their limitations and behaviors.
- Mainly a study of attitude and attitudinal changes, rather than actual behavior.

- Downplays institutional relations or the racialized system.
- Exaggerates racial progress.
- Emphasizes class stratification as the explanation for racism.
- Downplays the legacy of slavery and genocide.

Without explaining each 1 of the 10 tenets, color-blindness would have us forget history (both in the sense of a past and its continuity with the present), individualize racism without the benefit of a sociological understanding, and displace racial stratification with ideological explanations that obfuscate the reality of racism. The everyday expression of color-blindness assumes that slavery and genocide are legacies from long ago rather than as social facts that structure current relations. With that established, NCLB graduates to a more sophisticated form of color-blindness when it makes a casual pass at racism by naming its symptoms but not its structural causes. That is, NCLB recognizes the problems of race, such as uneven achievement among the races. It should be applauded for having the gumption to go this far, which makes racial patterns plain enough to see from the data gathered through the act's provisions. Under NCLB, race and racial inequality become a public, rather than a hidden, problem. This is progress; at the same time, it is not progressive enough. In NCLB, racism appears as happenstance because it allows the opportunity for educators and researchers to showcase racial patterns without the capacity to link them to racial relations of power, which is outside the purview of NCLB. Moreover, it makes the problem of White privilege and domination quite invisible. The following analysis attempts to uncover these color-blind and White referents of NCLB in order to realize its ostensive goals of leaving no child behind. It does not assert that NCLB is, by and large, better or worse than its predecessors. Rather, it places the act squarely within the context of its creation: the color-blind era. There are several lessons gained from placing NCLB within its historical context.

It is from within the historical condition of color-blindness that NCLB originated. Therefore, it is a symptom of our times. When NCLB received overwhelming support from both Democrats and Republicans in 2001, it was hailed as the most sweeping educational reform since the original Elementary and Secondary Education Act 40 years ago. The name was adopted from the Children's Defense Fund: "Leave No Child Behind" (Welner &Weitzman, 2005). Noble in its ostensive intent, NCLB reached across the political aisle when it recognized a pattern whereby certain groups of students were not succeeding compared with their counterparts. It sought out these groups and

enacted a federal mandate from a political party that usually favors state sov-
ereignty. Although Republican history certainly shows a proclivity for states'
rights, in his two terms, President Bush supported a particular deployment of
federal action as part of nation creation, sparked by the Supreme Court's decision giving the nod to President Bush's first term. NCLB is the educational cog-
nate of the Patriot Act following the terrorist attacks on the World Trade
Center in 2001, through its emphasis on nationhood and Americanism. It was
foreshadowed by A Nation at Risk, a report commissioned by the Reagan administration in the 1980s.

Consistent with the discourse of the War on Terror, if there are any failing schools in the United States, NCLB claimed to "smoke 'em out." In contrast to previous reforms where underperforming schools were provided
resources for remediation, NCLB introduces the threat of student exit from
schools and bleeding of moneys from low-performing schools (Sunderman &
Kim, 2005). It is the educational War on Terror that will show the rest of the
globe that Americans "mean business." In fact, NCLB contains Section 9528,
or a provision allowing military recruiters access to school campuses or lose
funding (Furumoto, 2005). One might ask what the military has to do with education. As part of nation building, social institutions (what Althusser [1971]
called Ideological State Apparatuses), such as schools, have always been part
of the military project, of inculcating militaristic values and their endorsement.
With the help of NCLB, the Pentagon wanted to double Latino presence in the
armed forces to 22%, which would increase the current 60% of soldiers of color
in a nation represented by roughly 70% Whites, a veritable dark wall of protection for Whiteness. As the educational Patriot Act, NCLB sends a message
to young children regarding what it means to act like a patriot: accept the right-
ness of Whiteness.

Insofar as it is difficult to put race on the nation's official agenda, NCLB
is welcomed by progressive thinking people across the political spectrum, by
both Whites and people of color, perhaps for different reasons. Despite NCLB's
problematic racial consequences, it does not mean that people of color who supported the act are inauthentic or suffering from forms of false consciousness. It
means that NCLB exists within the constraints of Whiteness, which requires
deliberate and critical sensibilities to detect. Without these interpretive safety measures, the Whiteness of NCLB becomes a hidden referent of the federal act. This fact does not make it sinister but racial. It becomes the guiding
ideology that frames how school failure will be explained and how it should be
remedied. As Melissa Da Silva (2005) puts it, "appealing to a white-normed

commonsense highlight[s] the real danger of NCLB, that is, all the ways in which it reinforces and contributes to color-blind racism . . . the preservation of white privilege—that is, the rational, material interests . . . of American [W]hites" (EducationNews.org). In other words, Whiteness is the default ideology that guides NCLB and many other educational initiatives before it. It ensures that White interests are preserved *even when people of color are recognized* within its logic. NCLB's color-blindness does not function by virtue of excluding people of color but precisely through the way that it problematically includes them in its rationale.

NCLB overtly targets improving four subgroups of student performance: minority children, students with disabilities, poor children, and English language learners. Regarding race, it would be tempting to dub NCLB as "No Color Left Behind." In principle, it is laudable to hold schools to higher standards with a promise of academic proficiency in at least the 3 Rs (i.e., reading, writing, and arithmetic). It is about time that someone insisted on an accountability system with an attitude and considered the 4th R (i.e., race). The degradation of students of color has lasted long enough, and NCLB represents the *chutspah* that educational reformers have been waiting for. However, consistent with a racial formation analysis, with NCLB it seems that "the color line has not been erased so much as it has been redrawn" (Freeman, 2005, p. 191). Insofar as NCLB is guided by an ideology of Whiteness, it depends on the continuation of racial differences as part of a logical rather than a social outcome. In other words, ostensibly giving public schools a chance to show progress, NCLB gives Whiteness the license to declare students of color failures under a presumed-to-be fair system.

On *prima facie*, NCLB seems to be driven by a racial understanding. After all, it recognizes race. But recognizing a problem does not equate with locating the source of that problem. In other words, NCLB acknowledges the symptoms but not the causes of the achievement problem affecting children of color. It frames race as incidental ("Whites and Blacks happen to experience an achievement gap"), rather than causal ("Students experience the achievement gap because they are racialized"), to student disparities in achievement. Welner and Weitzman (2005) declare that U.S. citizens have had a love affair with individual accountability. An equal appreciation for historical accounting is missing. NCLB does not make visible the structural obstacles that children of color and their families face, such as health disparities, labor market discrimination, and the like, processes that a class analysis alone cannot unmask (Brown et al., 2003). In fact, NCLB hides these dynamics even more efficiently, tucked away in the language of tough love, neo-liberalism, and harsh sanctions. Employment discrimination disappears in the abstract individualism of NCLB, where the threat of laissez-faire market forces becomes the final stop for persistently failing schools that will finally succumb to privatization under the voucher system. Some analysts have pointed out that NCLB is an attack on public schools, showcasing their hopelessness and moribund status (Darling-Hammond, 2004, 2007). This is what Kohn (2004) calls NCLB's "clever gambit" that forces educators and families either to be against public schools or accept mediocrity. This does not suggest that if NCLB were to acknowledge structural, racial inequalities, it would succeed in eliminating them, thereby saving public schools. But their absence signals its ultimate and perhaps predictable failure—its "conciliatory nature" (Freeman, 2005, p. 196)—like the fate of many reforms squeamish about race before it. The intractability of systemic school reform should not be underestimated, and we should not pretend that it will take less than a Herculean effort, but some of the causes of school failure are not a mystery either. A nation that supports an undeclared apartheid through color-blind policies produces foreseeable results. It is difficult to be surprised when such policies do not make a dent in narrowing the achievement gap. As Gillborn (2008) argues, we do not need a conspiracy; it is worse than that. If we let schools racially function the way they do, then the results are similar to a veritable conspiracy. Again, we can hardly be surprised.

It would be quite hopeful to expect major federal or even less ambitious educational policies to address these structurally determining factors. But such expectations would be a sign of either naïveté or blind optimism. That said, from an analyst's point of view, NCLB's inability to locate educational disparities within larger relations of power does not just betray its color-blind ideology but its *reinforcement of Whiteness and the protection of White privilege.* Ultimately, it subverts its own claims to "fix the problem" because it confuses symptoms for substance, implicating it in a certain performative contradiction. It is unable to deliver its own promise even as it annunciates it. All four subgroups targeted by NCLB implicate children of color. It is a well-known fact (or a dirty little secret) that African Americans, particularly boys, are diagnosed with difficulties overrepresenting them in special education; English language learning impacts more non-Whites; and NCLB's targeting of minority children speaks for itself. The fourth category of children who live in poverty includes White children, but their Whiteness is not responsible for their poverty, but rather their class status or their position in the relations of production.

White working-class people embody the contradictions of both race and class, but NCLB does not leave them behind because they are Whites but because they are poor. One of these contradictions is showcased by poor Whites' capacity to cope with their poverty due to the consolation provided by their membership in the White race. Living an exploitative, material life, poor Whites often displace their critique of the capitalist class with animosity toward poor minorities in particular and people of color in general. This leads Roediger (1994) to suggest that poor Whites' "correct" analysis of their impoverished condition is bound up with a racial analysis; that is, their economic liberation is at once their racial emancipation. That said, and without minimizing the exploitation that poor or working-class Whites experience, their Whiteness alleviates some of their suffering through what Du Bois (1935/1998) called Whites' "public and psychological wages" (see also Roediger, 1991). In other words, poor Whites are not poor *because* they are Whites but *despite* of it. It would be a bit like arguing that if Stephen Hawking were to become prime minister of England, it is due to his physical disabilities. Rather, Hawking would have to compensate for his physical disadvantages and the prejudice against them, such as being the brightest mind on the planet. He would earn the title despite his challenges.

Poor Whites have racial advantages despite their poverty. Whites register this contradiction, and it is not possible to separate out their White identity from their class experience. Poor or working-class Whites *feel* their exploitation as concrete White people. They cannot parse out the portion of their identity that is responsible for their suffering and that for their privilege. That established, analysis is poor without a sense of causality. As Brown et al. (2003) remark, "White Americans may face difficulties in life . . . but race is not one of them" (p. 34). Structurally speaking, policy analysis must be able to trace the origins of benefits and disadvantages. Without a discourse of causality, educators confuse epiphenomena with substance, correlations with causation.

In contrast to Whites, many people of color under White supremacy are poor *because* they are racialized minorities not despite of it. We may repeat the same reasoning for Whites with disabilities, whose Whiteness is not the source of their problem unlike students of color with disabilities, whose racial identity influences their overrepresentation in special education programs. Students of color diagnosed with disabilities face at least two strikes against them. If Novak and Fuller (2003) are correct in suggesting that NCLB comes with a "diversity penalty" by punishing schools with higher populations of students of color, then the opposite must also be true insofar as NCLB comes with a Whiteness reward for mostly White schools. Because the hidden referent of

NCLB is Whiteness and its ideology is color-blind, it is tempting to dub it "No Caucasian Left Behind."

NCLB's "pull yourselves up by your own schoolstraps" mentality betrays a certain lack of appreciation for the racial conditions in which schools exist. For example, it pretends that the achievement gap is ultimately a problem of both teaching and the educational state apparatus, something that could be addressed by putting pressure on teachers to "do their job." This is why NCLB defined funding for the Act in a manner that only covers testing costs because teaching grade and subject proficiency is already a teacher's job. It does not acknowledge the resources required to provide struggling students the opportunity to excel. Although it is common that authorized funds do not match appropriate funds, NCLB's appropriation for Title I, Part A for the first 4 years (2002–2005) of its enactment shows a $21.5 billion shortfall (or 31% missing) (Welner & Weitzman, 2005). This is tantamount to providing funds to test children but not to teach them, according to Senator Kennedy. Or as Darling-Hammond (2004) observes, NCLB "ignores the important inputs of resources the enable school quality, [which] mistakes measuring schools for fixing them" (pp. 8–9). Although President Bush was right to criticize the "soft bigotry of low expectations," this funding shortfall creates what Welner and Weitzman call the "soft bigotry of low expenditures." According to one conservative estimate, total national spending on education would need to increase by $137.8 billion, more than 11 times the current Title I funding. Even if schools continue the upward trend in progress evidenced in the 1990s, one analyst calculates that schools would take more than 100 years to reach the NCLB's target (see Darling-Hammond, 2004). Even this figure is conservative if reforms fail to address the structures of racism. It might be tempting to declare NCLB a naïve attempt to reform public schools. Nothing could be further from the truth. It is a well-informed and brilliant strategy of color-blind proportions. As it stands, NCLB's color-blindness ensures that school reform will proceed only at the snail's pace of Whiteness.

## Back to the Future

We now enter the post-NCLB reform climate but have not exited the color-blind era. President Obama's answer to leaving no child behind is to encourage schools and districts to "Race to the Top" through competitive funding. Some states have been successful in securing these funds but large states, like

California, failed to do so. We have had decades of school reform sweep through the nation, all of which arguably failed to bring the issue of race to the top. The latest trials and tribulations of NCLB provide more than ample evidence about the difficult task of changing the nation's schools. As part of the neo-liberal project, NCLB may not have been neo-liberal enough. To some, this means ramping up the business-model of education. To others, it signals the inappropriate commodification of education, which is less a market adventure and more a democratic venture. The long-standing issue of race is an intimate part of this struggle. To some, the election of our first Black president foreshadows its end; to others, it is only the beginning.

These are exciting times and President Obama is poised to either keep busy with clean up (e.g., the economic recession, the Gulf oil spill, and NCLB) or forge a new path and vision for the country. It would be unfair to form different and higher expectations for the first Black president to fix the nation's ills and spills. And despite the achievement of gunning down Osama Bin Laden, neither can we ask President Obama to fix a problem he had little part in creating (e.g., the War on Terror). But hopes are high and optimism is on the rise that the States can be united for reasons other than world domination. That we live in a color-blind era begs the question: Is it a White color-blindness or a Black color-blindness? The first is a feigning of sorts for Whites have proven time and again that they enjoy their racial privilege and blindness to race goes against these pretensions. It is not blindness to color at all but, like NCLB, its very opposite: Whiteness as policy and the continuation of racial disparities. However, Dr. Martin Luther King Jr. also aspired to color-blindness, arguably an authentic vision where righting the country meant moving it to left of our racial predicament. This requires bringing race to the top of our educational agenda, if not also our national agenda. To use Obama's campaign mantra: Yes we can!

## Note

1. This chapter is based on a longer 2007 essay, "The War on Schools: NCLB, Nation Creation, and the Educational Construction of Whiteness" in *Race Ethnicity & Education*, 10(3), 261-278.

## References

Althusser, L. (1971). *Lenin and philosophy* (B. Brewster, Trans.). New York: Monthly Review Press.

Brown, M., Carnoy, M., Currie, E., et al. (2003). *White-washing race*. Berkeley: University of California Press.

Darling-Hammond, L. (2004). "Separate but equal" to "NCLB": The collision of new standards and old inequalities. In D. Meier & G. Wood (Eds.), *Many children left behind: How the No Child Left Behind Act is damaging our children and our schools* (pp. 3–32). Boston: Beacon Press.

Darling-Hammond, L. (2007). Race, inequality, and educational accountability: The irony of "No Child Left Behind." *Race Ethnicity & Education, 10*(3), 245–260.

Da Silva, M. (2005). *How is NCLB a mechanism of the American racial project?* Retrieve October 20, 2005, from http://www.educationnews.org/how-is-nclb-a -mechanism-of-the-a.htm

Du Bois, W. E. B. (1935/1998). *Black reconstruction in America, 1860–1880.* New York: The Free Press.

Freeman, J. (2005). No Child Left Behind and the denigration of race. *Equity & Excellence in Education, 38,* 190–199.

Furumoto, R. (2005). No poor child left unrecruited: How NCLB codifies and perpetuates urban school militarism. *Equity & Excellence in Education, 38,* 200–210.

Gillborn, D. (2008). *Racism and education: Coincidence or conspiracy?* New York: Routledge.

Kohn, A. (2004). NCLB and the effort to privatize public education. In D. Meier & G. Wood (Eds.), *Many children left behind: How the No Child Left Behind Act is damaging our children and our schools* (pp. 79–97). Boston: Beacon Press.

Novak, J., & Fuller, B. (2003). *Penalizing diverse schools? Similar test scores but different students bring federal sanctions.* Berkeley: Policy Analysis for California Education.

Roediger, D. (1991). *The wages of whiteness.* New York: Verso.

Roediger, D. (1994). *Towards the abolition of whiteness.* New York: Verso.

Sunderman, G., & Kim, J. (2005). The expansion of federal power and the politics of implementing the No Child Left Behind Act. *Teachers College Record, 109*(5), 1057–1085.

Welner, K., & Weitzman, D. (2005). The soft bigotry of low expenditures. *Equity & Excellence in Education, 38,* 242–248.

whole life and at a frequency of about 8 to 12 flights per year. I don't have to instruct her on what to do when she approaches the conveyor belt; she gets her bin, throws in her shoes, coat, and belt, and puts her carry-on up on the conveyor belt before waiting in front of the metal detector to receive her instructions to walk through. She knows what she's doing.

It was 7 a.m., and the airport seemed to have more employees working the morning shift than there were departing passengers. We were rushing to make our 8 a.m. flight. We passed the first level of security, where our photo IDs were cross-checked with our boarding passes. Then as we proceeded, a very tall White woman with brown hair and broad shoulders rushed toward us and addressed me before we could even reach the conveyor belt. She was suited in a TSA security personnel uniform. She requested that I remove my headscarf. I looked her straight in her pupils and said, "No I will not remove my headscarf, but you are more than welcome to pat me down or do whatever you need to do in order to make yourself feel comfortable." Surprised by my response, the TSA female employee just turned away from me without saying anything further and went right back to her post.

Without instruction, Rayanah prepared herself at the conveyor belt to walk through the metal detector. On the other side of the metal detector, the same TSA woman was waiting for me. Although I passed through the metal detector without a sounding alarm, she still asked me to step over to the side. As always, I was cooperative and nonconfrontational. She began a full body search on me in public while my daughter and four other male TSA security personnel observed. She ran her hands up and down my body while my daughter and the male TSA personnel watched. The look in my daughter's eyes was heartbreaking. As familiar as she was with flying and airport security, the look in her eyes said something different. Seemingly incapable of verbal expression in the moment, Rayanah looked frightened and apprehensive about what was happening to mommy. Focusing on my daughter's horrific experience as she watched me go through a humiliating full-body, public pat down, I think I temporarily suspended my emotional concerns for myself.

**Sherick:** How did your emotional concerns for your daughter Rayanah influence the situation?

**Nadia:** After the public full-body search was complete, we proceeded to the back wall, where all of our carry-on luggage, shoes, coats, lap top, cell phone, games, books, markers, etc . . . all went through an additional search of their own; this time, "for bomb-making materials." "WHAT!" I burned from the inside. I was livid, yet I was still trying to convey an outward sense of composure for the sake of my child. One of the male TSA staff who observed and participated in the public search looked at me, and despite my attempt to maintain some semblance of composure, it seemed like he sensed that I was humiliated and angry. He was an older White gentleman, not too tall, with white hair, and he was wearing glasses. He tried to apologize by saying, "I'm so sorry, ma'am, for the inconvenience, but they changed procedures on us this morning." I replied sharply, "Please inform me of what those changes might be." He explained that TSA came out with a new ruling that morning which requires anyone "wearing a headscarf to be subjected to these new types of security measures and searches." I was baffled by his statement.

**Sherick Hughes:** What about his statement baffled you?

**Nadia Hassan:** Well, it's one thing to discriminate against a person or group of people based on sex, religion, or race, but it's a completely different thing to come right out with the "headscarf" comment to consciously or subconsciously say that you're doing it. At that moment and for the first time in my entire life, as the daughter of a U.S. Marine, I felt that I wasn't an American girl anymore. I often wondered if that gentleman, the TSA security personnel, knew what he was saying. I wonder if he would have said that statement had they not profiled me as racially Arab and religiously Muslim. Would he have spoken differently if I was wearing a sign on my shirt that read, "I'm the daughter of a U.S. Marine?" Would I have been treated differently if I was travelling with my father while he was suited in his Marine uniform?

**Sherick Hughes:** Can you talk a bit more about your U.S. family roots and ties to the U.S. military?

**Nadia Hassan:** I was born in Dearborn, Michigan, to a Middle Eastern, Muslim family. I grew up in sunny Southern California, Orange County to be specific, a place that is sometimes described by critics as "shallow, self absorbed, and on its own planet." Of course, I had no clue about this criticism the rest of the country had of us until I later left Orange County and moved to the East Coast. I lived in Villa Park, California, an affluent, upper-middle-class, predominantly White community. I attended elementary, middle, and high school in Villa Park, and to be completely frank and authentic, I was known as a Spazz. I had a lot of friends, and I was known around campus at Villa Park High School as the girl with a very outgoing and friendly personality; hence, the nickname "Spazz."

After graduating high school, I attended California State University Fullerton, where I received my Bachelor of Arts degree in Business and Finance. My father, who was a man with an entrepreneurial mind and spirit, played a huge role in my life by helping me to focus on business and the development of my entrepreneurial skills. Throughout my academic education, I would always think about different things that I could do or creative ideas that I could patent. At one point, I started my own business, and I began importing high-end clothing from Italy to the United States. I also worked closely with my father in his financial planning business. I learned a lot about business from him. As a former U.S. Marine, he was disciplined about his life, and he pretty much ran his personal life in much the same manner he ran his professional life. I truly believe that this formula was a U.S. prescription for "success" because it yielded much prosperity for our family throughout my father's lifetime.

**Sherick Hughes:** How did your father's death change your trajectory?

**Nadia Hassan:** After the death of my father, I applied to several graduate schools. I chose to attend Bentley University in Waltham, Massachusetts, for which I was accepted into the MBA program. I moved away from Orange County (The OC), and I lived in the Boston area for a little over 4 years. After graduation, I remained in Boston because I was hired by an accounting firm, as the Operations Manager, to manage the company and run the day-to-day operation of the firm. I never really recognized my true talent until after I left this company and moved back to California. I had completely revamped the company, collected all of its outstanding receivables, and I took the company from $200,000 to $1,000,000 in sales in the first year. After 3 years with the firm, I decided to leave and pursue other business and personal ventures. Years later, some of my colleagues from the firm called to inform me that I had left a legacy behind, of which I was very proud. The members of the firm still recognize my work today, more than a decade later.

Grad school was a turning point in my life. It was the first time I had ever lived alone and away from my family. For me, it was a time of solitude, solace, study, and deep reflection. I gained inner peace, strength, and a relationship with my Creator, God, that I never had before. Throughout my life, I've always had a passion for Islamic Theology. And although it may not have always been present from my public transcript, I recognize the miracles that have taken place in my life when I reflect on my past. Graduate school time was my time, a perfect opportunity for me to connect with the Supreme Being, without any interference or disruption from anyone. The passion from within me flowed like never before. I could feel the light in my face shine as it radiated my environment. Now more than ever, I recognize God's presence and protection in my life.

I continued to study Islamic Theology comparatively with Christian Theology. I made friends with my Christian brethren and shared our commonalities with them. As a woman, I became enormously present to the significance of the Virgin Mary in my life. She became my role model, and I aspired to live my life as she did. It was then that I decided to change my dress code to one that was more modest in order to emulate the Virgin Mary. As she always did, I began wearing the "Hijab," the headscarf.

**Sherick Hughes:** Growing up in the Protestant Christian faith, I never learned about this Muslim tie to Christianity, particularly the Virgin Mary.

**Nadia Hassan:** In the text of the Holy Qur'an, there are two very long chapters that discuss in detail the stories and the family of Jesus and the Virgin Mary. One chapter is titled "The Virgin Mary," and the other is titled "The Family of Imran," which talks about the Virgin Mary's family and lineage. With regard to the Hijab, God asked all the believing women (that includes Christians, Muslims, and Jews) to dress modestly and not display their beauty to strange men who are not their family members. Think about it, have you ever seen pictures of the Virgin Mary without her head covered? Have you ever seen any portraits of her dressed in sexually seductive clothing, such as tight jeans or a blouse that exposes her bosoms?

**Sherick Hughes:** No, I haven't. Can you talk more about this religious connection?

**Nadia Hassan:** The Virgin Mary was a pure, innocent, modest, chaste, and virtuous women as described in the Holy Qur'an, and she never exposed neither her hair nor her ornaments to anyone other than her immediate family members. She was the inspiration in my decision to change my wardrobe to one of modesty. This experience, of course, impacted my life in many ways. It had an effect on my character, and I found my personality changing from loud, opinionated, and stubborn to influential, outspoken, and humble. A very liberating experience, if I may say so myself. It completely changed my focus, my goals, and my outlook on life. I became a servant to my Lord, and I now want to spend the rest of my life perfecting my servitude to God.

Within a year and a half of leaving the Boston area, 2 weeks prior to 9/11, I was married to my husband, and I was right back on the East Coast again but this time in the DC area. Here I became more present to how people felt about The OC after I moved to the DC area to join my husband. But thankfully I had already experienced a spiritual transformation of my own prior to getting married and moving back east. I too began to feel somewhat disconnected from my Orange County roots. But ironically I had a difficult time assimilating to the DC area because I still felt rooted in Boston, where my spiritual transformation took place.

**Sherick Hughes:** How was your spiritual transformation challenged and/or enhanced by the events of 9/11?

**Nadia Hassan:** September 11, 2001, was a tragic event in the lives of the American people, particularly me. I was devastated by the news particularly because I was about to leave my hotel to go to Reagan International Airport in DC right when the first plane flew through the first Twin Tower and the news broke out to the public. I couldn't believe my eyes nor could I bare the pain. My heart was breaking; it was burning, and my heart felt like it had doubled in size and I couldn't tell if it was going to burst or just stop. I kept pinching myself to make sure that I wasn't dreaming. I kept thanking God, over and over, for not allowing me to be on one of those planes. You see, my husband and I had planned to take a trip up to Boston so that I could introduce my new groom to all of my friends that I had left behind there. And then I was going to fly back home to California from Boston to gather the rest of my things before I made the permanent transition to my new home in the DC area. I had informed my family members that I would be arriving back at LAX (Los Angeles, CA, airport) on September 11, coming in from Boston.

For whatever reason, our travel plans changed, and we did not go to Boston, and I ended up booking my ticket to California from DC. After both Twin Towers imploded and all cell phone services were cut off, I realized that I never informed my family members that I had changed my travel plans to leave from DC instead of Boston. And for the few readers who may not recall, the planes that hit the Twin Towers took off from Boston and were en route to land in LAX, exactly where I was headed. Naturally, my family members (and I have a very large family) thought that I was on one of those planes. Although unconfirmed, they reacted as if I was aboard one of those planes.

My connection to God became more real at that moment. I felt His love, His protection, His compassion. My heart was flaring, burning inside, and I couldn't make it stop. I was thankful to God for my life and the opportunities He bestowed upon me, yet I was mourning the lives of the American people who had lost their lives on that horrible day. I was feeling the agony of their family members who lost their loved ones. The pain was making me crazy. I was conflicted and confused, and I couldn't do anything about it.

I was a new bride on a honeymoon, and I was dealing with so much pain and so many different emotions on opposite sides of the spectrum. I couldn't help but reflect, Why this? Why now? I couldn't make sense of any of it. It was awhile before I was able to communicate and reconnect with my family members in Orange County. You can only imagine the sigh of relief that took place when my mother heard my voice through the phone. All she could say, repeatedly, over and over, is "Thank God, Thank God."

**Sherick Hughes:** You offer a counternarrative to what has been portrayed in popular media and to what filters into U.S. homes, including the homes of TSA workers and other government officials and leaders. If those TSA workers really had an opportunity to get to know you, the more complete and complex you that you have shared, how might they have treated you at the security check point?

**Nadia Hassan:** I think it's like with anyone else, if they really got to know me and how my life is tied to theirs, they would have and could have respected me more. In turn, I would have reciprocated that respect.

**Sherick Hughes:** What do you want readers to learn, to internalize, and to take home from the counternarrative you have shared?

**Nadia Hassan:** I would want them to recognize that I am an American, no different than any other American who travels and walks through the security check points. The female TSA employee seemed stunned by (a) me refusing to remove my Hijab, (b) my disobedience to her authority, and (c) the absence of a foreign accent that could justify her treatment of me by racializing me as an Arab and/or Muslim. Without continued education and information, Muslim women like me, who choose to wear the Hijab to display modesty, will continue to endure racialization, misrepresentation, and mistreatment in the post-9/11 American airport. I don't mind being checked or searched; in fact, I love that we have security, and I am in favor of added security. I want to feel just as safe and protected as any other American would want to be but not when it is selective. A more informed and educated TSA (and United States for that matter) would know to have a woman privately search the Muslim women in Hijab who are "randomly selected" for full-body searches. Being that my search was done in front of my little girl and four men watching not only humiliates me and mocks my Muslim identity, but also mocks my identity as a Lebanese American woman and the daughter of a respectable American entrepreneur and U.S. Marine.

**Sherick Hughes:** Thank you for sharing this painful and powerful story. Peace and be well.

**Nadia Hassan:** Thank you for your genuine concern and thank you for listening. May God Bless you, your family, and all of humanity. Peace!

# Afterword

## Selected Authors' Recommendations Toward a New Political Future of Race

## Sherick Hughes' Recommendations*

*I hope political leaders of the present and future will advocate for:*

1.  **A hits** (perceived threat of bias with confirming evidence), **misses** (no perceived threat of bias, with evidence to confirm the presence of a threat), and **false alarms** (perceived threat of bias without evidence to confirm the presence of a threat) **approach to intergroup communication.** A thoughtful and careful consideration of evidence to confirm or disconfirm whether a questionable experience is a hit, miss, or false alarm could (a) move us toward more informed and fulfilling responses that can decrease unwarranted knee-jerk reactions, and thereby (b) improve communication with individuals and groups inside and outside our own racialized, classed, gendered, sexualized, and religious communities.
2.  **A validation and commitment approach,** where validation is only as useful as our commitment to gaining more in-depth and broad interracial experiences, and where validation involves learning and unlearning, as well as working to know when and how to

appropriately shift the social center to address race. Related commitments would at least involve: (a) supporting folks committed to studying evidence and counterevidence of racialization; (b) supporting folks committed to maintaining the dignity of humanity and social justice, and to understanding the central role of race in a just and humane society; (c) supporting folks committed to reflexive self-critique; (d) supporting folks committed to challenging dominant narratives with counternarratives; and (e) supporting folks committed to exploring the potentiality of convergence and coalition building across and within racialized groups.

3.  **An ethic of respect for the voices of oppressed family pedagogy** with its counternarratives/counterevidence to challenge popular stereotypes and the myth of merit, as well as to challenge socially destructive, discursive innovations such as, "No Child Left Behind," "Freedom of Choice," "Race to the Top," and "Post-Racial America." Respecting the counternarratives of oppressed family pedagogy and respecting oppressed family members as legitimate authorities in teaching, teacher education, and education policy may offer an alternative opponent to challenge the type of misleading dominant discourse that misguides citizens and dissuades the political will to name and change oppressive living, learning, and teaching conditions.

4.  **More clarity and transparency regarding the philosophy of racial diversity** in Colleges of Education, universities, and society at large, including frank discussions about the evolving space for Whites on multicultural campuses and within multicultural communities.

5.  **Revisiting the aftermath of** *Brown v. Topeka,* **Replacing NCLB, and reconsidering race-conscious schooling** in light of the robust research regarding the anticipated and unanticipated negative consequences of resegregated schools.

6.  **A compassionate response to four decades of nationwide research suggesting the need for decreasing disproportionality and response biases** that inequitably place Blacks, Latinos, and the Impoverished in Special Education, Suspension, and Expulsion situations while inequitably pulling them away from Gifted Education and AP coursework.

7. **Critically reflexive autoethnography** and other forms of qualitative self-study that can reveal and name for the sincere participant the core of her or his response biases en route to eradicating them and promoting racial competence without a mandate for racial domination and competition.

8. **Giving equal weight to qualitative (interpretivist), quantitative (objectivist), and philosophical-theoretical (constructivist) epistemologies** and their accompanying methodologies for studying the evolving significance of race.

9. **A move toward more Type II (demonstrations) and Type III (long-term integrated) forms of assignments and assessments to evaluate students and teachers** and redirecting the national focus away from Type I (multiple-choice, timed, short answer) assignments/assessments.

10. **Dismantling Black-White testing gap ideology where Blacks (particularly Black mothers) become scapegoats** to mask larger problems linked to a history of White-male-property-owner privilege, and macro- and micropolitical economy issues.

11. **A system to offer more comprehensive, meaningful teacher education and professional development and resources for struggling prospective, novice, and veteran teachers** before redirecting folks who are either unwilling or unable to benefit from such development to other valuable community positions, where they may contribute to and benefit from the cultural commons.

12. **Diversifying the assessors, increasing the number of male and female K-16 teachers of color nationwide, and bussing in the knowledge, skills, and resources** prior to bussing in the people in order to promote the type of dispositions that may offer more support and constructive criticism during the transition into integrated settings.

13. **A dynamic, diverse, and bipartisan Federal Race Commission (FRC)** to address the evolving significance of living, learning, and teaching race. FRC members could be appointed to serve for limited terms during each presidential administration until Americans are neither judged by the color of their skin nor the height of their test scores.

*Authors listed in the order that they appear in the book.

## Tara Brown's Recommendations

*I hope political leaders of the present and future will advocate for:*

1.  **More authentic and experientially relevant learning experiences for students.** Since the implementation of NCLB, there is compelling evidence that public schools have been narrowing curriculum to reflect limited conceptions of what counts as school achievement, as outlined by the mandate. This is particularly true in schools that serve low-income children and children of color. Because these children are more likely to fail standardized tests for a variety of reasons originating both inside and outside of schools, they are also more likely to be inundated with remedial learning tasks, to the exclusion of more interesting and academically and personally enriching educational experiences. With about half of all African-American, Native-American, and Latino/a youth now dropping out of school, we need to seriously reconsider what they, our most vulnerable youth, are (not) getting in school. In many studies, youth say that what they are getting is boring curriculum that has little to do with the realities of their lives.

    Outside of school, many children living in low-income communities face other difficulties, such as persistent poverty, hazardous living conditions, criminalization, and social isolation. If the purpose of formal education is to foster leadership and civic participation and to help young people to improve the conditions of their lives, then public schools must prepare them to do this. We must provide especially marginalized youth with learning experiences that connect with and address the challenges in their everyday lives. This extends far beyond merely learning to read, write, and do mathematical equations. It requires learning in which young people come to understand the educational, socioeconomic, historical, and political realities that impact their lives and how to transform those realities to improve quality of life for themselves, their families, communities, and society at large. As demonstrated in this chapter, such authentic and experientially educational experiences can draw particularly disengaged youth into meaningful intellectual engagement and prepare them and others for the work of creating a more equitable and just society.

2. **Broader conceptualizations of scientific research.** In the 2002 report, *Scientific Research in Education*, the National Research Council upheld experimental and primarily quantitative methods as the "gold standard" in educational research. Since then, qualitative and liberatory research methods such as participatory action research and critical ethnography have come under increased scrutiny as "unscientific" and thus ineffective at understanding and solving problems in education. As such, funding, especially by the federal government, has increasingly dissipated for such research projects.

   Qualitative and liberatory research methods have long uncovered vital truths about social inequities and increased the involvement of marginalized communities in the production of knowledge, which greatly benefits their struggles to improve their quality of life. The current trend in educational research and funding amounts to an assault on these forms of inquiry that seek to build understanding about the real-life complexities of the human condition and to intervene into social inequities. It threatens to further subvert the participation of the least powerful to participate in the production of practices and policies that impact their lives, which is wholly undemocratic. Especially at this critical time of economic hardship and increasing educational inequity, we cannot afford to narrow conceptualizations of what counts as "scientific" research. If we are to genuinely use social science research to understand and ameliorate educational inequities, we must value and dedicate resources to research methods that have been at the forefront of work for social justice.

3. **Educational policy that takes racism into consideration.** Despite the trend toward "color-blindness," such as repeals of affirmative action laws and school desegregation mandates, it is clear that race still matters in educational policy. Whenever policies and/or practices result in unequal, racial/ethnic group-based outcomes, institutional racism is present. The fact that NCLB has had a disproportionately negative impact on children of color and the fact that most of our nation's worst public schools serve predominantly Latino/a and Black children are two examples among many. Despite the press to treat all children equally, we must take into consideration the impact of historical and contemporary racism,

which is manifest in hazardous living conditions, poor health care, political disenfranchisement, and substandard schooling among many children of color, particularly in urban areas. Thus, educational policy must instead strive for equity, explicitly and intentionally addressing the challenges faced by many children of color in order to create a more fair and just society.

## Sachi Feris' Recommendations

*I hope political leaders of the present and future will work to:*

1. **Continue a national, honest dialogue about the implications of being different in the United States today.** A dialogue that is not afraid of sadness, anger, frustration, guilt, or disempowerment— because these are feelings we must feel in order to empower ourselves to create real change around issues of inequity and racism in this country.

2. **Respond to the yet unfilled promise of *Brown v. Board of Education*** through efforts to legislate affordable housing, interracial neighborhoods, and interracial schools.

3. **Build bridges to create real understanding and alliances** between groups of people from different racial and socioeconomic backgrounds.

4. **Help increase the importance of teachers on a national level** by treating teachers as professionals and raising teacher salaries and investing in strong teacher education programs.

## Brian Schultz's Recommendations

*I hope political leaders of the present and future will address the legacy of racism.*

1. **There is not only an opportunity but also the responsibility to examine racial identities to understand how individual, institutional, and cultural racism manifest themselves.** As individuals and group members, we need to seek space, resources, and processes to challenge such racism.

2. **We have a responsibility to examine how race and racial identity is determined by our social location so that we can work toward understanding one another.** Everyone needs to attempt to

better understand how race complicates our roles both professionally and personally.

3. **No matter our personal backgrounds, we need to embrace the idea that many, especially historically-marginalized African-American youth from urban housing projects, may not have the same opportunities or choices as others.** And the persistent assumption about "picking oneself up by the bootstraps" is far more complicated than the simplistic saying.

4. **If we are to expect equity in student achievement across race and class, it is imperative that we provide equity across the educational funding landscape.**

5. **Encourage others to trouble race not in an effort to arrive at finite conclusions,** not to implicate whether the problematizing is good or bad, right or wrong, but with the intention to better understand our collective responsibility to make a difference in the lives and achievement of children.

6. **In dialoguing about race, open discussions about differences have opportunities to evolve.** Talking with young people about perspective and cultural differences can be one of the first steps in connecting and learning from students while broadening outlooks and increasing tolerance.

7. **Rather than choosing a "color-blind approach"** that relegates race as something that should be overlooked or is unimportant, irrelevant, or off-limits, interrogate these moments as opportunities to directly deliberate about differences.

## Hilton Kelly's Recommendations

*I hope political leaders of the present and future will consider the following notes toward electing and advising an "education" president:*

Newly elected presidents are compelled to articulate an educational vision and program that will affect the lives of individuals, families, communities, cities, states, and nations. For this reason, I have taken the time to jot down a few thoughts and suggestions inspired by my consideration of (double) consciousness in multicultural classrooms. Unless we, as a nation, deal with how we think and feel about marginalized individuals and groups, what we say and do in the name of "good" educational policy will make little difference in the everyday lives of marginalized students.

The popular image and discourse of no child being left behind needs a shift in focus from identities (marginalized bodies) to consciousness (thoughts about marginalized bodies). In a Du Boisian sense, the fundamental issue is not whether schools are segregated or desegregated (the proportion of marginalized bodies in a school), but whether schools are indeed caring, affirming, and equitable (the quality of the educational experience that students receive). Thus, we need an "education" president who:

1. **Provides tremendous leadership for social justice in education, which builds on previous efforts toward critical multiculturalism** (e.g., challenging and dismantling single Eurocentric curricula and school-wide programming) and toward anti-oppressive education (e.g., challenging and eradicating racism, sexism, classism, heterosexism, and ableism in schools). In this way, education has the potential to double the consciousness of all students and to reduce oppression in schools and society (for critical scholarship in this area, see Adams, Bell, & Griffin, 2007; Kumashiro, 2000; Ladson-Billings & Tate, 1995; Nieto & Bode, 2007).

2. **Uses new language to articulate contemporary educational problems.** More than new federal programs to replace the old, we need a shift in the attitudes, approaches, and concerns that some teachers, administrators, parents, and policymakers bring to their work. What would happen if our present or future president changed the discourse about school failure and achievement gaps from "accountability" and "testing" to "compulsory heteronormativity" and "complex inequalities?" Would it lead us to solve the invisible problem of gay, lesbian, bisexual, and transgender youth who drop out of school due to adult harassment and student bullying? Would it reveal that poor and working-poor White youth are not performing well on high-stakes tests, perhaps similar to their poor and working-poor Black and Brown peers? Toward a changing educational discourse, Mr. President and future Ms. President should focus less on "deficits" (what students do not possess) and more on "donations" (what students need). Indeed, how can we teach and nurture the whole child?

3. **Supports local efforts to increase teacher quality.** By "teacher quality," I mean the need for committed teachers who possess a double consciousness: They are sympathetic to the sociopolitical

and economic issues that their students face, they strive to teach knowledge that affirms every student, and they always tell the truth—carefully and responsibly. Any effort to increase teacher quality, as I have defined it, requires federal support for local- and state-level teacher recruitment programs, especially "Grow Your Own Teachers" initiatives. Quite different from national programs, such as "Teach for America," "Grow Your Own Teachers" identifies and selects candidates from the communities that they will serve. Current and future political leaders that comprise the "administration" of a U.S. presidency should push for federal funding to facilitate such local and state initiatives by introducing "loan forgiveness" programs as a financial relief to talented and committed teacher candidates who are rooted in communities where they teach (and saves us from lowering the standards for becoming a teacher). (For more information on "Grow Your Own Teachers" initiatives, visit the websites of programs in Illinois, Kansas, Idaho, Arizona, Washington, and other states.)

## References

Adams, M., Bell, L. A., & Griffin, P. (2007). *Teaching for diversity and social justice* (2nd ed.). New York: Routledge.

Kumashiro, K. (2000). Toward a theory of anti-oppressive education. *Review of Educational Research, 70*(1), 25–53.

Ladson-Billings, G., & Tate, W. F. (1995). Toward a critical race theory of education. *Teachers College Record, 97*(1), 47–68.

Nieto, S., & Bode, P. (2007). *Affirming diversity: The sociopolitical context of multicultural education* (5th ed.). New York: Allyn & Bacon.

## Cooper Thompson's Recommendations

*I hope White political leaders of the present and future will address the legacy of racism, but how?*

1. **In addition to ordinary White people exploring the legacy of racism in their lives, we need courageous White political leadership—from elected office holders, corporate leaders, and influential members of the media—to address institutional and cultural factors that have allowed White people to benefit from racism.** These White leaders need to educate themselves about their own family histories and the history of the United States,

share that history, and then work in collaboration with affected people of color to find solutions that redress the damage from racism.

2. **White leaders will have to do something that few White leaders have ever done: speak up about reality of racism and challenge White people in the United States to finally come to terms with our troubled history.** Candidates for public office have often talked about their own personal history in an effort to convince voters of their qualifications; in the 2008 presidential campaign, both candidates are doing just that, and it plays well with voters. Barack Obama also talked about the history of racism in the United States; His "A More Perfect Union" speech in March 18, 2008, in Philadelphia was well received by White people and people of color. Although conventional wisdom has suggested that it's too dangerous for a candidate to talk about racism—White people will be offended and the candidate will lose the support of White voters—the reaction to Obama's speech suggests that at least some White people are ready to hear about racism.

3. **Historically, it is people of color who have taken the risk to speak up about racism.** And too often they have paid a price for doing so, from loss of White support and being the target of White anger, to being killed for expressing their political views. Rather than leaving that work only to people of color, it is time for White political leaders to take a risk and do more of the "speaking up" against racism and for racial justice.

4. **If White political leaders are interested in that agenda, then there are many current, pressing issues for them to address that have more than a passing connection with racism.** I'll name a few: the disproportionately high imprisonment of people of color in the United States, U.S. immigration policy, rising prices and shortages of basic foods globally, the growing income and wealth gap between poor and rich people in the United States, health care, the occupation of Iraq, the impact of Hurricane Katrina in New Orleans, debt relief in Third World countries, the subprime mortgage crisis in the United States. In each of these, there is a history of racism that helped to create the situation, and there is a component in which White people have exploited people of color and profited financially. Unfortunately, White political leaders—including

elected officials, journalists, and corporate leaders—have not made the connections between these issues and race. Let me explore just one of these current issues in a little more detail and suggest its connections with racism and how White leaders might respond.

5. **Agents selling subprime mortgages intentionally targeted African Americans in some markets.** These agents in many cases knew that their customers could not repay or even understand the debts that they were taking on. Large financial institutions supported these mortgages and also knew how risky and untenable they were. The goal was short-term profit taking, and, not surprisingly, many White people made money from these transactions. The projected impact on the loss of aggregate Black wealth is staggering—perhaps hundreds of billions of dollars—and instead of wealth flowing from parents to children, as is the case for many current White Baby Boomers—wealth is flowing from children to parents in many Black families, as the children are forced to pay for their parents' mortgages. This contributes to the growing wealth gap between White and Black families.

6. **Some White political leaders have blamed African Americans for making bad financial decisions, for being "irresponsible" in taking on "risky" debt. Some White political leaders have defended White-led and White-dominated financial institutions.** Some White political leaders have simply remained silent. I believe that responsible White political leaders who care about racial justice need to honestly talk about the racism that set up this crisis and find solutions that repair the damage, hold financial institutions accountable, and ensure that this does not happen again through laws regulating the mortgage industry.

7. **Responsible White political leaders will "educate" the people of the United States about the history of federal complicity with racism in the real estate industry and how federally backed housing loans in the 20th century helped create White wealth while hindering the creation of wealth among people of color by denying loans to potential homeowners whose skin color was not White.** Responsible White political leaders will work with people of color to find solutions that compensate people of color for their losses, just like other White political leaders have worked to compensate White people for their losses—like "bailouts" for the loss-

es in the financial industry from this same crisis. Responsible White political leaders will have the courage to tell the leaders of White financial institutions that their actions were, intentionally or unintentionally, racist and then hold them accountable, emotionally and financially, for the damage they caused. And responsible White political leaders will face down the mortgage and financial services industry and pass laws that regulate the sale of mortgages even though the industry has fought against such regulations.

8. **It will take tremendous courage for White people to face up to the legacy of racism.** In my opinion, that is the work of current and future political leaders. But if we are to achieve the promise of equality and the challenge to oppression, on which this country was founded, do we have any other choice?

## Zeus Leonardo's Recommendations

*I hope political leaders of the present and future will consider the following notes toward a color-conscious presidential administration:*

1. **U.S. presidential administrations have an opportunity. Will race once again become the pink elephant in the room or will it continue on its path as one of the great U.S. anxieties?** Will color-blindness interpellate our president or will he or she act against the grain without underestimating the difficulties of doing so? It is not necessarily the case that a color-conscious president will further divide the country: The nation is already racially divided. This is not a pessimistic pronouncement as much as it is an observation that has been borne out through the best of empirical research from Myrdal to Hacker. It is not an exaggeration but an admission. It is not something to be feared but a risk worth considering in a thoughtful manner for the present and future presidency.

2. **In exchange for a color-blind discourse, my chapter in this volume argued for a color-conscious perspective.** Read as a racial text, NCLB is Whiteness turned into policy (Gillborn, 2005). As NCLB enters its second phase of reauthorization, it becomes even more imperative that critical discussions around its color-blindness occur among politicians and people in leadership positions. Bonilla-Silva (2005) outlines color-conscious analysis, and its contours include the following helpful list:

- Racial phenomena are regarded as the "normal outcome" of the racial structure of a society.
- The changing nature of what analysts label "racism" is explained as the normal outcome of racial contestation in a racialized social system.
- The framework of racialization allows analysts to explain over as well as covert racial behavior.
- Racially motivated behavior, whether or not the actors are conscious of it, is regarded as "rational"—that is, as based on the races' different interests.
- The reproduction of racial phenomena in contemporary societies is explained in this framework not by reference to a long-distant past but in relation to its contemporary structure.
- A racialization framework accounts for the ways in which racial/ethnic stereotypes emerge, are transformed, and disappear (pp. 21–22).

3. **No Child Left Behind (NCLB) does not signal the eventual disappearance of racism but its softened version.** Its color-blindness ensures the continuation of racial structures not their abolition. Because it is not guided by a race-conscious appreciation of U.S. society, it does not discredit Whiteness but ultimately people of color. When the year 2014 rolls around and the achievement gap has not been significantly narrowed, the nation's eyes will be on students and families of color. They, not Whiteness or White people, will be indicted. By and large, they already know this point. When American democracy falters in matters regarding race, color-blindness locates the problem in people of color as alibis for a condition they did not create. After all, NCLB gave public schools and people of color an opportunity to show their mettle. In the eyes of Whiteness, what more do we need? We must work deliberately against this mindset.

4. **Color-consciousness begins from the assumption that race matters, from womb to tomb.** Racialism is a natural part of a racial formation, something into which children grow. In the United States, it is not deviant to think and act in a racial manner; rather, feigning color-blindness is deviant (which is different from saying it is "normalized"). In other words, it takes a lot of energy and effort to perpetuate color-blindness because it is unnatural in a color-orient-

ed society. In a context of racial contestation, racial behaviors are rational insofar as they represent a racial subject's awareness of racial antagonisms and acts to secure or take away power. Seen this way, a racist person is not merely uninformed, ignorant, or misguided. That is, he is not irrational but behaves consistently with his racial interests (which is not the same as being guided by "reason"). Finally, racial formations, as Omi and Winant (1994) never tire of reminding us, shift and have no transcendental essence. They reflect the racial understandings of their time. History suggests that a good presidential administration is courageous; a great one is also hopeful. Color-blindness does not represent hope but surrender. It gives up trying to understand one of the fundamental structuring principles in U.S. society. A present or future presidential administration can set a precedent that changes the nation's course by bringing race to the top of the agenda.

## References

Bonilla-Silva, E. (2005). Introduction: "Racism" and "new racism": The contours of racial dynamics in contemporary America. In Z. Leonardo (Ed.), *Critical pedagogy and race* (pp. 1–36). Malden, MA: Blackwell.

Gillborn, D. (2005). Education policy as an act of white supremacy: Whiteness, critical race theory, and education reform. *Journal of Education Policy, 20*(4), 485–505.

Omi, M., & Winant, H. (1994). *Racial formation in the United States: From the 1960s to the 1990s* (2nd ed.). New York: Routledge.

# About the Authors

**Leticia Alvarez** is an Assistant Professor in the Department of Education, Culture, and Society, College of Education at the University of Utah. Leticia Alvarez began her professional career as a bilingual middle-school teacher and community educator in urban settings. After teaching middle school, she earned a master's degree in Education at Harvard University. Immediately following, she earned her doctorate in Educational Psychology at the University of Wisconsin–Madison and then completed the American Educational Research Association (AERA)/Institute of Education Sciences (IES) postdoctoral research fellowship at the University of Wyoming. During her postdoctoral research fellowship, she began to focus her research on understanding Latina(o) immigrant youth's everyday schooling experiences with particular emphasis on social interactions with mainstream youth and adults. Central to Alvarez's research is the identification of influences (both structural and cultural) and everyday experiences with peers and adults (e.g., teachers) that influence the psychosocial factors that contribute to youth's engagement in school and optimize their chances of social and academic success. Her research interests include peer relationships (both intra- and interrelationships), youth–adult relationships, and identity development and socialization of youth who are Latina/o, immigrant, and/or Second language learners in U.S. schools and society. Her research is closely linked with issues of immigration, ethnic identity, race, class, and gender. Dr. Alvarez's passion centers on making a difference in the everyday lives of marginalized and oppressed youth through relevant research that will benefit the education and socialization of students who are ethnic minorities, immigrants, and/or Second language learners.

**Theodorea Regina Berry** is an Assistant Professor at Mercer University. She has been a teacher, teacher-educator, and researcher for nearly 20 years with professional experiences in Germany, North Carolina, and Illinois. She has a Doctorate of Education degree from National-Louis University in Curriculum and Social Inquiry and completed a 3-year American Educational Research Association (AERA) postdoctoral research fellowship at the University of Illinois-Chicago. Dr. Berry's scholarship focuses on the intersections of curriculum theory, critical race feminism, and urban teacher education. Dr. Berry currently serves as the Chair, Critical Examination of Race, Ethnicity, Class, and Gender Special Interest Group of the AERA. She is an active member of the American Educational Studies Association (AESA) and the American Association for the Advancement of Curriculum Studies (AAACS). She has published several articles and book chapters and is lead editor and contributing author of *From Oppression to Grace: Women of Color and their Dilemmas Within the Academy* (2006, Stylus Publishing).

**Benjamin Blaisdell** is a faculty member in the Foundations Program of the Department of Curriculum and Instruction at East Carolina University, College of Education. Dr. Blaisdell's motivation in the field of education is to promote equity for culturally and linguistically diverse students. His research focuses on race and racism in education. His book, *Seeing With Poetic Eyes* (2009), discusses how Critical Race Theory (CRT) can be used dialogically with teachers to help teachers understand and counter their unintentional complicity in institutional and structural forms of racism. His ongoing work stems from this approach, and he is currently using CRT to work with teachers on understanding schools as racial spaces so they can better develop culturally responsive practices. Dr. Blaisdell received his PhD in Culture, Curriculum, and Change from the University of North Carolina at Chapel Hill. He was an English-as-a-Second-Language teacher and has lived and worked in North Carolina; Washington, DC; Spain; Colombia, and New York City.

**Thurman Bridges** earned his Doctorate of Philosophy in Curriculum and Instruction from the University of Maryland, College Park and both his Bachelors of Arts and Masters in Teaching Degrees from the University of Virginia. His dissertation: "Peace, Love, Unity and Having Fun: Storying the

Life Histories and Pedagogical Beliefs of African American Male Teachers from the Hip Hop Generation," examined the cultural context in which his participants' experiences with Hip Hop culture, their motivations to teach, and their pedagogical approaches emerged. At the University of Maryland, College Park, he was awarded the Promising Researching Fellowship by the Department of Curriculum and Instruction and honored as a Distinguished Teaching Assistant by the Graduate School and the Center for Teaching Excellence. Prior to enrolling in graduate school, he was a middle school social studies teacher in Richmond, VA where he was honored with the First Year Teaching Award. He was a post-doctoral fellow in the Department of Curriculum and Teaching at Teachers College, Columbia University, where he continued research on the life histories and identity development of African American male teachers from the Hip Hop Generation. His research expands upon the existing literature on teacher beliefs, which all but excludes the ontologies, epistomologies, and pedagogies of African American male educators. He is currently an Associate Professor at Morgan State University.

**Tara M. Brown** is an Assistant Professor of Education at Brandeis University. She holds a doctorate in education from Harvard University and is the recipient of a Spencer Research Fellowship and a Jacobs Foundation Dissertation Fellowship. She previously taught at the University of Maryland, College Park, where she received the 2008 College of Education Excellence in Teaching Award. Tara is a former secondary classroom teacher, having worked in alternative education. Tara's research and scholarship focuses on urban schooling, race, class, and gender in education, and school exclusion, including dropout and disciplinary exclusion, using participatory research methodologies. Her most recent research project examines the educational, socioeconomic, and emotional experiences of young adults in urban low-income communities, who are no longer in school and do not have a secondary credential.

**Rod Carey** is a PhD student in the Minority and Urban Education program in the Department of Curriculum and Instruction at the University of Maryland, College Park. He received his BA in English and Secondary Education from Boston College, and he earned his EdM in Human Development and Psychology from the Harvard University Graduate School of Education. Most recently, Rod spent 4 years as a coach, mentor, and high school English teacher in Washington, DC, urban charter schools. Rod is currently interested in researching issues of equity in classroom practice, student motivation, and, more specifically, how Black and Latino adolescent students form and sustain academic identities in urban schools.

**Summer Clark** is a doctoral candidate in Minority and Urban Education at the University of Maryland, College Park. Her current research examines literacy education, social justice, and teacher development in urban schools. Other research interests include critical theory, feminist perspectives, participatory action research, new literacy studies, literacy assessment, and emancipatory possibilities in education.

**Chuck Collins** is a senior scholar at the Institute for Policy Studies (IPS) and directs IPS's Program on Inequality and the Common Good. He is an expert on U.S. inequality and author of several books, including *Economic Apartheid in America: A Primer on Economic Inequality and Insecurity*, co-authored with Felice Yeskel. (New Press, 2005). He co-authored with Bill Gates Sr. *Wealth and Our Commonwealth*, (Beacon Press, 2003), a case for taxing inherited fortunes. He is co-author with Mary Wright of *The Moral Measure of the Economy*, a book about Christian ethics and economic life. He is co-founder of Wealth for the Common Good, a network of business leaders, high-income households and partners working together to promote shared prosperity and fair taxation. In 1995, he co-founded United for a Fair Economy (UFE) to raise the profile of the inequality issue and support popular education and organizing efforts to address inequality. He was Executive Director of UFE from 1995-2001 and Program Director until 2005.

**Josh Diem** is a Clinical Assistant Professor in the Department of Teaching and Learning, Social Foundations, University of Miami. Dr. Diem joined the University of Miami in 2004 after receiving his PhDin Education from the University of North Carolina. Diem's research interests primarily focus on qualitative research methods and theories and social theory praxis. Some of his particular research interests include race/racism in public schools, education for social justice, immigration, community-based research, multicultural education, gender and sexuality, homelessness and education, urban education, and popular culture and youth identity formation. Prior to completing his PhD in education, Diem was a social worker. He received his BSW from the University of Texas and his MSW from the University of North Carolina. His social work experiences focused primarily on issues related to poverty, low-income housing, and homelessness. He spent time in Texas, Georgia, and North Carolina as a practitioner, activist, lobbyist, and program administrator.

**Sachi Feris** is founder and director of Border Crossers, an organization that brings together young students from segregated neighborhoods in New York City to explore issues of discrimination, inequality, and social justice, and to develop student leadership toward lasting social change (www.bordercrossers.org).

**Nadia Hassan** grew up in Orange County, California, where she finished high school and her undergraduate university studies. She received a Bachelor of Arts degree from California State University Fullerton. Nadia later received an MBA from Bentley University in Waltham, MA. She married her husband, Jamal, in August 2001, and they have a 5-year-old daughter named Rayanah. Currently, Nadia works across different disciplines. She runs a real estate business and works with a nonprofit organization that belongs to a world-renowned author and scholar. She has proofread, edited, and designed some of the 65 books that he has written. Nadia also offers counsel to women who are displaced, abused, or destitute. Furthermore, she works with her husband, who is an entrepreneur. He has three businesses in the areas of real estate development, architecture, and corporate brand strategy and marketing. Nadia is part owner in one of his businesses, and she offers management and accounting support to his companies. She has acquired a newfound love of journalism. Nadia's exposure to the media has allowed her to redirect her talents toward writing, education, speaking, and public awareness.

**Sherick Hughes** is Assistant Professor of Education at University of Maryland, College Park. He earned a BA from University of North Carolina-Wilmington, an MA from Wake Forest University, and an MPA and a PhD from University of North Carolina-Chapel Hill. He teaches several graduate courses in the Department of Curriculum and Instruction, including: Introductory and Advanced Qualitative Research Methods; Power, Privilege, and Diversity in Teaching; and Urban Education. He has recently developed an undergraduate, innovative "I" Series award-winning course focused upon cultural competence, leadership, and critical self reflexivity. He serves on the editorial boards of the *Urban Review*, *Educational Studies*, and *Educational Foundations*. His research generally involves: (a) social context of schooling and urban education; (b) critical race studies and Black Education; and (c) interdisciplinary foundations of education; and (d) diversity education/response bias. He has published numerous articles, book chapters, and two books, including the 2007 AESA Critics' Choice Award-Winning title, *Black Hands in the Biscuits Not in the Classrooms: Unveiling Hope in a Struggle for Brown's Promise*.

**Hilton Kelly** is an Assistant Professor of Education at Davidson College. Dr. Kelly researches in the areas of Sociology of Education, Education in African American History and Culture, Teachers' Work, Lives and Careers, and Critical Race Theory in Education. Dr. Kelly holds a PhD in Sociology from the University of Massachusetts at Amherst and has published articles in such journals as *The American Sociologist* and *Educational Studies*.

**Rita Kohli** is a faculty member within the Teacher Education Program atthe University of California, Los Angeles (UCLA). Dr. Kohli earned a PhD from UCLA's Graduate School of Education and Information Studies in 2008, with a focus on the role of race and racism in the educational experiences, observations, and perspectives of teachers of color. Her work is generally concerned with the intersections of race, class, gender, teaching and learning, and the integration of research and practice. Using frameworks of Critical Race Theory and Internalized Racism, her research specifically investigates racism, racial hierarchies, and cross-racial dynamics within K-12 and teacher education contexts. Dr. Kohli's research has appeared in such journals as *Race, Ethnicity, and Education*, *Teacher Education Quarterly*, and the *Chicano-Latino Law Review*.

**Zeus Leonardo** is Associate Professor of Social and Cultural Studies in the Graduate School of Education and Affiliated Faculty of the Critical Theory Designated Emphasis at the University of California, Berkeley. Leonardo has published many articles and book chapters on race, class, and educational theory. He is the author of *Ideology, Discourse, and School Reform* (Praeger), the editor of *Critical Pedagogy and Race* (Blackwell), and the co-editor (with Tejeda and Martinez) of *Charting New Terrains of Chicano(a)/Latino(a) Education* (Hampton). His articles have appeared in *Educational Researcher*; *Race, Ethnicity, and Education*; and *Educational Philosophy and Theory*. Some of his articles include: "The Souls of White Folk," "Critical Social Theory and Transformative Knowledge," and "The Unhappy Marriage between Marxism and Race Critique." His recent book is *Race, Whiteness, and Education* (Routledge).

**Goodwin Liu** currently serves as Associate Justice of the Supreme Court of California. Before his appointment by California Governor Jerry Brown, Liu was Associate Dean and Professor of Law at the University of California, Berkeley School of Law. He has been recognized for his writing on constitutional law, education policy, civil rights, and the Supreme Court. On February 24, 2010, U.S. President Barack Obama nominated Liu to fill a vacancy on the U.S. Court of Appeals for the Ninth Circuit. Although this nomination did not reach fruition, it would be only a few months before Governor Jerry Brown nominated Liu to a seat on the Supreme Court of California, succeeding Associate Justice Carlos R. Moreno. Judge Liu was sworn in on September 1, 2011. His chapter represents a reprint of a powerful letter to the editor of the Washington Post. Dr. Sherick Hughes, lead editor of this volume, contacted the then, Professor Liu via telephone to obtain his permission to reprint that powerful educational narrative in this volume.

**Marvin Lynn** is an Associate Professor and Associate Dean at the University of Wisconsin at Eau Claire. Dr. Marvin Lynn conducts qualitative research on the work, lives, and experiences of African-American male urban school teachers and the role of urban teacher education programs in developing teachers for racial justice. In addition, he charts and studies the development of the Critical Race Studies in Education movement in the United States and Europe. He has a forthcoming book titled *What's Race Got to Do With It? Critical Race Theory and the New Sociology of Education*. He cofounded and organized the first-ever Critical Race Theory and Education Conference in the United States. The year prior, he was a keynote speaker at the first-ever Critical Race Theory seminar in the United Kingdom. He has published articles in several well-respected academic journals, including *Teachers College Record*, *Qualitative Studies in Education*, and *Review of Research in Education*. He also serves on the editorial boards of several education journals. Professor Lynn was previously Associate Professor and Founder/Director of the Minority & Urban Education Program at the University of Maryland, College Park and the Director of the Department of Curriculum and Instruction in the College of Education at the University of Illinois at Chicago. He also taught in public and private elementary schools in New York City (Harlem) and Chicago. Dr. Lynn teaches courses on urban education, multicultural education, African-American education, critical race theory and education, and methods of elementary teaching in urban schools.

**Dedrick Muhammad** is currently serving the NAACP as the Sr. Director of the Economic Department and Executive Director of the Financial Freedom Center. In 2011 the NAACP re-launched it's economic department with a new headquarters in Washington DC, an enlarged staff, and new programmatic work focused on financial and economic education, fair lending, and diversity and inclusion efforts. Dedrick's past civil rights experience includes his time at Reverend Al Sharpton's National Action Network where he first worked as the National Crisis Coordinator and then as the National Field Director. Dedrick's professional work in economic equity began at United for a Fair Economy (UFE) where he was coordinator of the Racial Wealth Divide Project. While at UFE, Dedrick co-founded the State of the Dream report and has been a co-author of this annual report for five years. Pursuing his work in economic and racial equity Dedrick went on to the Institute for Policy Studies (IPS) where he worked in the Inequality and Common Good Program, under the leadership of Chuck Collins. At IPS, he cofounded the "Race and Economy Forum" with the Economic Policy Institute's Algernon Austin. During this time, Dedrick also produced the reports "40 Years Later: The Unrealized American Dream" and "Challenges to Native American Advancement: The Recession and Native America". Dedrick received his Bachelors of Arts Degree in Political Science from Williams College where he was awarded the Political Science Krouse Award and the William Bradford Turner Citizenship Prize. He went on to receive his Masters of Arts in Systematic Theology from Union Theological Seminary. While at Union Theological Seminary Dedrick was twice elected president of the student council.

**Connie North** manages multimedia projects for the various departments at WIDA. Prior to joining WIDA, Dr. North taught diversity, equity, and qualitative research methods courses in the College of Education at the University of Maryland, College Park. Earning a Ph.D. from the University of Wisconsin-Madison's Department of Curriculum and Instruction and Education Policy Studies, she specialized in teacher and anti-oppressive education and queer theory. She is the author of the 2009 Paradigm Publishers book, *Teaching for Social Justice: Voices From the Front Lines*, and her articles have appeared in such journals as *Curriculum Inquiry*, *Teachers College Record*, and *Review of Educational Research*.

**Francisco Rios** is the Dean of the Woodring College of Education at Western Washington University. Prior to this appointment, Dr. Rios was a faculty member at the University of Wyoming, where he served as Professor and Chair, Department of Educational Studies. Professor Rios' research interests are learning and teaching, preservice teacher education, multicultural education, and Latinos/Chicanos in education. In fact, Dr. Rios is a nationally known figure in the field of multi-cultural education and he has worked as professor and chair of the Educational Studies Department in the College of Education. Moreover, Dr. Rios was the founding director of the Social Justice Research Center at the University of Wyoming, where he also served as co-editor of the acclaimed *Multicultural Perspectives*, a highly respected peer-reviewed journal.

**Brian D. Schultz** is Associate Professor, Honors Faculty, and Chair, Department of Educational Inquiry and Curriculum Studies at Northeastern Illinois University. His research focuses on students and teachers theorizing together, developing integrated curriculum based on the students' priority concerns, and curriculum as social action and public pedagogy. He is particularly interested in encouraging preservice and practicing teachers to create democratic and progressive educational ideals in historically marginalized neighborhoods. Prior to his role at Northeastern, Brian taught in Chicago's Cabrini Green neighborhood.

**Dale Snauwaert** is Associate Professor of Educational Theory and Social Foundations of Education at the University of Toledo. He received his BA in Philosophy at the University of Illinois at Chicago in 1983, and he completed an MEd in Educational Policy and a PhD in Philosophy of Education from the University of Illinois at Urbana-Champaign in 1990. He is the author of *Democracy, Education, and Governance: A Developmental Conception* (State University of New York Press, 1993), which received an American Educational Studies Association Critics' Choice Award in 1995. He has published in such academic journals as *Educational Theory, Journal of Educational Thought, Peabody Journal of Education, Holistic Education Review, Current Issues in Comparative Education*, and *Encounter* on such topics as democratic education, the nature of teaching, moral education, holistic education, and international ethics. He is currently working on a book on the ethics of war and peace and human rights education. His research interests focus on two areas: moral and political philosophy as they pertain to educational theory, especially the ethics of war and peace, democracy, and human rights, and the nature of spirituality and holistic education. He teaches courses in the philosophy and social foundations of education.

**Cooper Thompson** has been leading workshops, consulting, organizing, and writing about sexism, homophobia, and racism for 30 years. For a decade beginning in the 1980's, he helped found and then led an international educational project, The Campaign to End Homophobia. As a senior consultant with VISIONS (visions-inc.org), he worked with hundreds of organizations in the United States and Europe to challenge oppression and promote multiculturalism. In 2003, he moved to Nürnberg, Germany, where he is a member of Diversity Works (www.diversity-works.de), an elected representative on the Immigration Council in Nürnberg, and a counselor and coach (www.cooper-thompson.com). He is the author of many essays and educational materials on oppression and a co-author of *White Men Challenging Racism: 35 Personal Stories* (2003, Duke University Press; all author royalties go directly to fund antiracist work.). He is currently writing a book about his experience as an older adult learning and using German.

# Index